RESOURCES FOR WRITERS

THE MAGILL BIBLIOGRAPHIES

Other Magill Bibliographies:

American Drama 1918-1690—R. Baird Shuman
American Theatre History—Thomas J. Taylor
Biography—Carl Rollyson
Black American Women Novelists—Craig Werner
Classical Greek and Roman Drama—Robert J. Forman
English Romantic Poetry—Bryan Aubrey
Shakespeare—Joseph Rosenbloom
The Modern American Novel—Steven G. Kellman
The Victorian Novel—Laurence W. Mazzeno
The Vietnam War in Literature—Philip K. Jason

RESOURCES FOR WRITERS

An Annotated Bibliography

R. Baird Shuman

*Professor of English
University of Illinois at Urbana-Champaign*

SALEM PRESS
Pasadena, California   Englewood Cliffs, New Jersey

Copyright © 1992 by SALEM PRESS, INC.
All rights in this book are reserved. No part of this work may be used or reproduced in any manner whatsoever or transmitted in any form or by any means, electronic or mechanical, including photocopy, recording, or any information storage and retrieval system, without written permission from the copyright owner except in the case of brief quotations embodied in critical articles and reviews. For information address the publisher, Salem Press, Inc., P.O. Box 50062, Pasadena, California 91105.

∞ The paper used in these volumes conforms to the American National Standard for Permanence of Paper for Printed Library Materials, Z39.48-1984.

Library of Congress Cataloging-in-Publication Data

Shuman, R. Baird (Robert Baird), 1929-
   Resources for writers / R. Baird Shuman
      p. cm.—(Magill bibliographies)
   Includes index
   ISBN 0-89356-673-X
   1. Authorship—Bibliography. 2. Publishers and publishing—Bibliography. I. Title. II. Series.
Z5165.S55   1992
[PN145]   91-36214
016.808'02—dc20   CIP

In memory of

GEORGE WILLIAM SHUMAN
March 6, 1904—January 2, 1951

and

ELIZABETH EVANS DAVIS
July 13, 1903—February 22, 1983

EDITORIAL STAFF

Publisher
FRANK N. MAGILL

Advisory Board　　　　　　　　*Series Editor*
KENNETH T. BURLES　　　　　　JOHN WILSON
DAWN P. DAWSON

Production Editor　　　　　　　*Copy Editor*
CYNTHIA GREEN　　　　　　　　CHRISTINA J. MOOSE

CONTENTS

	page
Acknowledgments	xi
Introduction	1
General Studies	3
Chapter 1: Writing Short Fiction	9
General Studies	9
Creating Characters	19
Science-Fiction Stories	21
Chapter 2: Writing Novels	22
General Studies	22
Creating Characters	38
The Adventure Novel	39
The Mystery, Crime, and Horror Novel	40
Science Fiction	43
Romance	47
The Western Novel	48
Chapter 3: Writing Nonfiction for Commercial Publication	50
Chapter 4: Writing Plays	61
Chapter 5: Writing Poems	69
Chapter 6: Writing for Film and Television	86
Chapter 7: Writing for, with, and about Juveniles	94
Chapter 8: Writing Autobiography, Biography, and Family History	108
Autobiography	108
Biography	113
Family History	116

RESOURCES FOR WRITERS

 page

Chapter 9: Writing for Magazines and Journals 117

Chapter 10: Preparing, Marketing, and Promoting
  Manuscripts and Books 122
    General Studies 122
    The Letter of Inquiry 132
    The Literary Agent 132
    Promotion 135

Chapter 11: Parting Words 137
    Writing Programs 137
    Writers' Conferences and Workshops 144
    Writers' Colonies 155
    Additional Print Sources 156

Index 163

ACKNOWLEDGMENTS

Many people helped with the birthing of this book. I do not know the names of all the librarians who helped me, but I am grateful to those who allowed me to take down whole shelves of books to browse in and make notes about. My research travels took me to libraries in the following communities:

>Albuquerque, New Mexico
>Beatty, Nevada
>Blacksburg, Virginia
>Boulder City, Nevada
>Brinkley, Arkansas
>Cairo, Illinois
>Casa Grande, Arizona
>Danville, Virginia
>Gallup, New Mexico
>Glen Rock, New Jersey
>Granville, Ohio
>Hawthorne, Nevada
>Independence, Kansas
>Kankakee, Illinois
>Kingman, Arizona
>Los Gatos, California
>Monterey, California
>Norfolk, Virginia
>Paso Robles, California
>Perrysburg, Ohio
>Portsmouth, Virginia
>Reno, Nevada
>Richmond, Indiana
>Roxboro, North Carolina
>Sapulpa, Oklahoma
>San Luis Obispo, California

Santa Barbara, California
Santa Fe, New Mexico
Santa Maria, California
Somerset, New Jersey
South Hill, Virginia
Tucumcari, New Mexico
Walton, New York
Xenia, Ohio
Zanesville, Ohio
Zephyr Cove, Nevada

Ann Trombley, Assistant Marketing Manager of Writer's Digest Books/Northern Lights Books in Cincinnati, Ohio, responded to my call for help and provided me with information about recently published books, alerting me to the imminent appearance of forthcoming books so that this bibliography could be as up-to-date as possible.

Various friends helped me as I traveled to and worked in collections, among them Professor and Mrs. Omer Abdelrasoul of Shaker Heights, Ohio; Mrs. E. C. Bolles of Carmel, California; Professor John Marshall Carter of Atlanta, Georgia; Mr. and Mrs. James J. Clark of San Jose, California; Professor Martha H. Cox of San Francisco, California; Professor James Davis and Ms. Lisa Minklei of Granville, Ohio; Mr. and Mrs. Peter Kirchmaier of Perrysburg, Ohio; Mr. Bao Nguyen of Lancaster, California; Ms. Caroline Somerville of Warrensville, Ohio; Professor and Mrs. Joseph B. Trahern, Jr., of Knoxville, Tennessee; Professor and Mrs. Denny T. Wolfe, Jr., of Portsmouth, Virginia.

For good advice and moral support, I am grateful to Cindy and Gideon Schlessinger, ever-faithful friends. Casey Diana, Scott Glander, Deostello Palomares, Faisal S. Razzaq, and Michael Yonan also served as responsive sounding boards.

Finally, John Wilson of Salem Press has proved to be a sensitive and responsive editor. He has made invaluable suggestions and has been as much a friend as an editor to me during the creation of this book.

RESOURCES
FOR
WRITERS

INTRODUCTION

When I agreed to prepare this volume, I had only a vague notion of the kinds and extent of resources available to writers and would-be writers. I had frequently used such books through the years, but I had never thought of them as the comprehensive group that I was now about to organize into the sort of bibliography that would provide an overview of the field.

I had my initial introduction to books about writing in the early 1940's, when, as a budding adolescent, I needed someone to tell me how to write poetry. As I recall, I was in love at the time and was desperate to express that emotion on paper. To reveal my emotions to anyone I knew would have been unthinkable, so I darted furtively around the sprawling library of Central High School in Scranton, Pennsylvania, where I lived then, seeking a book that might offer the help and advice I needed.

I found Robert Hillyer's *First Principles of Verse*. It offered exactly what I was looking for. I checked the book out and devoured the advice it offered. I even went so far as to buy the book—in hard cover for something like $2.50, as I recall. I mustered my courage to the point of writing to Robert Hillyer in care of his office in the Department of English at Harvard University in Cambridge, Massachusetts, certain that he, a publishing professor, would not respond to me, a kid who wanted to write poetry. I was not even sure at the time that people who wrote books were really human. Certainly, I had never met one.

Within a week, however, an envelope with a purple three-cent stamp in the upper-right-hand corner arrived, addressed to me with an unaccustomed "Mr." before my name, bearing a return address that read "Cambridge, Mass." Hillyer was encouraging, jovial, and chatty in his letter. I still have it stashed away somewhere among my collected treasures.

Hillyer told me about his dog and about his sloop—the *Glorianna*—and about his obsession with sailing off the Cape. I was elated to have a new friend who wrote books. My appreciation to Hillyer, now long dead, has not diminished through the years, and I still value his book and the advice it offers so gently.

As I began to gather material for this bibliography, I thought I would work mostly in the library of the University of Illinois, where I teach, the fifth-largest library in the world. I presumed I would be able to gather most of the material I needed without straying far from home. A graduate student, awed by the University Library, had once said to me, "Just think. All the information that has ever existed anywhere in the world is somewhere in that building. All you have to know is how to get at it!" Years of using this library have led me to accept that student's observation as about ninety-nine percent accurate.

After several days at work in our excellent collection, however, I did what all writers have to do before they proceed very far: I asked myself, "Who is my who will use this book—people in places with such enchanting names as Tesuque, New Mexico; Sedona, Arizona; Laughlin, Nevada; Houghton, Michigan; Wanamingo, Minnesota; Coffeeville, Kansas; Bird-in-Hand, Pennsylvania; Meddybemps, Maine; Wicktunk, New Jersey; Lowgap, North Carolina; Malesus, Tennessee; and Trilby, Florida—will not be able to go to major research libraries to find the sources they need.

As a result, I set out on several long drives that over the year this book was in preparation took me to small- or medium-size towns and to out-of-the-way places all over the United States. I found the local library in each place and checked all of its holdings on how to write—in most cases, Dewey Decimal number 808.02 or 808.025. My travels took me to public and/or college libraries in the places listed under my acknowledgments. I am grateful to their staffs for allowing me to take down whole walls of books to browse in and make notes about.

As I originally conceived this book, I decided that I should probably exclude from it any resource that was more than twenty years old. Having reached that decision, I asked myself, "But where does that leave Hillyer?" I decided that perhaps, for both sentimental and substantive reasons, I should let him be an exception.

As I moved, however, from community to community, I discovered that some libraries had extensive collections of books about writing published in the 1950's and 1960's but, for various reasons, had few current books on the subject. I also discovered as I looked at the circulation histories on the backs of these books that many of them, although they were quite old, had circulated briskly in the past five years. Therefore, I decided to include relevant books that I actually found in libraries if they had circulated four times in the past five years.

Obviously, an older book is hopeless if someone needs to find the names and addresses of literary agents and publishers or the current needs of magazine publishers. For those who want information about writing, however, many of these books are still serviceable and well worth reading. The advice they give about how to write short fiction, novels, plays, poems, nonfiction, and juvenile literature is often sound, although it may have been superseded by later books.

A bibliography of this sort is never totally complete and is outdated before it appears in print. A flood of books appears regularly in this field, with new titles appearing, quite literally, every week. I hope, though, that this resource will be helpful to the people for whom it is chiefly intended: writers, would-be writers, and librarians.

Below is a list of general studies that do not fit gracefully into the categories around which the book is organized—short fiction; novels; nonfiction; drama; poetry; film and television; juvenile literature; autobiography, biography, and family history; magazines and journals; and preparing, marketing, and promoting manuscripts and books. Within the bibliography itself, I have attempted to make appropriate cross-references in an effort to facilitate the book's use.

General Studies

Barzun, Jacques. *Simple and Direct: A Rhetoric for Writers.* Rev. ed. New York: Harper & Row, 1985.
This revision of Barzun's 1975 version of his rhetoric has the virtue of being well written and realistic. It discusses clearly and directly such matters as diction, linking (transition and coherence), tone and tune (sound), meaning, composing, and revision. Chapter 8, "Time Out for Good Reading," suggests that one way to learn to write effectively is to read, as critically as possible, good writing. Twenty helpful exercises are interspersed among the chapters.

Bennett, Hal, and Michael Larson. *How to Write with a Collaborator.* Cincinnati: Writer's Digest Books, 1988.
Bennett and Larson cite some of the most effective writing collaborations of all time and show how collaborations work best. They discuss how matters of temperament can be dealt with. Acknowledging the idiosyncratic nature of all collaborations, they nevertheless suggest some techniques that will help a collaboration to survive. Before the actual work begins, it is essential to outline the project sufficiently to allow for a reasonable distribution of labor. This distribution will be based upon the unique abilities, interests, and enthusiasms of each collaborator. Means of communicating must be decided upon, and specific times for communicating should be established. This book, itself a collaboration, is a fine example of what a fruitful collaboration can produce.

Cassill, Kay. *The Complete Handbook for Freelance Writers.* Cincinnati: Writer's Digest Books, 1981.
Cassill does not focus on any single genre of writing, but gives excellent general information not easily available elsewhere on such matters as organizing oneself for problem-solving techniques, doing research, making money directly and indirectly from writing, and finding agents and publishers. Cassill also discusses how writers can provide for their futures through establishing Keogh plans, contributing to Social Security, and other such means. Although this information is now outdated, these benefits are still generally available. Current specific regulations regarding them are available through government agencies.

Flesch, Rudolf. *The Art of Readable Writing.* New York: Harper & Row, 1949.
Flesch's books on reading and writing found enthusiastic audiences in the 1940's and 1950's. In this one, Flesch begins with Aristotelian theory about writing and moves in easy stages up to modern writing theory. His best chapters are chapter 8, "Drama in Everyday Life," chapter 9, "An Ear for Writing," and chapter 13, "R_x for Readability." The suggestions in these chapters have lasting value for writers, as does the somewhat whimsical chapter 6, "From False Starts to Wrong Conclusions."

Fluegelman, Andrew, and Jeremy Joan Hewes. *Writing in the Computer Age: Word Processing Skills and Style for Every Writer.* Garden City, N.Y.: Anchor Press/Doubleday, 1983.
The most creative chapter in this book is chapter 4, "Wordplay: Editing Texts." It demonstrates the flexibility that composing on the computer offers writers. Chapters 5 and 6 deal with formatting and are also useful, although much of what is said here has been superseded by more recent books in the field.

Freeman, William. *Dictionary of Fictional Characters.* Boston: The Writer, Inc., 1985.
Freeman's collection is a useful reference resource for writers. It presents information about more than twenty thousand fictional characters from all genres of writing. It covers the full range of literature written in English, from classic to modern works. This book belongs on the writer's shelf along with the dictionary, thesaurus, and other such indispensable reference tools. The writer whose work depends on literary allusions cannot function well without this exhaustive study, which is accurate and cogent.

Gibson, Walker. *Tough, Sweet, and Stuffy: An Essay on Modern American Prose Styles.* Bloomington: Indiana University Press, 1966.
A remarkable book because it identifies the three styles noted in the title, then draws examples from literature to illustrate each. Gibson makes his generalizations by identifying preferences in the vocabularies, grammars, and syntax of various authors. Appendix A deals with styles and statistics; appendix B is a style sampler.

Golding, William. *A Moving Target.* New York: Farrar, Straus & Giroux, 1982, rev. ed. 1984.
A collection of essays by William Golding, the 1983 winner of the Nobel Prize in Literature and author of *Lord of the Flies*, this volume's second half is particularly relevant to writers. In such essays as "Surge and Thunder," "Rough Magic," "My First Book," and "A Moving Target" Golding explores his essential motivations for writing and reveals valuable insights into the creative process. In its revised edition, the book also contains Golding's Nobel lecture, which deals valuably with the question of what makes a successful writer tick.

Howells, James F., and Dean Memering. *Brief Handbook for Writers.* Englewood Cliffs, N.J.: Prentice-Hall, 1986.
Although this book is essentially aimed at college students in freshman composition courses, its chapters 3, "Revising and Editing," 19, "Sentence Consistency," 42, "Figurative Language," and 43, on writing effective paragraphs, are especially useful to all writers—creative writers as well as writers of nonfiction.

Kane, Thomas S. *The NEW Oxford English Guide to Writing.* New York: Oxford University Press, 1988.
Designed for the freshman writing course in colleges, this book has splendid advice to offer on looking for and exploring subjects to write about (part 1, sections 4 and 5). Parts 5, on diction, and 6, on description and narration, are also worth looking into. The author has a good sense of the need to use language concisely, to control emphasis, to be aware of rhythm, and to use a variety of both subject matter and form.

Klauser, Henrietta Anne. *Writing on Both Sides of the Brain: Breakthrough Techniques for People Who Write.* New York: Harper & Row, 1986.
The fundamental aim of this book is to help people overcome writing problems by helping them find ways to invite the right brain, which is essentially intuitive and holistic, to work harmoniously with the linear, rational left brain, which most people have been schooled to depend upon. Klauser discusses the uses of daydreaming, the need for rumination, and the value of procrastination when it is used to evoke ideas that reside deep within the human psyche. Chapter 5 contains practical suggestions for organizing one's writing through branching, a technique that works well for some people who have trouble getting started and think, probably mistakenly, that they are suffering from writer's block.

Leader, Zachary. *Writer's Block.* Baltimore: The Johns Hopkins University Press, 1991.
Leader understands in depth the psychological factors that account for what is commonly referred to as "writer's block," tracing the problem in poets William Wordsworth and Samuel Taylor Coleridge. He shows clearly that the phenomenon does not have a single cause and that it is of the utmost importance for those who experience it to isolate the source(s) of their own inability to write. The author classifies possible causes into sensible categories and suggests ways to deal with the problem. Leader's analysis is penetrating and well informed.

Mack, Karin, and Eric Skjei. *Overcoming Writing Blocks.* Los Angeles: J. P. Tarcher, 1979.
Although this book focuses on writing such things as letters, technical reports, and term papers, its first 164 pages are useful to writers in all fields. In these pages, the authors deal with writer's block—what it is and why it happens. They then present specific techniques that writers can use to overcome such blocks in chapters entitled "Preparing to Write," "Organizing Your Material," "Writing the Rough Draft," and "Revising and Polishing." By breaking writing down into these steps, many can overcome the paralyzing fear that overtakes would-be writers who think of writing in terms only of the finished product. By realizing that many books in print have grown from severely flawed and fragmented drafts, anyone can gain control over the elements that constitute writing.

Perlmutter, Jerome H. *A Practical Guide to Effective Writing*. New York: Random House, 1965.
The most helpful advice in this book is found in the "Before You Write" and "After You Write" checklists on pages 169 and 170. Each checklist considers the message, the reader, and the treatment. Chapter 9, on tone, is brief and direct. The fifteen-page portion that provides samples of good writing of various sorts is also useful. It provides much information in its abbreviated presentation.

Polking, Kirk, ed. *Writing from A to Z*. Cincinnati: Writer's Digest Books, 1990.
This book is a revision of Polking's *Writers' Encyclopedia* (Cincinnati: Writer's Digest Books, 1983) and is little changed from it. The more than twelve hundred entries packed into its 539 pages remain useful, including such items as the code of ethics of the Society of Travel Writers, a sample news release, an application form for copyrighting a work, and other such items that are of immediate use. The 1990 edition differs from the earlier one in that the entries are alphabetized, which makes the information easily accessible for quick and ready reference.

Polking, Kirk, and Leonard S. Meranus. *Law and the Writer*. Cincinnati: Writer's Digest Books, 1981.
Despite its age, this book will heighten its readers' awareness of the legal aspects of dealing with literary agents and publishing companies. The information on contracts—what they must include and what they should not include—is still quite relevant. Questions about copyright law and about how to protect literary properties are raised and answered practically and directly. The issue of who should hold copyrights is also addressed. Readers who use this book should not take everything in it as gospel, because laws change, and they are not the same in all states. Given this small caveat, however, the book is an important one for anyone who aspires to a career in writing.

Shedd, Charlie W. *If I Can Write, You Can Write*. Cincinnati: Writer's Digest Books, 1984.
The early chapters of this book consider motivation, including chapter 4, "What Are You Burning With?" Shedd stipulates certain rules for writers to follow: no more than fifteen words per sentence; do not use the same word twice in one sentence; use adjectives one at a time; limit yourself to two commas in each sentence; write the way you talk; and do not insult the reader by stating the obvious. This book has a friendly, supportive tone that should appeal to beginning writers.

Strunk, William, Jr., and E. B. White. *The Elements of Style*. New York: Macmillan, 1959 and subsequently.
This much-heralded book is essentially the class notes from a writing course that E. B. White took under Strunk when he was a student at Cornell University. The

approach is authoritarian but delights most readers. White contributed the last chapter, "An Approach to Style," to later, revised editions of this thin book. The chapter is puckish but relevant to anyone who wants to write well. Strunk's recommendations—"mandates" would be a more accurate word—include admonitions to write with nouns and verbs, to revise and rewrite, not to overstate or overwrite, to avoid using qualifiers, not to explain too much, to place oneself in the background as writer, not to break sentences in two, to make paragraphs the basic unit of composition, and to keep related words together. Part 4 discusses words and expressions commonly used and misused in writing. *The Elements of Style* has been a perennial best-seller in the field.

Sypher, Wylie. "Introduction and Appendix: The Meanings of Comedy." In *"Comedy: An Essay on Comedy," by George Meredith, and "Laughter," by Henri Bergson*. Baltimore: The Johns Hopkins University Press, 1956.
The volume in which Sypher's thoughts appear contains Henri Bergson's noted work on laughter and, as such, is of considerable philosophical interest to writers in many genres, particularly in fiction and in drama. The choice sections of the book for writers, however, are found in the four chapters of the appendix, particularly in chapter 1, "Our New Sense of the Comic," in chapter 3, "The Guises of the Comic Hero," and in chapter 4, "The Social Meanings of Comedy." Sypher has rendered a considerable service in updating two important works on comedy, relating much in them to contemporary writing and adding his own intelligent comments to the two works that are the centerpieces of the book.

White, Eric Charles. *Kaironomia: On the Will-to-Invent*. Ithaca, N.Y.: Cornell University Press, 1987.
Although this book does not deal directly with any one form of literary production, it has significance for all forms of creative endeavor, for all the arts, but particularly for the writer. The first chapter concerns the paradox of the liar, which is, in essence, a literary question. Chapter 2, "The 'Reflexive' Is (Not) the Middle Voice,'" is less significant to the creative writer than the third chapter, "Interpretive Mobility and the Sublimation of Desire," and the fourth chapter, "An Image of Change." This study is philosophical and profound. It is the sort of book potential writers will read, put aside, and reread.

Williams, Joseph. *Style: Toward Clarity and Grace*. Chicago: University of Illinois Press, 1990.
One of Williams' several books on writing style. It considers how to achieve clarity, emphasis, cohesion, coherence, elegance, and grace in writing. Williams' comments on English usage are apt and will be valuable to those who are interested in dialogue. This is a solid standard resource for writers in all fields.

Zinsser, William. *Writing with a Word Processor*. New York: Harper & Row, 1983.

    The most useful chapter of this well-written book is chapter 14, which details the methods of manuscript preparation that the word processor allows. Chapters 16 and 17, "The Act of Writing: One Man's Method" and "The Act of Writing: Other Methods," are also of considerable practical value.

Chapter 1
WRITING SHORT FICTION

General Studies

Ballanger, Bruce, and Barry Lane. *Discovering the Writer Within: Forty Days to More Imaginative Writing*. Cincinnati: Writer's Digest Books, 1989.
The authors write generally enough that this book will assist all writers, not merely writers of short fiction. Nevertheless, the information given for Day 7 (the book is divided into forty days rather than into chapters), "Going out on a Limb," Day 8, "Breaking the Habits of Seeing," Days 18 and 19, "Getting the Draft" and "Divorcing the Draft," and Day 32, "Weed a Sentence and Make It Bloom," speak directly to techniques that writers of short fiction must develop if they are to succeed. The exposition is clear and concise, with most sections (days) ranging from three to seven pages.

Barkas, J. L. *How to Write Like a Professional*. New York: Arco Publishing, 1985.
This book deals with such questions as writer's block (chapter 2), the content of one's writing (chapter 4), style (chapter 5), and how to get published (chapter 7). The book begins with a chapter on diction, word choice, and the effectiveness of words. It is, perhaps, the best chapter in a book that has many virtues. The writer obviously has faced the problems that the book's chapters depict. This entry also appears in chapter 2 of this bibliography.

Bentley, Phyllis. *Some Observations on the Art of Narrative*. New York: Macmillan, 1948.
Writers of short fiction and of novels will find Bentley's comments on narrative in this brief book apt. For purposes of analysis, she breaks narrative down into its various types, giving examples of each and discussing its virtues and limitations. Her chapters on the use of summary and the use of scene are brief, direct, and cogent, remaining relevant despite the book's age. The chapter entitled "The Art of Narrative" is the heart of the book; the brief chapter that follows it and discusses the limitations of narrative is valuable in helping writers make necessary decisions in their writing. Obviously, Bentley's discussion, in chapter 8, of contemporary trends is badly outdated, but it has some historic interest.

Bernays, Anne, and Pamela Painter. *What If? Writing Exercises for Fiction Writers*. New York: HarperCollins, 1990.
This book, arranged in twelve subsections, consists of eighty-three chapters that deal with such matters as plot, characterization, and dialogue. Section 12, "Learning from the Greats," contains analyses of works by such major writers

as Franz Kafka. Section 7, "Story Elements as a Given," is also worth reading because it gets to the heart of invention and development.

Bishop, Leonard. *Dare to Be a Great Writer: 329 Keys to Powerful Fiction*. Cincinnati: Writer's Digest Books, 1988.

Bishop presents 329 direct, succinct lessons that will lead sequentially to better writing and to effective strategies for crafting stories. The approach seems deceptively simple. The exercises are easy to do, but the impact of completing this many of them will have lasting effects upon how one writes.

Boles, Paul Darcy. *Storycrafting*. Cincinnati: Writer's Digest Books, 1987.

Anyone who writes short fiction will benefit from the sequential, step-by-step process through which Boles takes his readers as they work toward increasing their writing skills in this genre. Boles does a fine job of relating written language to spoken language, showing how effective writers capture dialogue accurately and how, through such dialogue, they make their stories succeed.

Brady, John, and Jean M. Fredette, eds. *Fiction Writer's Market*. Cincinnati: Writer's Digest Books, 1981.

Three essays in this collection are of particular use to writers of short fiction. André Maurois' essay, "The Writer's Craft," Wright Morris' essay, "On Being True to Life," and Flannery O'Connor's essay, "Lecture on the Nature and Aim of Fiction," all focus on much that is at the heart of writing imaginative fiction, either short stories and novellas or novels. Other essays that address short fiction specifically are found in essays by W. Somerset Maugham, Vera Henry, and James D. Lucey. Bob Jacobs also has a useful essay on the science-fiction short story. See additional comments on this book under "General Studies" in chapters 2, 7, and 10 of this bibliography.

Burnett, Whit, and Hallie Burnett. *The Modern Short Story in the Making*. New York: Hawthorne Books, 1964.

What makes this collection of twenty-two short stories valuable is that each story is accompanied by comments their authors make about their creation. Among those represented in the anthology are Tennessee Williams, who discusses the subjective duologue in "The Important Thing"; Truman Capote, who discusses the objectivized subjective as used in "My Side of the Matter"; Katherine Anne Porter, who deals with writing longer fiction in relation to her story "Noon Wine"; and Mary O'Hara, who discusses "My Friend Flicka" as a craftsman's story.

Campbell, Walter S. *Writing: Advice and Devices*. Garden City, N.Y.: Doubleday, 1950.

Despite its age, Campbell's advice to love your subject, love your reader, and take your reading into the ear and mind of your characters is still sound. Chapters

8, 9, and 10 (part 3 of the book) deal respectively with devices of beginning, middle, and end. The pieces for analysis in part 5 are well chosen and valuably discussed. The only section that has been superseded by later works and later philosophies of writing is part 1, chapter 1, "Qualifications of a Writer."

Dibell, Ansen. *Plot: How to Build Short Stories and Novels That Don't Sag, Fizzle, or Trail Off.* Cincinnati: Writer's Digest Books, 1988.
Dibell's advice about grand openings (chapter 2), early middles (chapter 5), and endings (chapter 10) makes this book well worth reading. Other chapters give such salient information as how to harness melodrama and limit coincidence (chapter 7) and how to handle exposition (chapter 4). His comments about subplots in chapter 5 are also of immediate use to writers of short fiction. For further comments on this entry, look under the same heading in chapter 2 of this bibliography.

Dickson, Frank A., and Sandra Smythe, eds. *The Writer's Digest Handbook of Short Story Writing.* Cincinnati: Writer's Digest Books, 1987.
This is the seventeenth printing of the handbook since its first appearance in 1971. It is as comprehensive a book as one can find on the subject. This edition has a worthwhile introduction by Joyce Carol Oates. Among the other contributors are Thomas Uzzell, Pearl Hofgrefe, Dennis Whitcomb, Harry Golden, William Peden, Jean Z. Owen, Muriel Anderson, and Peg Bracken. Among the topics presented are getting started, where to find story ideas, characterization, dialogue, description, plotting, conflict, and point of view. Later chapters deal with the beginnings, middles, and ends of stories.

Dowis, Richard. *How to Make Your Writing Reader-Friendly.* White Hall, Va.: Betterway Publications, 1990.
This book is notable for its upbeat, optimistic approach to the writing of both fiction and nonfiction. The author urges direct, exact, and concise expression as a means of energizing writing. He reminds writers to keep in mind who their audiences are likely to be and what their expectations likely will be. The information on overcoming writer's block is apt.

Duncan, Lois. *How to Write and Sell Your Personal Experiences.* Cincinnati: Writer's Digest Books, 1979.
Duncan's book begins with a chapter that identifies the most reliable vehicles for placing stories based on personal experience. The second chapter discusses ways in which writers can accommodate the marketplace. Other chapters deal with religious markets, confessions, and kinds of fiction that pay well. Chapter 5 discusses how to mold personal experience into fiction. For additional comments about this book, see chapters 7 and 8 of this bibliography.

Feldman, Gayle. "Is There a Short Story Boom?" In *Novel and Short Story Writer's Market*, edited by Laurie Henry. Cincinnati: Writer's Digest Books, 1989.
Citing such encouraging factors as the growth of small presses, the reemergence of small literary magazines and journals, and the rapid growth in writing schools and writing workshops, Feldman concludes that the future looks promising for writers of short fiction. She cites seven sources that require large numbers of manuscripts: mass-audience magazines, literary magazines, publications from small presses, annual collections of short fiction, ad hoc anthologies, university press collections by a single author, and single-author collections by mainstream presses. This essay is upbeat and encouraging.

Fulton, Len, ed. *The International Directory of Little Magazines and Small Presses*. 26th ed. Paradise, Calif.: Dustbooks, 1990.
The twenty-sixth edition of this valuable book, which covers 1990-1991, is the most comprehensive alphabetical listing of most of the little magazines and small presses available to writers in the United States. The book, at 939 pages, is huge and detailed. Each page is packed with valuable information for writers and potential writers. Toward the end of the book there is a cross-referencing of the items contained in it according to geographical location. This book has endured through the years and continues to be invaluable. For additional comments about it, refer to "General Studies" in chapter 5 of this bibliography.

Harris, William Foster. *The Basic Formulas of Fiction*. Norman: University of Oklahoma Press, 1944.
This book, as old as it is, is still valuable for its analysis of stories from *The Saturday Evening Post* issue of August 2, 1938. This section makes the book timeless. Its comments on what a story is and on point of view, characterization, process, and finishing touches are pedestrian, but the story analyses are pure gold.

Henry, Laurie, ed. *Novel and Short Story Writer's Market*. Cincinnati: Writer's Digest Books, 1989.
While the information on markets in this volume has been superseded by subsequent annuals, the more general articles are still useful. Especially valuable are chapters by Valerie Martin and Gayle Feldman, discussed separately in chapters 1 and 2 of this bibliography, and a chapter by Susan Shreve on writing for young people, discussed in chapter 7 of this bibliography. Henry's section on small presses is especially welcome, as is her close-up of two such presses. These close-ups provide readers with realistic view of how small presses operate and of what they hope to achieve. Contains a useful list of markets by categories. Strongly recommended. See additional comments in chapter 2 of this bibliography; see also chapter 10 for comments on the 1992 edition of this annual, edited by Robin Gee.

Hill, Wycliffe A. *The Plot Genie: General Formula*. 5th ed. Hollywood, Calif.: The Gagnon, 1935.
This book had a striking success in the 1930's, and much of it is still of interest today. The first thirty-eight pages give a general, in-depth discussion of plot. The remaining ninety-one pages consist essentially of a list of possible plots under such headings as "Male [Female] Characters," "Unusual Male [Female] Characters," "Obstacles to Love," and "Crises." For further information about this book, see chapter 2 of this bibliography.

Hughes, Riley. *Finding Yourself in Print: A Guide to Writing Professionally*. New York: Franklin Watts' Vision Books, 1979.
This book, which deals with all kinds of writing, has good advice for short-story writers. Chapter 3, on language, discusses selecting the exact word, constructing the clear sentence, and using the so-called "fog index," a guide to sentence complexity. Chapters 7 and 8 deal with matters germane to writers of short fiction—description, summary, scene—and angles of narration. Chapter 7 presents a structural analysis of Stephen Crane's "The Open Boat." Chapter 9 addresses fiction and action and differentiates between literary fiction and popular fiction. The book also suggests markets—advice that, although dated, is of general use.

Knight, Damon. *Creating Short Fiction*. Cincinnati: Writer's Digest Books, 1985.
Damon Knight has fashioned a series of exercises that will help those who work through them to recognize and eliminate the weaknesses that creep into their own writing, making them their own most effective editors. The exercises lead to the writing of a short story and controlling it every step along the way to its production.

Macauley, Robie, and George Lanning. *Technique in Fiction*. New York: Harper & Row, 1964.
In this book, two former editors of *The Kenyon Review* draw from their experience in publishing quality short fiction to reveal what makes such writing effective. The organization is quite conventional, addressing invention (which they call "conception") first, then going on to discuss such topics as style and speech, characterization, point of view, background (place, setting, milieu), time and pace, plot and story, and organic form and final meaning. Despite its age, this small volume is still serviceable because of the basic intelligence and perceptions of its authors. They provide fifteen pages of helpful exercises and writing suggestions as well as a bibliography of books that deal with writing technique.

McLarn, Jack Clinton. *Writing Part-Time for Fun and Money*. Wilmington, Del.: Enterprise Publishing, 1978.
Writers of short fiction will find considerable valuable material in this book, especially in the chapter that deals with writing fiction. In chapter 7, the author

examines writing for children and ghostwriting. Appendix 3 focuses on the juvenile story. For additional comments about this book, see chapters 2, 7, 9, and 10 of this bibliography.

Marks, Percy. *The Craft of Writing*. New York: Grosset & Dunlap, 1932.
Of historical rather than immediate interest, Marks's essay on the technique of the short story (chapter 6 of the book) offers some insights that are still quite applicable to those writing short fiction. For further comments about this book, see chapter 2 of this bibliography.

Marston, Doris Ricker. *A Guide to Writing History*. Cincinnati: Writer's Digest Books, 1976.
This book is as relevant today as it was when it was written. Broad in scope, it addresses nonfiction, novels, poetry, and writing for young people, all with a historical base. After chapters on audience and research, Marston provides an excellent essay in which she categorizes the kinds of articles that have historical bases. Chapter 12 focuses on historical poetry and short fiction, suggesting places that publish such work. For additional comments about this book, see chapters 2, 3, 5, and 7.

Martin, Valerie. "Waiting for the Story to Start." In *Novel and Short Story Writer's Market*, edited by Laurie Henry. Cincinnati: Writer's Digest Books, 1989.
Martin is concerned with one of every writer's chief difficulties, that of invoking the muse. One cannot sit passively and wait for it to arrive. By following some of Martin's suggestions, the writer will find a way to get the creative juices flowing. Probing the unconscious mind is fundamental to most imaginative writing, and Martin has good ideas about how this can be done. See additional comments in chapter 2 of this bibliography.

Mathieu, Aron M., ed. *The Creative Writer*. Cincinnati: Writer's Digest Books, 1961.
Mathieu's chapter on writing short fiction stresses the need for compression and focus if stories are to succeed. Ann Finlayson's "Writing a True Story" and Albert Delacorte's "Modern Romances" should also interest writers of short fiction. This is a most comprehensive book, which, although dated in some specifics, holds much of interest to modern readers. For additional comments about this book, refer to chapters 2, 4, and 7 of this bibliography.

Muth, Marcia. *Writing and $elling: Poetry, Fiction, Articles, Plays, and Local History*. Santa Fe, N.Mex.: Sunstone Press, 1985.
Although this book may strike some readers as more concerned with commerce than with art, chapter 2 makes interesting observations about the writing and marketing of fiction, particularly short fiction suitable for periodicals. One must

read beyond the dollar signs to realize that some of the advice given in this chapter is quite astute. For additional comments about this book, look under "General Studies" in chapters 4, 5, 9 and 10.

Nyberg, Ben. *One Great Way to Write Short Stories.* Cincinnati: Writer's Digest Books, 1988.
Nyberg's title is too modest. This book is a comprehensive approach to formulating, writing, revising, and marketing short fiction. Nyberg knows the industry and understands what makes short fiction publishable for mass markets. His suggestions are clear and detailed, following a step-by-step process from invention to the production of a final, marketable manuscript. Nyberg pays considerable attention to the necessity of close observation and the accurate recording of such observation in order to transform events and ideas into a coherent, well-focused, and gripping story.

Oates, Joyce Carol. "Building Tension in the Short Story." In *The Writer's Handbook, 1987*, edited by Sylvia K. Burack. Boston: The Writer, Inc., 1987.
Oates realizes the limitations of short fiction. The points must be made quickly and memorably. She suggests that they must communicate directly, that the forward thrust must never be lost, and that the building of tension must be continuous and must not waver because of the limitations set by the genre. In order to achieve what Oates thinks is necessary, writers of short fiction will reduce details and will not let what she terms "secondary material" intrude into the main narrative. There is in this kind of fiction no room for digression because to digress is to lose momentum. She illustrates her points by citing one of her own stories, one by Anton Chekhov, and one by Franz Kafka. She emphasizes that tension must be inherent but must not exist only for its own sake.

O'Connor, Flannery. "The Nature and Aim of Fiction." In *The Writer's Craft*, edited by John Hersey. New York: Alfred A. Knopf, 1974.
This popular southern novelist and short-story writer understands that fundamental to structuring any piece of fiction is a decision about how best to achieve the progression that keeps any story moving. O'Connor fixes on the English sentence as the vehicle through which progression is necessarily achieved and suggests ways in which writers can control their sentences and, thereby, their progressions. For further comments about this essay, look under the same heading in chapter 2 of this bibliography.

Peck, Robert Newton. *Secrets of Successful Fiction.* Cincinnati: Writer's Digest Books, 1980.
The tone of this book is breezy and will likely offend some readers. Those who do not object to a chapter title like that of chapter 2, "How to Write Good with Swell Adjectives," may find some value in this book, whose information on plot,

description, dialogue, and promotion are not bad. The book, however, is marginal at best. For additional comments about this book, refer to chapter 10 of this bibliography.

Percy, Bernard. *The Power of Creative Writing: A Handbook of Insights, Activities, and Information to Get Your Students Involved.* Englewood Cliffs, N.J.: Prentice-Hall, 1981.
Chapter 7 of this book is concerned with the writing of short fiction. In its eleven pages, it packs a great deal of information about how to structure short stories and how to make the characters that populate them convincing. Chapters 2, about creativity and art, and 3, on motivation, are also relevant to writers of short fiction. A glossary of terms used in the profession of writing and a list a resources for writers, both at the end of the book, are also serviceable. The exercises are fun to do and are instructive. For additional comments on this book, see chapter 5 of this bibliography.

Poe, Edgar Allan. "The Philosophy of Composition." In *The Writer's Craft*, edited by John Hersey. New York: Alfred A. Knopf, 1974.
Among the best-controlled short fiction writers of all time, Edgar Allan Poe in this essay discusses how one writes authentically, where one begins a story, how one brings in necessary background details, and how an author builds suspense and expectation in the reader. Poe is fundamentally concerned with tone and style as they pertain to the development of works of short fiction. For further comments about this collection, see other entries in this chapter as well as in chapters 2 and 5 of this bibliography. For additional comments about the Poe essay, see chapter 5 under "General Studies."

Polking, Kirk, ed. *A Beginner's Guide to Getting Published.* Cincinnati: Writer's Digest Books, 1987.
This broad-ranging book contains a valuable contribution by Helen Hinckley Jones entitled "Writing the Story of Accomplishment," which deals with how to structure a convincing and appealing short story. The advice is practical and cogent. It emphasizes the need to present believable characters in interesting situations. For additional comments on this book, refer to "General Studies" in chapters 4, 5, and 7 of this bibliography.

Provost, Gary. *Make Every Word Count: A Guide to Writing That Works—for Fiction and Nonfiction.* Cincinnati: Writer's Digest Books, 1980.
Part 2 of this book gives good advice about writing style, emphasizing that it is preferable to say things in a positive way. Part 4 considers characterization (see below); part 5, creating dialogue; part 6, description and detail; and part 7, point of view—all necessary ingredients of fiction writing. For additional comments about this book, see the section of this chapter entitled "Creating Characters."

Rosen, Michael. *Did I Hear You Write?* London: André Deutsch, 1989.
Aimed essentially at children and their teachers, this book has excellent suggestions that will help writers of any age. The author discusses how to capture speech and transform it into written form and gives a list of starting points for what he labels "oral writing." The book's five chapters are enhanced by four extensive appendices with some examples of various sorts of writing. For further comments on this book, look under "General Studies" in chapter 5 of this bibliography.

Sanders, Linda S. *Best Stories from New Writers.* Cincinnati: Writer's Digest Books, 1991.
Sanders' approach is rich and imaginative. She has selected twelve stories, each the first publication of its author, and after presenting the story, she comments on it and has its author comment on it. The insights into the creative process are varied and at times profound.

Simons, George F. *Keeping Your Personal Journal.* New York: Paulist Press, 1978.
Chapter 5, on specific applications of journal-keeping for fiction and nonfiction writers, is still valuable, although much of the rest of the book has become dated. The information on starting a journal is rather *pro forma*, but the advice about how to maintain one is excellent. The information about sharing the journal with others is also practical. For additional comments about this source, refer to chapter 8 of this bibliography.

Steward, Joyce S., and Mary K. Croft. *The Leisure Pen: A Book for Elderwriters.* Plover, Wis.: Keepsake Publishers, 1988.
This upbeat and encouraging book suggests ways in which older people can write short memoirs (chapters 1 and 2) and short stories (chapter 11). The approach is supportive and the suggestions given are practical and realistic. For further comments on this book, refer to chapters 5 and 8 in this bibliography.

Surmelian, Leon. *Techniques of Fiction Writing: Measure and Madness.* Garden City, N.Y.: Doubleday, 1968.
The advice in this book has held up extremely well over the years. The tone, as Mark Schorer notes in his introduction, is relaxed and casual. The information given about such matters as setting the scene for stories, using summary and description, achieving aesthetic distance, using first- and third-person narration, and what Surmelian calls "the challenge of chaos" are exceptionally well done and thorough. The information provided is of value to short-fiction writers as well as to novelists. For additional comments about this book, see chapter 2 of this bibliography.

Weber, Olga S., and Stephen J. Calvert, eds. *Literary and Library Prizes.* 10th ed. New York: R. R. Bowker, 1980.

This frequently published volume lists international, American, British, and Canadian literary and library prizes. It gives the year and the names of the prizes and the names of winners. In this edition of the book, twelve pages were devoted to prizes for short stories. For additional comments about this book, see chapters 4 and 7 of this bibliography.

Welty, Eudora. *The Eye of the Story: Selected Essays and Reviews*. New York: Random House, 1977.
This collection of essays, by one of the most successful writers of short fiction in the United States, is divided into two parts. Part 1, comprising 163 pages, presents essays in which Welty writes about such writers as Jane Austen, Henry Green, Katherine Anne Porter, Willa Cather, and Anton Chekhov. Part 2, which is 187 pages long, focuses on problems of writing and is especially strong on dealing with elements of time and place in writing short fiction. Welty's essay "Some Notes on Time in Fiction" is uniquely valuable. Implicit in many of the essays is the importance of point of view.

_____. *One Writer's Beginnings*. Cambridge, Mass.: Harvard University Press, 1984.
Best known as a consummate short-story writer, Welty presented the 1983 William E. Massey, Senior, Lectures in History and American Civilization at Harvard University. This thin volume contains her three lectures, one on listening, one on learning to see, and one on finding a voice. Probably the most useful of these lectures for beginning writers is the one on learning to see, in which Welty gives excellent specific advice on how to observe closely and use the details of that observation in one's writing.

Wharton, Edith. *The Writing of Fiction*. New York: Octagon Books, 1966, 1970.
Chapter 2 of this book focuses on the writing of short fiction, showing the similarities to and differences between the novel and the short story. Chapter 1, "In General," is also relevant to short-story writing because it sets the stage for understanding what transforms actual, everyday life experiences into compelling fiction. Wharton's techniques of observation, her depiction of detail, and her ability to handle suspense and surprise make her work notable, as does her controlled use of dramatic irony—as seen, for example, in her novella *Ethan Frome*.

Whitney, Phyllis A. *Guide to Fiction Writing*. Boston: The Writer, Inc., 1988.
Phyllis Whitney shares with her readers some of the techniques that have made her a successful and much-published writer of fiction. Part 1, "Methods and Process," discusses various approaches to the writing of fiction, from organizing a writer's notebook to planning and plotting short stories and novels. She gives good advice about how to generate ideas and about how to use one's inspirations

productively in the writing process, sometimes as a means of overcoming writer's block. Part 2, "Techniques," focuses on such practical matters as point of view, writing beginnings and endings, sustaining middles, controlling conflict, building suspense, using surprise, establishing goals, handling the time elements of narratives, using flashbacks, and building effective transitions.

───────────. *Writing Juvenile Stories and Novels.* Boston: The Writer, Inc., 1976.
Whitney's greatest contribution, in this classic work on the topic of writing for young people, is in suggesting how potential authors can discover the kinds of juvenile writing they, individually, are best able to do. She suggests ways to assess one's abilities, experience, interests, and background and to use such an assessment as a guide to writing. She also mentions taboos in literature for young people, although some of the taboos in effect when the book was written have subsequently ceased to exist as constraints upon writers. Whitney identifies the main areas in which juvenile literature is written—fantasy, mystery, animal stories, stories of modern American life, science fiction, and stories that explore ethnicity.

Willis, Meredith Sue. *Personal Fiction Writing: A Guide to Writing from Real Life for Teachers, Students, and Writers.* Urbana, Ill.: National Council of Teachers of English, 1985.
Willis explores the ways in which writers can draw from all that is around them and turn the commonplace into uncommon fiction. The book is aimed at young writers, but writers of any age will profit from reading it. The author has a keen sense of how autobiography is part of any writing. For additional comments about this book, see chapters 7 and 8 in this bibliography.

The Writing Business: A Poets and Writers Handbook. Edited jointly by the editors of *Coda: A Poets and Writers Newsletter.* New York: Poets and Writers, 1985.
The early material on writer's block, using word processors, and revision is informative. Part 6 lists the fourteen major magazines, what they want, and what they pay. The writer's guide to reference books is valuable, as is the checklist for giving readings. The list of publishers' addresses is minimal but accurate. For further comments on this book, see chapters 2, 3, 5, 9, and 10 of this bibliography.

Creating Characters

Leavitt, Hart Day. *An Eye for People: A Writer's Guide to Character.* New York: Bantam, 1970.
For a discussion of this book, refer to chapter 2 under "Creating Characters."

Provost, Gary. *Make Every Word Count: A Guide to Writing That Works—for Fiction and Nonfiction.* Cincinnati: Writer's Digest Books, 1980.
   Part 4 of this book focuses on characterization and on the need to bring characters to life on the printed page. The advice, particularly that about developing techniques of observing human behavior, is solid. The book is concerned more with the commercial aspects of writing than with its artistic aspects, but the two areas overlap sufficiently that some of the advice given is aesthetic. For additional comments about this book, see the "General Studies" section of this chapter.

Rico, Gabriele Lusser. *Writing the Natural Way: Using Right-Brain Techniques to Release Your Experience.* Los Angeles: J. P. Tarcher, 1983.
   Although the intended audience of this book seems to be college students in writing courses, the methods Rico suggests for allowing the right brain to broaden the scope of what one can address in writing is of use to anyone who wishes to write. This book will help get its readers in touch with their inmost selves, enabling them to enhance the memory and work with the unconscious mind. This source is listed also in chapter 2 of this bibliography.

Swain, Dwight V. *Creating Characters.* Cincinnati: Writer's Digest Books, 1990.
   In particularly precise, direct, and lucid language, Swain takes readers through a step-by-step approach to inventing characters and building them into believable literary personages. The materials on physical detail and on creating dialogue are particularly vibrant. The author urges the reader to show rather than tell, and his exercises are all aimed in the direction of showing writers how to achieve this vital skill. The examples drawn from literature are well selected and completely pertinent to what is being discussed in each section of the book. Swain succeeds better than most authors in presenting rationales for the generally accepted rules of characterization.

Turco, Lewis. *Dialogue.* Cincinnati: Writer's Digest Books, 1989.
   Turco teaches by example: His book is in dialogue form and covers a broad variety of dialogic structures, demonstrating how dialogue is the essence of strong characterization. In chapter 2 he explores how to use speech in narration, and in chapter 5 he discusses genre dialogue. Chapter 4 focuses on types of speech, including dialects and how to represent them in written form. Any writer of short fiction will benefit practically from reading Turco's interestingly presented book. For further discussion of this title, look under "Creating Characters" in chapter 2 of this bibliography.

Science-Fiction Stories

Asimov, Isaac, and Martin Greenberg. *Cosmic Critiques: How and Why Ten Science Fiction Stories Work.* Cincinnati: Writer's Digest Books, 1990.
In this book, one of the world's most prolific and successful writers and his collaborator review analytically ten science-fiction stories and show clearly the elements that make them effective and marketable. They demonstrate how accurate information lends believability to stories, and they demonstrate the intimate relationship that exists between theme and plot in successful writing. The fictional characters in science fiction are unlike the conventional, realistic characters that one finds in much literature. This fact is not lost on these authors, who have especially incisive advice to impart about shaping science-fiction characters.

Bova, Ben. *Notes to a Science Fiction Writer.* New York: Charles Scribner's Sons, 1975.
Bova analyzes four of his own science-fiction stories—"Fifteen Miles," "Men of Good Will," "Stars, Won't You Hide Me," and "The Shining Ones"—discussing both the theory and the practice of writing science fiction in relation to each. He focuses particularly on character, background, conflict, and plot.

Bretnor, Reginald, ed. *The Craft of Science Fiction.* New York: Harper & Row, 1976.
Bretnor's opening essay, "SF: The Challenge to the Writer," both defines the market and suggests its difficulties. Jack Williamson's "Short Stories and Novelettes" is specifically relevant, as is Frank Herbert's essay, "Men on Other Planets." For further comments about this book, see chapters 2 and 6 of this bibliography.

Chapter 2
WRITING NOVELS

General Studies

Abbe, George, ed. *Stephen Vincent Benét on Writing*. Brattleboro, Vt.: The Stephen Greene Press, 1964.
Abbe has gathered from Stephen Vincent Benét's letters and publications information and advice about writing that Benét gave to the young writer. Among the topics Benét touched on are how to choose and test a theme, construction, plot, balance, characterization, overwriting, avoiding clichés, and revision. The material on overwriting is particularly engaging and important. In the book's second section, Benét discusses the commercial aspects of writing: how one learns writing by the act of writing, how to select and deal with publishers, how to select an agent, and how to make enough money as a writer to support oneself. Much of the advice is still timely, although it was given several decades ago.

Ames, Van Meter. *Aesthetics of the Novel*. New York: Gordian Press, 1966.
Originally published in 1928, this book has become a classic of sorts among those who write. The initial metaphor compares athletes and artistic works, which the author claims are admired for similar reasons. Ames devotes thirty pages to defining personality, then shows how the novel ministers to the personality. If the book speaks directly to modern readers, it does so in its last two chapters, "The Technique of the Novel" and "The New Novel," which is now the not-so-new novel but is of historical interest. Readers will find that Ames's views are in sharp contrast to those of modern and postmodern critics, but that they are of interest as a reflection of how the novel was viewed in the first third of the twentieth century.

Aristotle. *On the Art of Poetry*. Edited by Lane Cooper. Ithaca, N.Y.: Cornell University Press, 1962.
Because Aristotle's use of the word that is usually translated *poetry* is broader than its use today, one should not be misled by this book's title. *Poetry* in the Aristotelian sense encompasses most creative acts and certainly includes prose fiction, which in Aristotle's day was largely oral. This book is carefully translated. Cooper's introduction considers epic poetry and problems in criticism. It also defines *tragedy* in the Greek sense. For additional comments about this book, see chapter 5 of this bibliography.

Asimov, Janet, and Isaac Asimov. *How to Enjoy Writing: A Book of Aid and Comfort*. New York: Walker, 1987.
The Asimovs have produced an upbeat book for writers and have illustrated it

with beguiling cartoons. Much of the material in the book is in the form of an extended pep talk, but as such it succeeds well. Chapter 3, which addresses in four pages the problem of writer's block, and chapter 10, "Imagination: The Joys of Writing Fiction," are particularly relevant to novels and to writers of short fiction. Because each chapter in the book is brief, the authors make their points quickly and directly without preaching. See also the comments for this listing in chapter 7 of this bibliography.

Barkas, J. L. *How to Write Like a Professional.* New York: Arco Publishing, 1985.
This book deals with such questions as writer's block (chapter 2), the content of what one writes (chapter 4), style (chapter 5), and how to get published (chapter 7). The book begins with a chapter on diction, word choice, and the effectiveness of words. It is, perhaps, the best chapter in a book that has many virtues. The writer obviously has faced the problems that the book's chapters depict. This entry also appears in chapter 1 of this book.

Bentley, Phyllis. *Some Observations on the Art of Narrative.* New York: Macmillan, 1948.
Writers of short fiction and of novels will find Bentley's comments on narrative in this brief book apt. For purposes of analysis, she breaks narrative down into its various types, giving examples of each and discussing their virtues and limitations. Her chapters on the use of summary and the use of scene are brief and direct, and they remain cogent despite the book's age. The chapter entitled "The Art of Narrative" is the heart of the book; the brief chapter that follows it and discusses the limitations of narrative is valuable in helping writers make necessary decisions in their writing. Obviously, Bentley's discussion of contemporary trends, in chapter 8, is badly outdated, but it has some historic interest.

Block, Lawrence. *Spider, Spin Me a Web: Lawrence Block on Writing Fiction.* Cincinnati: Writer's Digest Books, 1988.
Block, himself a best-selling novelist, shows in this book how to create stories that can be turned into novels. He pays special attention to the use of specific, carefully observed detail. His discussion is far-ranging, covering even such mundane matters as how to survive financially in the economically uncertain world of novelists.

_____. *Writing Fiction.* Cincinnati: Writer's Digest Books, 1990.
This book is broader than Block's *Writing the Novel,* listed below. It also is updated and has valuable information about marketing manuscripts. The overall structure is quite similar to that in the earlier book, but this book will be useful to writers of short fiction as well as to novelists. As usual, the style is controlled and clear. The book is a pleasure to read for its effective use of the English language.

_____. *Writing the Novel: From Plot to Print.* Cincinnati: Writer's Digest Books, 1985.

Block covers comprehensively matters related to writing novels, from plot progression to research. His greatest contribution, however, is in his carefully thought-through suggestions about how to produce a book that in every respect is ready for the editor once it is out of the word processor. Following Block's suggestions should obliterate some of the roadblocks that stand between writers and editors.

Bocca, Geoffrey. *You Can Write a Novel.* Englewood Cliffs, N.J.: Prentice-Hall, 1983.

Bocca's first chapter, on getting started, has little new in it, but the following chapter, "The Rules of the Game," is fresh and lively. Bocca covers the usual areas of plot development, action, dialogue, unity, and style well enough, but his chapter on description (chapter 5) is particularly satisfying in the specificity with which he details how writers can use physical reality and feelings in arriving at descriptions that reverberate with authenticity.

Brace, Gerald Warner. *The Stuff of Fiction.* New York: W. W. Norton, 1969.

Following the introduction, which is chapter 1, Brace continues in chapter 2 to discuss talent and its relationship to writing. Chapter 3 is the title chapter. Following it are eight quite straightforward, if slightly unimaginative, chapters on plan, plot, theme, characters, points of view, setting, dialogue, and style. What Brace says is sound but not sparkling, and much of it has been said more effectively since this book was published.

Brady, John, and Jean M. Fredette, eds. *Fiction Writer's Market.* Cincinnati: Writer's Digest Books, 1981.

In his essay on the writer's craft, André Maurois gets to the very heart of what imaginative fiction is and of how it succeeds. This thoughtful essay is among the best in a book of strong essays. Also of interest to novelists will be Flannery O'Connor's "Lecture on the Nature and Aim of Fiction." Wright Morris, in "On Being True to Life," calls for accuracy of observation and presentation. An accomplished photographer as well as an able novelist and short-story writer, Morris has always striven to achieve a camera-like verisimilitude in his own writing, and he conveys in this essay some of his means of doing so. See additional comments about the Brady-Fredette collection in chapters 1, 7, and 10 of this bibliography.

Campbell, Walter S. *Writing: Advice and Devices.* Garden City, N.Y.: Doubleday, 1950.

For a discussion of this book, see chapter 1. The advice given applies equally to short fiction and to novels.

Collier, Oscar, with Frances Spatz Leighton. *How to Write and Sell Your First Novel*. Cincinnati: Writer's Digest Books, 1990.
This 240-page book touches on every aspect of writing convincing and marketable novels, putting valuable emphasis on point of view, characterization, transforming common experiences and background into imaginative literature, using dialogue, and capturing authentic physical details. The potential writer is urged to keep a notebook in which to record events that might be incorporated into stories. Such notebooks should also contain one's musings and imaginings, which might in time yield raw material for writers. The examples of effective writing have been chosen thoughtfully and are directly relevant to each topic under discussion.

Conrad, Barnaby, et al. *The Complete Guide to Writing Fiction*. Cincinnati: Writer's Digest Books, 1990.
The celebrated author Barnaby Conrad, assisted by the staff of the Santa Barbara Writers' Conference, touches on writing all kinds of fiction but is especially strong in his comments on writing novels and short fiction. Special attention is focused on invention and on how to invite the muse when one is trying to write but finds it difficult to get started. Such topics as writer's block, dealing with literary agents, direct submissions of material, preparation of manuscripts, multiple submissions, and protecting one's original writing are discussed in sufficient detail to give writers better control over the business aspects of their profession. The 320 pages of this book are filled with the sage advice of experienced writers that every writer will benefit from reading and following.

Daigh, Ralph, ed. *Maybe You Should Write a Book*. Englewood Cliffs, N.J.: Prentice-Hall, 1973.
Writers in several genres can benefit from looking into this book, although it is aimed primarily at novelists. The advice given is varied and authoritative, coming as it does from such well-known writers as James Michener, Joyce Carol Oates, John D. MacDonald, Saul Bellow, Taylor Caldwell, Isaac Asimov, Norman Vincent Peale, Jessamyn West, and Bruce Catton. Because of the broad range of writers represented in the book, the overview the text provides is unusually rich. The level of writing is, as might be expected given the accomplishments of the authors represented, superb.

Dibell, Ansen. *Plot: How to Build Short Stories and Novels That Don't Sag, Fizzle, or Trail Off*. Cincinnati: Writer's Digest Books, 1988.
In this book, the author painstakingly details how to formulate plot in such ways as to make short stories and novels credible and to keep reader interest high. His step-by-step development makes it easy for users of the book to adopt its suggestions, ranging from grand openings (chapter 2) to pacing and transition (chapter 9), in practical ways. The chief emphasis in this book is that of keeping interest levels high as stories proceed. A tightly interwoven plot succeeds in doing this

more than any other single element in imaginative writing, and the skill is one that can be learned through the processes suggested in this clear, coherent book, which is discussed further in chapter 1 of this bibliography.

Dillard, Annie. *Living by Fiction*. New York: Harper & Row, 1982.
By referring to specific pieces of fiction, Annie Dillard shows how various writers have handled such questions as characterization, point of view, narration, and time elements, particularly in extended fictions such as novels. She addresses the effect that literary critics have on literary production and upon authors' success. Her chapter 9, entitled "Can Fiction Interpret the World?," is particularly engaging, especially her allusions to *Moby Dick* in "How a Whale Means." She ends with a chapter, the eleventh in the book, that asks the question "Does the world have meaning?" Dillard'suggestion is that literature and the people who write it help to give meaning, or at least refine the meaning inherent within it.

_____. *The Writing Life*. New York: Harper & Row, 1989.
Less structured than *Living by Fiction*, this book essentially contains Dillard's informal, intensely personal musings about writing. This short book, which uses parable and metaphor to make its most important points, was aimed at writers but reached a wide general audience and became a best-selling nonfiction item. Notable in what Dillard writes is her obvious geographical interest: She writes with considerable feeling about the area of northwest Washington State with which she is intimately familiar, and about Cape Cod.

Elwood, Maren. *Characters Make Your Story*. Boston: The Writer, Inc., 1987.
The sequential development of this book from the simplest techniques of characterization to the most complex helps writers to master the broad variety of ways they can add flesh to their basic characters. The focus is most directly on the novel, although the book has implications for all genres of writing. The presentation is analytical and demonstrates that satisfactory characterization is the primary source of all effective writing. The examples are well chosen and show specifically how effective characterization is achieved.

Foster, E. M. "Aspects of the Novel." In *The Writer's Craft*, edited by John Hersey. New York: Alfred A. Knopf, 1974.
This essay, by the author of *A Passage to India*, is a classic among works that concentrate on the novel as a genre. Foster is especially strong in suggesting how authors can find the topics about which they are best equipped to write and how they can stimulate their writing by drawing from their experience, which must be unlocked from their unconscious minds in sufficiently accurate detail to enable them to mold it into stories that have a ring of truth and accuracy—both physical and mental. Individual chapters in Forster's book by the same title, which was

published in 1927, deal with story, people (characterization), plot, fantasy, prophecy, and pattern and rhythm. For further remarks about this collection, see other entries in this chapter as well as in chapters 1 and 5 of this bibliography.

Gardner, John. *The Art of Fiction: Notes on Craft for Young Writers.* New York: Alfred A. Knopf, 1984.
The late John Gardner, author of such powerful novels as *Grendel* and *The Sunlight Dialogues*, was also a gifted and inspiring teacher of creative writing; in this book, he synthesized principles tested over many years in the classroom and in his own writing. The first part of the book presents a general theory of fiction, while the second part focuses on specific technical matters. A number of exercises are included at the end of the book.

_____. *On Becoming a Novelist.* New York: Harper & Row, 1983.
Gardner completed this book only weeks before his death in a motorcycle accident. In it he addresses the three consuming questions that most of his writing students had when they began to work with him: (1) Am I talented enough? (2) How should I educate myself? and (3) Can I make a living from writing fiction? Gardner spends the first half of the book answering the first question, because he considered it fundamental. Besides sensitivity to language and an eye for significant detail, writers must, according to Gardner, have curiosity, self-awareness, detachment, and the kind of nerve that enables them to inhabit the lives and worlds of other people and to communicate these lives and worlds to disparate audiences.

Goldberg, Natalie. *The Wild Mind.* New York: Bantam, 1990.
This book contains extremely perceptive essays on what it is to be a writer. Its chapter on the novel is particularly searching and insightful, perhaps one of the best available anywhere. The treatment, although it covers such essentials as characterization, plot development, and dialogue, is not narrow in its focus. It gets to the essence of what it is to write novels, of what novelists set out to do, and of what their audiences demand. A first-rate, highly imaginative book.

Guthrie, A. B., Jr. *A Field Guide to Writing Fiction.* New York: HarperCollins, 1991.
Such Guthrie novels as *The Big Sky* were painted with a broad brush. This thin volume is valuable especially to those who aspire to be novelists because in it Guthrie pays special attention to creating scene and atmosphere, to capturing the physical realities about which one is writing. A major virtue of Guthrie's writing is the utter authenticity of scene that he creates. In this book, he provides insights into how he worked to achieve the verisimilitude that is the hallmark of his writing.

Hall, Oakley. *The Art and Craft of Writing a Novel.* Cincinnati: Writer's Digest Books, 1989.
Hall pays special attention to structure in this book, although he touches on invention, characterization, plot, theme, and point of view, all of which contribute in their own ways to the overall structure. The presentation is sequential and easy to follow. The process followed here will build the self-confidence of beginning writers in many subtle ways. Hall has, as a creative artist, wrestled with the problems tackled in the book. The practical approaches he suggests for dealing with them should put readers at ease as they work toward implementing the book's ideas.

Henry, Laurie, ed. *Novel and Short Story Writer's Market.* Cincinnati: Writer's Digest Books, 1989.
Chapters by Valerie Martin and Gayle Feldman, cited elsewhere in this chapter, are of particular use to writers of novels, as is the editor's section on small presses, which includes an in-depth discussion of two such presses. This book contains a considerable amount of material that is of lasting value, even though any book of this kind necessarily becomes dated quickly. Strongly recommended. For additional comments about this book, see chapter 1 of this bibliography; see also chapter 10 for comments on the 1992 edition of this annual, edited by Robin Gee.

Hill, Wycliffe A. *The Plot Genie: General Formula.* 5th ed. Hollywood, Calif.: The Gagnon, 1935.
This book was highly successful in the 1930's, and much of it is still of interest to novelists today. The first thirty-eight pages offer a general, in-depth discussion of plot. The remaining ninety-one pages consist essentially of a list of possible plots that fiction writers use, under such headings as "Male [Female] Characters," "Unusual Male [Female] Characters," "Obstacles to Love," and "Crises." For further information about this book, see chapter 1 of this bibliography.

Holinger, William. "Turning Experience into a Novel." In *The Writer's Handbook, 1987,* edited by Sylvia K. Burack. Boston: The Writer, Inc., 1987.
Defining fiction as heightened reality, Holinger acknowledges the role of exaggeration in writing fiction. Rather than outlining his first novel, *The Fence-Walker,* Holinger dredged up vivid scenes from his memory and wrote them, not paying much attention initially to where the discrete scenes would fit within the total work. He became greatly concerned with the climax of the novel, which he defines as the answer to the work's major dramatic question. He works toward his dramatic climax and then ends the novel as quickly as he can, realizing the drawn-out denouement, for which Charles Dickens was renowned, is not welcome in most modern fiction.

Hughes, Riley. *Finding Yourself in Print: A Guide to Writing Professionally.* New York: Franklin Watts' Vision Books, 1979.
In chapter 10 of this wide-ranging book, Hughes presents valuable general information about getting ideas for writing novels and offers specific information about writing historical novels. Its discussions of angles of narration, point of view, characterization, and the use of the flashback—all in chapter 8—will be useful to writers, as will the material on the resources of language in chapter 3. Particularly cogent is the advice on overwriting. The author urges writers and would-be writers to become practiced and accurate observers who write with verve, reminding readers that prose lives when it moves. The material on multiple submission of manuscripts and on marketing manuscripts is outdated.

James, Henry. "The Art of Fiction." In *The Writer's Craft*, edited by John Hersey. New York: Alfred A. Knopf, 1974.
In this landmark essay by one of the most renowned American writers, Henry James discusses the demands fiction places upon novelists. The essay is brief (eight pages) but pithy and specific. James is especially concerned with point of view, with the ethics of writing, and with the depiction of character. He is especially concerned with the question of how much omniscient authors should tell. They have a responsibility to their readers, but they also have an obligation not to violate completely the privacy of their characters, even though those characters are fictional. For further comments about this book, see chapters 1 and 5 of this bibliography.

_____. *The Complete Notebooks of Henry James.* Edited by Leon Edel and Lyall H. Powers. New York: Oxford University Press, 1987.
This carefully edited volume contains a treasure trove of materials that will be of extraordinary use to potential novelists. Of special interest besides the notebooks themselves are the pocket diaries (part 2 of the book) that James kept from 1909 to 1915. These reveal his distress with World War I and the artistic purposes to which he put his suffering during the difficult period. James's deathbed notes, dictated in December, 1915, the last month of his life, show his concerns and the continuing sharpness of his mind.

Koontz, Dean R. *How to Write Best-Selling Fiction.* Cincinnati: Writer's Digest Books, 1981.
Chapters 7 and 8, "Creating Believable Characters" and "Achieving Plausibility Through Character Motivation," respectively, are among the most interesting and useful ones in this book. Chapter 2, "Writing the Great American Novel," will puncture a few balloons, shatter a few long-held myths. For additional comments about this book, see below under "Science Fiction," as well as chapters 7 and 10 of this bibliography.

Lubbock, Percy. "The Craft of Fiction." In *The Writer's Craft*, edited by John Hersey. New York: Alfred A. Knopf, 1974.

This well-known essay by Lubbock places great emphasis on establishing point of view early in a story and on keeping a consistent point of view throughout. Lubbock stresses also the importance of close observation and accurate depiction of events and of physical props. He notes the importance of characterization and shows how dialogue and descriptive detail enhance the creation of characters within a story. For further comments about this collection, see chapters 1 and 5 of this bibliography.

McCormack, Thomas, ed. *Afterwords: Novelists on Their Novels*. New York: 1969.

Comments by authors about the creation of their own works can be extremely illuminating to writers. This collection is well balanced. It covers each of the following authors, who discuss the book that follows his or her name: Wright Morris (*One Day*); Mary Renault (*The King Must Die*); William Gass (*Omensetter's Luck*); Reynolds Price (*A Generous Man*); Truman Capote (*Other Voices, Other Rooms*); Norman Mailer (*Deer Park*); and others.

McLarn, Jack Clinton. *Writing Part-Time for Fun and Money*. Wilmington, Del.: Enterprise Publishing, 1978.

Writers of fiction will find considerable valuable material in this book, especially in chapter 9, which deals with writing fiction, including the novel. Appendix 1, which is about writing confessions, is also relevant. For additional comments about this book, see chapters 1, 7, 9, and 10 of this bibliography.

Mann, Thomas. "The Story of a Novel." In *The Writer's Craft*, edited by John Hersey. New York: Alfred A. Knopf, 1974.

Thomas Mann, whose writing brought him the Nobel Prize in Literature in 1929, discusses in some detail the making of his prodigious and complex novel, *Joseph the Provider*. He traces a historical idea as it progresses through the creative machinery he, as author, brought to it. In this compelling essay, Mann shows the kinds of judgment successful authors use as they decide the course their work will take, revealing the changes that took place during some of the revisions of the manuscript and explaining the reasons for these alterations. For further comments about this collection, see other entries in this chapter, as well as items in chapters 1 and 5 of this bibliography.

Marks, Percy. *The Craft of Writing*. New York: Grosset & Dunlap, 1932.

Of historical rather than immediate interest, Marks's comments on the purpose, material, and characters of fiction (chapter 5) and on the novel, including the psychological and realistic novel (chapter 7), are worth looking into. For further comments about this book, see chapter 1 of this bibliography.

Marston, Doris Ricker. *A Guide to Writing History*. Cincinnati: Writer's Digest Books, 1976.
Marston offers early chapters that deal with audience, motivation, and research, including interviewing. Chapter 10, on opening paragraphs, is directly relevant to novelists and short-fiction writers, and chapter 16, which identifies four kinds of history in fiction, is absolutely essential. Marston suggests how to market manuscripts, but her chief contribution is in her suggestions about how to produce them. For further comments on this title, see the entry under "The Adventure Novel," as well as chapters 1, 3, 5, and 7 of this bibliography.

Martin, Valerie. "Waiting for the Story to Start." In *Novel and Short Story Writer's Market*, edited by Laurie Henry. Cincinnati: Writer's Digest Books, 1989.
Martin offers ways for writers to stimulate their imaginations and probe their unconscious minds to draw forth memories on which they can build their creative writing. The recommendations are practical and should work for people who have difficulty getting started. For additional comments, look under "General Studies" in chapter 1 of this bibliography.

Mathieu, Aron M., ed. *The Creative Writer*. Cincinnati: Writer's Digest Books, 1961.
Patricia McGerr's contribution, "How I Plot a Novel," speaks directly to a topic that all novelists must consider carefully. The entire first section of the book focuses on the novel. For additional comments about this book, see below, as well as chapters 1, 4, and 7 of this bibliography.

Maugham, W. Somerset. *Strictly Personal*. Garden City, N.Y.: Doubleday, Doran, 1941. Reprint. New York: Arno Press, 1977.
In this autobiographical work that tells about Maugham's experiences during the first two years of World War II, which he spent in France and later in England, one learns how a sensitive novelist relates to the chaos that surrounds him and from this experience gains insights that will inform his later writing. For additional comments about this book, see chapter 8 of this bibliography.

_____. *The Summing Up*. Garden City, N.Y.: Doubleday, Doran, 1938. Reprint. New York: Penguin, 1978.
Among the autobiographical works that Maugham produced, this is perhaps the one that best shows him as the budding novelist. Chapter 43 tells about his early work, including his first novel, *Lisa of Lambeth* (1897). Chapters 62, 63, and 64 are especially relevant to novelists. In them, Maugham asks about the value of what one has written and suggests how to evaluate one's own work. Chapter 64 focuses particularly on the interconnections between philosophy and literature in writing. For further comments about this source, see chapter 8 of this bibliography.

Meredith, Robert C., and John D. Fitzgerald. *Structuring Your Novel: From Basic Idea to Finished Manuscript.* New York: Barnes & Noble Books, 1972.

Although this book is now dated in some of its information, the exercises are still useful and stimulating, and the two chapters on craftsmanship in writing are classics. It is helpful to read the short exposition on the common elements of the structure in a traditional novel (appendix 1). The exercises in chapter 1 that have to do with invention are good motivators for those who have trouble getting started with their writing. In a similar vein, chapter 10, "How to Write the First Chapter of a Novel," should help any writer to move into the process of writing rather than fretting about getting started.

Morris, Wright. *About Fiction: Reverent Reflections on the Nature of Fiction with Irreverent Observations About Writers, Readers, and Other Abuses.* New York: Harper & Row, 1975.

Among the chapters of this book (which are not numbered) the first, entitled "What Is Fiction?," and the second, "What Good Is It?," are challenging. However, the fifth chapter, "Fiction as Truth Maker and Life Enhancer," and the seventh, "On Being True-to-Life," have the most pertinent advice for writers and would-be writers. Morris is particularly strong in his powers of observation and in applying principles of photographic composition, in which he was well schooled, to writing.

Naylor, Phyllis Reynolds. *The Craft of Writing the Novel.* Boston: The Writer, Inc., 1989.

Naylor, herself a successful novelist, guides the reader through the steps of practicing the craft of writing novels. The process described is well sequenced and moves slowly and interestingly enough to help readers apply the techniques discussed to their own creative enterprises. To a large extent, Naylor demystifies the daunting task of planning a novel and executing the plan. The author shows potential writers how to use what they know best—the commonplaces of their lives and environments—as the substance of their writing. The material on point of view demonstrates how a story told from one perspective might fail, while a shift in point of view might rescue it from obscurity.

Nin, Anaïs. *The Future of the Novel.* New York: Macmillan, 1968.

The title chapter of this book is chapter 7 and does not fully represent what the book is about. Most of the book gives knowledgeable advice to novelists, beginning with chapter 1, which encourages writers to proceed from the dream (conception) outward. Of particular use are chapters 4, 5, and 6, which deal, respectively, with the genesis of a story idea, the genesis of a writer's diary, and diary versus fiction. Nin clearly understands the autobiographical nature of much writing in this field, and these three chapters take that tendency into full account. For further comments about this source, see chapter 8 of this bibliography.

O'Connor, Flannery. "The Nature and Aim of Fiction." In *The Writer's Craft*, edited by John Hersey. New York: Alfred A. Knopf, 1974.
In this essay, O'Connor is much concerned with the compelling question of progression in fiction, of how successful writers craft their sentences in such ways that they move gracefully from point to point, constantly orienting their readers to where they are and to where they are going. At only ten pages, the essay is brief, but the subject on which it focuses is significant to anyone who is concerned with achieving unity and well-controlled emphasis in the piece of writing. For additional comments on this essay, look under "General Studies" in chapter 1 of this bibliography.

Orvis, Mary Burchard. *The Art of Writing Fiction*. New York: Prentice-Hall, 1948.
It is interesting to compare this book from the past with more recent ones, many of which address similar topics. Orvis is more authoritarian than most recent writers in this field, as can be seen in chapter 3, which deals with the central point of command in a story. Chapters 7, which deals with the "angle of narration," and 10, "Digging Beneath the Surface," are still worth reading. Chapter 11, which deals with social communication in fiction, is ahead of its time.

Paris Review. Writers at Work: The Paris Review Interviews. New York: Viking Press, published periodically.
These volumes appear annually and have been edited by such luminaries as Alfred Kazin, Van Wyck Books, Malcolm Cowley, and Joyce Carol Oates. Each volume contains extensive, in-depth interviews with such authors as Edward Albee, Ernest Hemingway, Arthur Miller, Norman Mailer, Evelyn Waugh, E. B. White, E. L. Doctorow, Lawrence Durrell, Robert Frost, T. S. Eliot, and Harold Pinter. Each volume is extremely worthwhile and helps readers and writers to develop a realistic view of how major writers write and of how they view their writing. See further comments on this series in chapter 8 of this bibliography.

Polking, Kirk, Jean Chimsky, and Rose Adkins, eds. *The Beginning Writer's Answer Book*. 2d ed. Cincinnati: Writer's Digest Books, 1978.
Listed also in chapters 4 and 6, this book pays particular attention to fiction in chapter 12, which demonstrates how to build and sustain conflict, how to create believable characters, and how to market fiction. Chapter 16, "Creating the Novel," makes some deceptively simple suggestions that can result in more polished writing. Among them, the first admonition is to know the mechanics of expression. The writers then consider how to switch point of view effectively, how to handle the passage of time, techniques of heightening suspense, and the art of developing characters that convince and entice readers. The chapters on working with collaborators and finding agents are useful and practical.

Polti, Georges. *The Thirty-six Dramatic Situations*. Boston: The Writer, Inc., 1988.
Polti's remarkable analysis of what constitutes plot has been of great help to many playwrights and novelists. Polti narrows the types of dramatic situations down to thirty-six basic plots upon which, he contends, all plays and novels are based. The book is not formulaic, but it is thought-provoking and provides a fine stimulus to the creative imagination. Polti's extensive knowledge of dramatic literature and of prose fiction makes it possible to arrive at significant generalizations about the nature of literature and of the creative process.

Price, Reynolds. *Clear Pictures: First Loves, First Guides*. New York: Atheneum, 1989.
Reynolds Price's autobiography is extremely interesting in terms of methodology. Price's most remote memory was unlocked when he underwent hypnosis to control pain following spinal surgery and the hypnosis brought forth in him a surge of memory that resulted in this book. Price reveals an incredible flood of details about his past. Those familiar with his novels can easily see how he transformed the realities of his early life into the stuff of which most of his novels have been made. For further comments about this book, see chapter 8 of this bibliography.

Rees, Clair F. *Profitable Part-Time/Full-Time Freelancing*. Cincinnati: Writer's Digest Books, 1980.
Chapter 9 of this book discusses moving from the writing of articles to the writing of full-length books. Although it does not necessarily focus on the novel, much that it says has relevance for that genre. For additional comments on this entry, see chapters 3 and 9 of this bibliography.

Rico, Gabriele Lusser. *Writing the Natural Way: Using Right-Brain Techniques to Release Your Experience*. Los Angeles: J. P. Tarcher, 1983.
Rare is the novelist who will not benefit from reading this book, because a major part of the novelist's job is to retrieve from the unconscious mind the stuff of which novels are made. The book, although directed toward college students in writing courses, has much to offer a broader audience, notably anyone who is serious about learning how to devise and structure stories. Rico's methods of clustering are excellent. Chapters 5, "Discovering Design," and 6, "Recurrences: The Unifying Web," seem particularly fruitful, as is chapter 9, "Wedding Word to Image." For further comments on this book, refer to chapter 1 of this bibliography.

Rinehart, Mary Roberts. *Writing Is Work*. Boston: The Writer, Inc., 1939.
Despite its age, this book, by a prolific writer, has relevance to contemporary readers and to those who write fiction. Rinehart devotes twenty-five pages to answering the important question, "Where do writers get ideas?" She notes how

writers' prospects improved after World War I, before which they were largely at the mercy of publishers who paid them whatever they wanted to pay them and exploited them unmercifully. Rinehart's comments about the writing methods of Arnold Bennett and O. Henry are revealing and fascinating. They indicate quite clearly that there is no one way to write, despite the generalizations one can make about the writing process and about writing techniques.

Stern, Jerome. *Making Shapely Fiction.* New York: W. W. Norton, 1991.
Stern's advice is particularly relevant to writers of long fiction because it demonstrates well how precise and accurate description, dialogue, and conflict sustain fiction that deals at length with complex situations. The sections on characterization, conflict (including climax), plot structure, and thematic impact are well presented. Stern emphasizes the need for balance in works of longer fiction and demonstrates how balance is achieved. A classic simplicity is inherent in an artistically balanced work; Stern shows how to achieve this simplicity. For further comments about this book, see chapter 1 of this bibliography.

Strickland, Bill, ed. *On Being a Writer.* Cincinnati: Writer's Digest Books, 1989.
The advice Strickland has gleaned from thirty-one notable writers should be of help to fiction writers, particularly novelists. Among the authors represented in this collection are Ernest Hemingway, Erica Jong, William Faulkner, and Ellen Goodman, all of whom go into the technique and technicalities of their writing in considerable detail.

Surmelian, Leon. *Techniques of Fiction Writing: Measure and Madness.* Garden City, N.Y.: Doubleday, 1968.
This comprehensive book, whose tone is informal and relaxed, covers such important matters as the uses of first and third person narration, how to set the scene and the components of scene, the development of fictional characters, and the handling of time, including stream of consciousness and the flashback. Despite its age, the book still offers cogent advice to those who wish to write fiction. The information provided is of value to novelists as well as to short-fiction writers. For additional comments on this book, see chapter 1 of this bibliography.

Tobias, Ronald B. *Theme and Strategy.* Cincinnati: Writer's Digest Books, 1990.
Tobias rises above the obvious in this book and focuses on the intellectual approach to writing, on how to develop general, socially significant themes in forms more appealing for the political or social essay. This book is for writers who are careful planners, writers with ideas they wish to ventilate in a literary form that will make them appealing to readers. Tobias is very much concerned with structure. He tests various thematic approaches, demonstrating which ones work and which ones do not, always suggesting the small alterations that make

the unworkable more workable, more likely to succeed. This book, at times profound, is intellectually solid and stimulates its readers to think nonlinearly and deeply about their motives for investing large amounts of time in their writing.

Turco, Lewis. *Dialogue*. Cincinnati: Writer's Digest Books, 1989.
Dialogue does more to add verisimilitude to any fictional work than any other single factor. Because characters are best revealed by showing them rather than telling about them, they are best revealed through what they say. Their dialogue must be clear and consistent if they are to be credible as characters. Turco, through the use of valuable illustrative examples, discusses dialogue in all its forms, from the short, staccato speech used to build tension to the thoughtfully delivered soliloquy that reveals the inmost feelings, fears, and wishes of fictional characters. Turco understands the ways in which dialogue among characters must be balanced, and he is especially effective in revealing the interrelationships among the speeches given by characters in any work of fiction.

Uzzell, Thomas H. *The Technique of the Novel: A Handbook on the Craft of Long Narrative*. Rev. ed. New York: Citadel Press, 1959.
This revision of Uzzell's book from the 1947 original is of particular interest and value for two of its chapters: chapter 2, which considers the question of internal demand, or how writers' temperaments affect the kinds of writing they will do, and chapter 3, which considers the external demands, the demands of the marketplace. All authors must reach an accommodation between these two sometimes conflicting demands if they are to succeed. Much of the rest of the book has been superseded by more recent considerations, but much that Uzzell says still has a ring of truth about it.

Wharton, Edith. *The Writing of Fiction*. New York: Octagon Books, 1966, 1970.
This posthumous publication of renowned novelist Edith Wharton's reflections on the writing of fiction deals in chapter 3 with the writing of novels and in chapter 4 with characterization and situation in novels. The fifth chapter analyzes some of the novels of Marcel Proust from an analytical and structural viewpoint. Wharton, a great storyteller, shows how a sensitive writer develops the ears and eyes of the novelist and uses the senses to transform commonplace experience into something unique and interesting to a broad range of readers, bringing to them the vicarious illusions that novels at their best create. The writing in this book is a model of careful construction and polished presentation.

Whitney, Phyllis A. *Guide to Fiction Writing*. Boston: The Writer, Inc., 1988.
Phyllis Whitney shares with her readers some of the techniques that have made her a successful and much-published writer of fiction. Part 1, "Methods and Process," discusses various approaches to the writing of fiction, from organizing a writer's notebook to planning and plotting short stories and novels. She gives

good advice about how to generate ideas and about how to use one's inspirations productively in the writing process, sometimes as a means of overcoming writer's block. Part 2, "Techniques," focuses on such practical matters as point of view, writing beginnings and endings, sustaining middles, controlling conflict, building suspense, using surprise, establishing goals, handling the time elements of narratives, using flashbacks, and building effective transitions.

———————. *Writing Juvenile Stories and Novels*. Boston: The Writer, Inc., 1976.
See "General Studies" under chapters 1 and 7 of this bibliography.

Wilbur, L. Perry. *How to Write Books That Sell*. Chicago: Contemporary Books, 1979.
Wilbur's treatment is comprehensive. The information moves from an initial chapter, "What It Takes to Write a Novel," through a discussion of how to get ideas for best-sellers and how to construct chapters. Wilbur discusses the juvenile market, the market for religion and inspirational books, and the historical romance (see "Romance," below). The chapters on marketing and on literary agents are worth reading. For further comments about this book, see chapters 7 and 10 of this bibliography.

Williams, Nan Schram. *Confess for Profit: Writing and Selling the Personal Story—A Comprehensive Guide*. Los Angeles: Douglas-West Publishers, 1973.
Williams discusses various methods of planning, plotting, and writing stories as first-person narratives, all methods that have worked for her. Chapter 4, "Sex Themes Without Obscenity," is among the strongest in the book. Also noteworthy is chapter 7, "The Short Story vs. the Novelette." Williams presents information about how to prepare and market manuscripts. Her guide to book publishers and magazines, useful in its day, is now dated. For more information about this book, see chapters 8 and 10.

Wolfe, Thomas. "The Story of a Novel." In *The Writer's Craft*, edited by John Hersey. New York: Alfred A. Knopf, 1974.
Thomas Wolfe, whose work was overtly autobiographical despite its fictional trappings, discusses in detail the making of a huge novel, the first of several that essentially focus on his own life. Looked upon in his lifetime as a quite undisciplined writer whose work required substantial editorial revision, Wolfe wrote using a whirlwind of detail. His work leaves little out, as can be seen, for example, in the minute-by-minute detail of the death of Ben Gant, the protagonist's brother in the novel and Wolfe's brother in real life.

Woolf, Virginia. "A Writer's Diary." In *The Writer's Craft*, edited by John Hersey. New York: Alfred A. Knopf, 1974.

These excerpts from Virginia Woolf's diary for the years 1929 to 1931 focus on the responsibility of fiction writers. Woolf gives insights into her own method of crafting her delicate stories, such as *To the Lighthouse* and *Mrs. Dalloway*. Woolf shows how restraint and subtlety—what is left unsaid and unshown rather than what is said and shown—can add to the impact of fiction. For additional comments about this collection, see other entries in this chapter as well as in chapters 1 and 5 of this bibliography.

The Writing Business: A Poets and Writers Handbook. Edited jointly by the editors of *Coda: A Poets and Writers Newsletter*. New York: Poets and Writers, 1985.
Part 3 of this book is its most comprehensive section. It is concerned primarily with the novel and gives good advice for marketing a first novel. It also discusses the second novel and beyond. It offers sections on such underground topics as screenwriting, pornographic writing, ghostwriting and collaboration, novelizations of works from other genres, young adult novels, and genre fiction in general. The book also contains valuable information about small presses and advice about how writers can establish their own presses. For additional comments on this source, see chapters 1, 3, 5, 9, and 10 of this bibliography.

Zinsser, William, ed. *Paths of Resistance: The Art and Craft of the Political Novel*. Boston: Houghton Mifflin, 1989.
This book is exceptionally interesting for what it has to say about the rhetoric of politics and for the broad range of markets it suggests. The selections are pithy and direct, written in all cases by people who have had considerable experience and have enjoyed considerable success in writing major works of political significance.

Creating Characters

Leavitt, Hart Day. *An Eye for People: A Writer's Guide to Character*. New York: Bantam, 1970.
This book is part of Bantam's useful Stop, Look, and Write series. It is concerned primarily with the important question of achieving historical accuracy in presenting fictional characters. Section 5 of part 1 considers costumes, background, and props. Section 7 focuses on how to deal with contradictions within a single image, and section 8 addresses the problem of dealing with changes in time. In part 2, section 2 deals with the presentation of children, section 3 with presenting members of another generation, section 4 with presenting the interactions between generations, and section 6 with presenting burlesques and grotesques in writing.

MacDonald, John D. "How a Character Becomes Believable." In *The Mystery Writer's Handbook*, edited by Lawrence Treat. Cincinnati: Writer's Digest Books, 1984.
MacDonald discusses the limitations of first-person narration but shows ways to handle it if the occasion calls for it. His chief objection is that in first-person narration it is more difficult to show than to tell, so the maxim to show what characters do rather than tell about it is hard to observe. MacDonald considers the third-person-singular form of narration the most versatile to use. It gives authors a freedom not enjoyed in the first-person narrative. He also cautions against oversimplifying characters; villains should not be all bad, heroes not all good. The personalities of the characters should be balanced and authentic, as they are in real people.

Peck, Robert Newton. *Fiction Is Folks: How to Create Unforgettable Characters*. Cincinnati: Writer's Digest Books, 1987.
This short book is fun to read. The writer is imaginative and writes with clarity and with an appealing wit. He is well attuned to the nuances of human behavior as reflected not only in speech and surface appearance but also in small elements of dress and action. What small physical anomalies do characters have? What habits do they reveal by their actions? What are their sensitivities, and how are they revealed nonverbally? How does word choice help to depict and define characters? Peck's own success as a writer stems largely from his lifelike characterization, a skill that he practices quite naturally but here analyzes in the kind of detail that makes it accessible to other writers.

Swain, Dwight V. *Creating Characters*. Cincinnati: Writer's Digest Books, 1990.
In particularly precise, direct, and lucid language, Swain takes readers through a step-by-step approach to inventing characters and building them into believable literary personages. The material on physical detail and on creating dialogue is particularly vibrant. The author urges writers to show rather than tell, and his exercises are all aimed in the direction of showing writers how to achieve this vital skill. The examples drawn from literature are well selected and completely pertinent to what is being discussed in each section of the book. Swain succeeds better than most authors in presenting rationales for the generally accepted rules that govern characterization.

The Adventure Novel

Cussler, Clive. "Writing the Suspense-Adventure Novel." In *The Writer's Handbook, 1987*, edited by Sylvia K. Burack. Boston: The Writer, Inc., 1987.
Cussler notes that writing is hard work and that when he finishes a piece of writing, it is as though the clouds part and he is free again. He emphasizes the need for writers always to consider their readers above all else. His first step is

always to grab a concept that captures his readers' fancies. He realizes that what once appealed to readers of adventure stories will not appeal today. Therefore, writers in this genre must keep attuned to what readers are willing and able to accept. He considers structure the most important element in any novel, more important certainly than characterization, plot, or setting, fundamental as those elements are. However, a strong structure must underlie everything else in a novel.

Marston, Doris Ricker. *A Guide to Writing History*. Cincinnati: Writer's Digest Books, 1976.
Because much adventure writing has a base in history, this book will be of use to practitioners in this genre. Of special relevance is chapter 16, which outlines four types of history in fiction. For a fuller discussion of this book, see above. Also see chapters 1, 3, 5, and 7 of this bibliography.

Newton, Michael. *How to Write Action Adventure Novels*. Cincinnati: Writer's Digest Books, 1989.
Michael Newton has frequently demonstrated in his own writing his ability to create swashbuckling characters and to place them in situations of high adventure. He demonstrates in this book how writers can use suspense and surprise to their distinct advantage in creating novels that bristle with excitement. This book does much to stimulate the creative imagination. It invites the combination of daydreaming and solid research that results in gripping adventure novels, some of them based upon historical incidents. Newton assesses realistically the markets for writing of this sort.

The Mystery, Crime, and Horror Novel

Brady, John, and Jean M. Fredette, eds. *Fiction Writer's Market*. Cincinnati: Writer's Digest Books, 1981.
Specific information about writing mystery novels is provided in Ross Macdonald's essay in this book. Macdonald discusses such matters as how to build and sustain suspense, the uses of coincidence, and developing characters for mystery novels. Phyllis Whitney's essay on the gothic novel is also relevant, as is Steven King's essay on horror fiction. See an additional listing for this collection in the "General Studies" section of this chapter.

Burack, Sylvia K., ed. *How to Write and Sell Mystery Fiction*. Boston: The Writer, Inc., 1990.
Burack has assembled twenty-one chapters—by such successful mystery writers as Joan Aiken, Robert Barnard, Rex Burns, Max Byrd, Mary Blount Christian, Stanley Ellin, P. D. James, Ian Stuart, Michael Underwood, and Phyllis A.

Whitney—that focus on writing police procedurals, detective stories, spy thrillers, true-crime fiction, psychological suspense novels, and other types of fiction in this genre. The advice on how to solve the technical problems unique to mystery fiction is of particular benefit to the fledgling mystery writer, although it is also appropriate to experienced writers in the field.

Macdonald, Ross. *On Crime Writing*. Santa Barbara, Calif.: Capra Press, 1973.
This slim volume consists of two essays: "The Writer as Detective Hero" and "Writing the Galton Case." Macdonald was a consummate writer of crime novels, and his advice is doubly valuable, informed by an artist's sensibility as well as a sharp awareness of the realities of the marketplace. These two essays are reprinted in a collection of Macdonald's essays, reviews, and occasional pieces, *Self-Portrait: Ceaselessly Into the Past*, edited by Ralph B. Sipper (Santa Barbara, Calif.: Capra Press, 1981).

Mathieu, Aron M., ed. *The Creative Writer*. Cincinnati: Writer's Digest Books, 1961.
This is a most comprehensive book, which, although dated in some specifics, has a great deal of interest for modern readers. Edward Aswell's contribution, "Plotting a Mystery Novel by the Question and Answer Method," is gripping. It can be read profitably in concert with Patricia McGerr's chapter, "How I Plot a Novel." For additional comments about this book, see "General Studies" above, as well as chapters 1, 4, and 7 of this bibliography.

_____. *Armed and Dangerous: A Writer's Guide to Weapons*. Cincinnati: Writer's Digest Books, 1990.
This book is based upon excerpts from the most widely recognized mystery writing and is factually dependable. Anyone who wishes to write mystery fiction needs to read this book, as well as Serita Stevens' *Deadly Doses* (see below), both of which will keep the budding mystery writer from making technical and logistical mistakes. This book is extremely specific in its survey of weapons and of the effects of these weapons under a broad variety of circumstances. This book is the first in the "Howdunit Series," of which Stevens' book is also a part. The books in this series are major reference works for writers of mystery fiction.

Newton, Michael. *How to Write Action-Adventure Novels*. Cincinnati: Writer's Digest Books, 1989.
The most valuable portion of this book is the part of chapter 4 that deals with outlines versus inspiration. Newton, himself a successful, publishing writer of adventure novels, knows that writers do not sit passively and wait for inspiration. Rather, they set themselves research and writing tasks and work doggedly to complete those tasks. Newton has good suggestions on writing the hook, defining

the quest, establishing believability, and achieving clarity. For additional comments about this book, refer to chapter 10 of this bibliography.

Nolan, William F. *How to Write Horror Fiction*. Cincinnati: Writer's Digest Books, 1991.
The lesson mystery writers will learn from this book is the information it offers about how much gore to include in stories about how far to go. The book is also strong on pacing and suspense, providing practical information on how to keep stories frightening from beginning to end.

Norville, Barbara. *Writing the Modern Mystery*. Cincinnati: Writer's Digest Book, 1986.
Norville is well versed on trends in mystery writing and suggests ways to produce writing in this genre that will immediately attract the attention of editors and agents. The modern mystery is fast-moving and often high-tech. It is in many ways slick, and the basic formula for writing it is defined in this book in such a way that one can master the craft with a reasonable expenditure of effort. The material on building suspense and on characterization and point of view is particularly useful and applicable to modern writing techniques in this clearly defined field.

O'Cork, Shannon. *How to Write Mysteries*. Cincinnati: Writer's Digest Books, 1989.
This book is strong in its suggestion of invention techniques in the formulation of engaging mysteries, but its chief strength is in its advice on how to structure plot, which is essential to writing mysteries that are not filled with contradictions and inconsistencies. A mystery is a closely woven fabric that can easily become unraveled if small details do not add up to a consistent and coherent part of the complicated structure that every mystery story is. O'Cork has mastered the art of mystery writing well herself, and this book has grown out of her background in writing and reading extensively in the field.

Provost, Gary. *How to Write and Sell True Crime*. Cincinnati: Writer's Digest Books, 1991.
Provost realizes that ideas float around in the air that surrounds everyone. All the writer has to do is pluck them out. Local crime stories, reported usually in detail in both newspapers and police reports, are the stuff of which best-selling crime novels are made, and the basic information is easily available to the resourceful writers who seek it out. He tells how anyone can gain access to police reports, court records, and court transcripts.

Stevens, Serita Deborah. *Deadly Doses: A Writer's Guide to Poisons*. Cincinnati: Writer's Digest Books, 1990.

Writing Novels

This book, along with Michael Newton's *Armed and Dangerous*, is a basic reference work for anyone who wishes to write mystery fiction and also makes interesting reading for those who enjoy mysteries. In 320 pages, *Deadly Doses* covers every conceivable kind of poison, indicating the dosages and kinds of effects in which each of them results. It indicates the time it takes for each poison to take effect, the physical manifestations of poisons in the systems of their victims, and antidotes to the poisons. The book is remarkably comprehensive and accurate, wholly consistent with similar information given in recognized textbooks in physical diagnosis and toxicology.

Treat, Lawrence, ed. *Mystery Writer's Handbook, by the Mystery Writers of America*. Cincinnati: Writer's Digest Books, 1990.
This useful handbook, much of it based on responses to questionnaires distributed to members of the Mystery Writers of America, has appeared in many editions, all of them serviceable, although the later editions have the best information about markets. The first chapters in most editions focus on the writer and quote responses from the questionnaire; the second section addresses preparing to write; the third is on getting down to writing; the fourth discusses how to write; the fifth addresses types of mysteries, and the sixth analyzes how to prepare and market manuscripts and how to engage a literary agent. Among contributors to most volumes are such notable mystery writers as Rex Stout, Phyllis A. Whitney, Aaron Mark Stein, Dorothy Salisbury Davis, Hillary Waugh, and Pauline Bloom. The writing is direct and lucid; the suggestions are eminently practical.

Waugh, Hillary. *Hillary Waugh's Guide to Mysteries and Mystery Writing*. Cincinnati: Writer's Digest Books, 1991.
Waugh, a mystery writer himself, reviews the history of the genre from Edgar Allan Poe to Mickey Spillane. He analyzes some of the most renowned mysteries of all time and in so doing suggests many ploys that current mystery writers can use. He understands well what makes a mystery succeed, and he shares this information gracefully with readers.

Science Fiction

Asimov, Isaac. "Science Fiction Today." *The Writer's Handbook, 1987*, edited by Sylvia K. Burack. Boston: The Writer, Inc., 1987.
One of the most prolific science-fiction writers of his day, Asimov reflects on the status of the genre from the time he, as an eighteen-year-old, submitted his first story. At the time (the late 1930's), there were only three magazines in the field, but pulp magazines existed in profusion, giving writers many outlets for the stories they produced. Now—although, as Asimov says, science fiction is "big time"—the magazine field is not much larger than it was in the 1930's. The difference is that, whereas earlier science-fiction writers usually kept writing

stories and a small group virtually monopolized the field, people who currently make their mark with science-fiction stories usually have the opportunity to turn to writing novels, so that there is movement in the field.

Bradbury, Ray. *Zen in the Art of Writing: Essays on Creativity.* Santa Barbara, Calif.: Capra Press, 1989.

Ray Bradbury is seen by many readers of both mainstream and science fiction as the dean of the latter genre. In this book, he addresses the question of creativity in ways that will be interesting to all fiction writers, but particularly to those who wish to write science fiction. The thirteen-page essay on the secret mind, the following fifteen-page essay on Zen in the art of writing, and the subsequent nineteen-page essay on creativity are the best portions in the book, all of which is engaging and thought-provoking.

Brady, John, and Jean M. Fredette, eds. *Fiction Writer's Market.* Cincinnati: Writer's Digest Books, 1981.

Besides the comments on science fiction in this book (mentioned earlier in chapter 2 as well as in chapter 1), James Gunn's essay on the topic is thoughtful and offers sound guidance to would-be science-fiction novelists.

Bretnor, Reginald, ed. *The Craft of Science Fiction.* New York: Harper & Row, 1976.

Bretnor's essay, "SF: The Challenge to the Writer," both defines the market and suggests the difficulties that lurk in it. His recommendations are practical, as are John Brunner's in "The SF Novel." Frank Herbert's essay, "Men on Other Planets" (its sexist language notwithstanding) is also useful. For further comments about this book, see chapters 1 and 6.

Card, Orson Scott. *How to Write Science Fiction and Fantasy.* Cincinnati: Writer's Digest Books, 1990.

This brief book is worth its weight in royalty checks. Into its 144 pages it crams practical and easily applied information about how to write in the two genres it addresses. Card identifies markets, indicating what the current needs of many of them are. He gives helpful information about query letters, the preparation of manuscripts, and their submission. His information about remuneration is current for 1990 and will be updated as the need occurs. Card has an intimate and comprehensive knowledge of a field in which he has succeeded as a writer.

Clareson, Thomas D., ed. *SF: The Other Side of Realism—Essays on Modern Fantasy and Science Fiction.* Bowling Green, Ohio: Bowling Green University Popular Press, 1971.

In Clareson's title essay, this frequent contributor to the field presents an interesting perspective on the antirealism of science fiction. Other noteworthy essays are those by Lionel Stevenson, "The Artistic Problem: Science Fiction as Romance," which takes a point of view quite similar to Clareson's; James Blish's "On Science Fiction Criticism," which packs a great deal into its four pages; and Samuel R. Delany's "About Five Thousand One Hundred and Seventy-five Words," which also appears in his *The Jewel-Hinged Jaw*, reviewed below. For additional comments about this source, see chapter 6 of this bibliography.

Delany, Samuel R. *The Jewel-Hinged Jaw: Notes on the Language of Science Fiction.* Elizabethtown, N.Y.: Dragon Press, 1977.
The imagination with which this book bristles makes it good reading. Of special interest are parts 3, "Writing S-F," and 5, "Autobiographical Postscript." Part 3 has subsections on the thickening plot (pages 163-170), on characters (pages 171-178), and "On Pure Story Telling" (pages 179-190). Each of these subsections is well presented. The autobiographical postscript that comprises part 5 is whimsical and witty, yet filled with insight.

Giblin, James Cross. *Writing Books for Young People.* Boston: Mass.: The Writer, Inc., 1990.
This highly practical book about writing for young people devotes considerable space to a discussion of science fiction and fantasy as genres that are important in young people's literature. Giblin identifies what children at various age levels accept easily, and in chapter 6 he addresses the matter of common pitfalls that face writers in this field. For further comments about this book, refer to chapter 7 of this bibliography.

Jarvis, Sharon, ed. *Inside Outer Space: Science Fiction Professionals Look at Their Craft.* New York: Frederick Ungar, 1985.
Each of the ten essays in this collection is valuable in its way. Among the most penetrating are the editor's "What Does a Woman Know About Science Fiction, Anyway?," David Stuart Schiff's "The Glorious Past, Erratic Present, and Questionable Future of Specialty Presses," and Ron Goulart's "Historical Hysteria or Humor in Science Fiction." The suggestions about how to get science fiction published are sensible and should be of great use to novice writers.

Koontz, Dean R. *How to Write Best-Selling Fiction.* Cincinnati: Writer's Digest Books, 1981.
Chapter 12 focuses specifically on writing science fiction and mysteries. The material is presented succinctly and well. Science-fiction and mystery writers may also want to look at chapter 3, "The Changing Marketplace." For additional comments about this book, see above as well as chapters 7 and 10 of this bibliography.

Malzberg, Barry N. *The Engines of Night: Science Fiction in the Eighties.* Garden City, N.Y.: Doubleday, 1982.

Malzberg, author of more than one hundred books, including nearly thirty science-fiction novels, presents interesting comments about science fiction and the academy. Malzberg also goes into the history of science fiction, the golden age of the pulps, in which much contemporary science fiction had its origins, the conventions of writing science fiction, and a view of the future of this genre. Malzberg is exceptionally well informed in the field.

Myers, Robert E., ed. *The Intersection of Science Fiction and Philosophy: Critical Studies.* Westport, Conn.: Greenwood Press, 1983.

Among the most intriguing chapters in this excellent collection is Alexandra Aldridge's "Science Fiction and Emerging Social Values," which raises extremely searching questions. Chapter 10, Paul Rice's "Metaphor as a Way of Saying the Self in Science Fiction," is penetrating and provocative, as is Frans van der Bogert's "Nature Through Science Fiction." Chapter 14, David E. White's "Medical Morals and Narrative Necessity," raises interesting ethical questions and is thoughtfully presented.

Scithers, George H., Darrell Schweitzer, and John M. Ford. *On Writing Science Fiction.* Philadelphia, Pa.: Owlswick Press, 1981.

These three editors of Isaac Asimov's *Science Fiction Magazine* have an encompassing view of the field they are writing about, and they explore knowledgeably such matters as where to get ideas (chapter 3), how to establish and sustain conflict (chapter 4), how to develop character (chapter 5), how to build plot (chapter 6), and how to create background (chapter 7). Most interesting, though, is chapter 8, "Science: The Art of Knowing," which is spirited and specific. The book is rich with examples that are discussed in intelligent detail.

Silverberg, Robert, ed. *Robert Silverberg's Worlds of Wonder: Exploring the Craft of Science Fiction.* New York: Warner Books, 1987.

A distinctive combination of anthology and how-to manual, this book, while primarily directed at aspiring writers of science fiction, will be of value to anyone studying the craft of fiction in general. Silverberg begins with a long autobiographical essay, "The Making of a Science-Fiction Writer," which focuses on his evolving understanding of the art of storytelling. This is followed by a selection of thirteen outstanding science-fiction stories (among the authors represented are Alfred Bester, C. L. Moore, Cordwainer Smith, and Philip K. Dick). Appended to each story is an analysis by Silverberg, again focused on matters of craft. The volume concludes with suggestions for further reading.

Williamson, J. N., ed. *How to Write Tales of Horror, Fantasy, and Science Fiction.* Cincinnati: Writer's Digest Books, 1987.

Writing Novels 47

Among his cast of contributors, Williamson numbers such luminaries as Ray Bradbury (on new ghosts from old minds), Mort Castle (on setting and character in horror fiction), Dean R. Koontz (on building and sustaining suspense), Colin Wilson (on fantasy), and Patrick Lo Brutto (on marketing). Williamson's own essay in the book is an excellent one on the supernatural. This is a well-balanced study of three overlapping forms of fiction writing. For additional comments about this book, refer to chapter 10 of this bibliography.

Romance

Falk, Kathryn, ed. *How to Write a Romance and Get It Published.* New York: Crown, 1983.
A centerpiece of this book is the interview in part 5 with Barbara Cartland, certainly the most prolific and successful writer of romances in the twentieth century, if not ever. Part 1 offers advice from published romance writers on how to write and publish work in this genre. Part 2 focuses on how to write a historical romance. Part 3 considers science-fiction romances, gothic romances, the contemporary romance novel, fantasy, and teen romances. For additional comments about this book, see chapter 7 of this bibliography, under Johnson and under Zuckerman.

Lowrey, Marilyn M. *How to Write Romance Novels That Sell.* New York: Rawson Associates, 1983.
In chapter 3, Lowrey urges writers of romances to establish the identities of the romantic hero and heroine early in a work. She devotes the next two chapters to characterization, moving in chapter 6 to the development of the story and in chapter 7 to dialogue. Chapters 8 and 9 are devoted to sensuous description and sex scenes, respectively. The book covers all sorts of romances: the regency romance, the gothic romance, the gay romance, the historical romance, the romantic soap opera, the contemporary romance, and the young adult romance. An extremely comprehensive book. For further comments about it, refer to "General Studies" in chapter 7 of this bibliography.

Pianka, Phyllis Taylor. *How to Write Romances.* Cincinnati: Writer's Digest Books, 1988.
The romances that jam the displays of drugstores and supermarkets represent an incredibly brisk market in prose fiction, and account for a major percentage of the book sales in the United States. Pianka, herself a successful practitioner in the field, has written a quite formulaic book, but this perhaps is appropriate to the topic—the writing of romances is formulaic and requires a special form of invention that, once mastered, can be practiced regularly, with prolific results. Chapter 10, "Sensuality vs. Sexuality," is indispensable reading for writers in

this genre. Pianka goes into the economic side of writing romances, many of which bring lump-sum payments rather than the continuing royalties that most novels command. Although many romances are really works for hire rather than works of great artistic value, the market for such books is seemingly insatiable. For additional comments about this source, refer to chapters 7 and 10 of this bibliography.

Wilbur, L. Perry. *How to Write Books That Sell*. Chicago: Contemporary Books, 1979.
Chapter 19 of this book is entitled "Hooked on Historical Romances." It gives solid advice about how to break into this field, which is in constant need of new manuscripts. The information on marketing and on literary agents is worth reading. For further comments about this book, see chapters 7 and 10 of this bibliography.

Wimberley, Mary. *To Writers with Love: On Writing Romantic Novels*. Sunrise, Fla.: The Spot Press, 1985.
Wimberley provides information about materials for and methods of writers in this field. She touches on such areas as getting ideas, researching one's ideas, building characters, setting, plot development, and beginnings and endings. Her most interesting chapter is "Beyond the Bedroom Door," which advises writers about how much to tell in explicit detail, particularly about sexual encounters. She also goes into the matters of remuneration and taxes.

The Western Novel

Braun, Matt. *How to Write Western Novels*. Cincinnati: Writer's Digest Books, 1988.
Braun focuses particular attention on the faithful and credible depiction of locale and on developing point of view, both of which place special demands upon writers who contribute to this genre. He indicates in chapter 3 how characterization in westerns, while similar to that in other forms of prose fiction, has its own peculiarities, to which he alerts his readers in specific ways. Chapter 6, "Craft Your Own Voice," and chapter 7, on the mechanics of storytelling, are particularly apt. Braun's discussion of markets that publish this kind of fiction is extensive and provides an invaluable guide to those who wish to write stories based in the American West. The examples in this book are drawn from the best western literature of the nineteenth and twentieth centuries. For additional comments about this source, see chapter 10 of this bibliography.

Collins, James L., ed. *The Western Writer's Handbook*. Boulder, Colo.: Johnson Books, 1987.

Collins' broad-ranging book is especially strong for its directions about how to shape characters for books in the three genres under scrutiny. Subtle ways of building suspense and maintaining reader interest direct the would-be writer into practice activities that will strengthen the tight structure of these forms of writing. Williamson and those who provided essays for this book are adamant about the need to control point of view carefully so that stories maintain their consistency and veracity. Despite its stated emphasis, anyone writing imaginative fiction of any sort will benefit from what the book has to offer. For additional comments about this book, see chapter 7 of this bibliography.

Kelton, Elmer. "Writing Realistic Western Fiction." In *The Writer's Handbook, 1987*, edited by Sylvia K. Burack. Boston: The Writer, Inc., 1987.

Kelton favors the western that is firmly based in history. He contends that realism is the benchmark of the genre and that complicated plots are generally to be avoided in this sort of fiction, which has yet to find its full audience. For modern readers, Kelton believes that the simplistic good guy/bad guy westerns of the past are passé. Contemporary readers demand more searching characterization than the old western typically offered; therefore, the genre is now developing in new directions. Much of the conflict in this sort of writing has to do with change versus resistance to change.

Chapter 3
WRITING NONFICTION
FOR COMMERCIAL PUBLICATION

Andersen, Richard. *Writing That Works: Practical Guide for Business and Creative People*. New York: McGraw-Hill, 1989.
This book will help writers of nonfiction, particularly through the information it provides in chapter 1 on "prewriting" and in chapter 2 on "freewriting." The material on revision (called "rewriting" in this book) is also useful. The intended audience is business people, but the information is generally valuable to a broader audience.

Baker, Samm Sinclair. *Writing Nonfiction That Sells*. Cincinnati: Writer's Digest Books, 1986.
Baker concentrates early in the book on where to get writing ideas. His chapter on work methods (chapter 6) is sensible and should lead to productive results. In chapter 8, he shows how writers can, by thinking like editors, enhance their chances of publication. The essential focus of the book is on how to market manuscripts. For additional comments on this source, see chapter 10.

Benedict, Helen. *Portraits in Print: A Collection of Profiles and the Stories Behind Them*. New York: Columbia University Press, 1990.
Benedict offers profiles of such people as Isaac Bashevis Singer, Beverly Sills, Jessica Mitford, and Joseph Brodsky and follows each profile with an essay in which she tells in detail the circumstances of each profile, such as whether it was based on one or more interviews with the subject, interaction with editors, and material gleaned from information in print. Benedict shows clearly how one can write profiles and provides useful detail about marketing them. For further comments on this source, see chapters 8 and 10 of this bibliography.

Biagi, Shirley. *How to Write and Sell Magazine Articles*. Englewood Cliffs, N.J.: Prentice-Hall, 1981.
Biagi does a fine job of helping writers to discover and develop potential topics for their writing. She also suggests how to approach the physical task of writing: how to organize both one's thoughts and one's time so that the writing process will become a regular part of one's daily routine, as it must for serious writers. In reading this book, potential writers will realize that the regularity with which writers write has much to do with their success or failure. Writing, if it is to assume professional proportions, cannot be indulged in sporadically. Just as good athletes or musicians keep in tone through daily practice, so must writers stick to a routine that will contribute to their fluency and competence. See also chapter 9 of this bibliography.

Boggess, Louise. *How to Write Fillers and Short Features That Sell.* 2d ed. New York: Harper & Row, 1981.

Popular magazines often require short pieces to fill the space left on a page on which a longer piece ends. These fillers are usually nonfiction pieces of between 100 and 350 words. Many of them report factual oddities or small pieces of news, usually offbeat news with some human interest element. Boggess suggests topics and ways of discovering topics, as well as providing a twelve-page list of markets for such material. She suggests that such items benefit by being short, witty, and pithy. Among the types of filler she addresses are self-help articles, how-to-do-it pieces, profiles, nostalgia, personal opinion pieces, and humorous bits. Writing such items is a good starting point for many beginners. See also chapter 9 of this bibliography.

Brooks, Terry. *Word's Worth: A Handbook on Writing and Selling Nonfiction.* New York: St. Martin's Press, 1989.

The information in this book is forthright, working from writing the lead to selling the piece one has written, with intervening chapters on transitions, verbs, descriptions, and quotations. Each chapter (except 9 and 10) has useful exercises. Chapter 10 deals well with the rights and responsibilities of nonfiction writers.

Cassill, Kay. *The Complete Handbook for Freelance Writers.* Cincinnati: Writer's Digest Books, 1981.

This handbook is relatively complete, as the title promises, but it is beginning to be dated. Nevertheless, it presents considerable useful material for writers, especially those who wish to write articles commercially. Of most use are chapter 3, "Assessing the Markets," and chapter 12, which gives good advice about approaching agents. A glossary of writing, editing, and production terms and symbols provides an added dimension to the book. Despite its age, this information is still quite relevant. See also chapter 10 of this bibliography.

Collier, Oscar, with Frances Spatz Leighton. *How to Write and Sell Your First Nonfiction Book.* New York: St. Martin's Press, 1990.

The authors give advice about what kinds of nonfiction are in demand and about the markets in which books of this nature can be placed. They identify the areas that are selling most briskly today, and they suggest how to produce a manuscript with enough appeal to make it salable.

Cook, Claire Kehrwald. *The MLA's Line by Line: How to Edit Your Own Writing.* New York: Houghton Mifflin, 1985.

The major focus of this book is nonfiction writing. It is an amazing resource in that it provides more than seven hundred examples of original and edited sentences. Besides the examples, the author provides valuable comments on basic grammar and usage; on loose, baggy sentences; on verb/noun/pronoun agreement; on punctuation; and on questionable usage. Kehrwald, who has worked in publishing and is now on the staff of the Modern Language Association, provides a forty-four-page glossary of usage that should be helpful to anyone who writes.

Cool, Lisa Collier. *How to Sell Every Magazine Article You Write.* Cincinnati: Writer's Digest Books, 1989.
Cool knows how to identify markets and write specifically for them. Her own students have been highly successful in placing their work, and those who use this book will have revealed to them the tactics that work when one writes and markets articles. For additional comments about this book, refer to chapter 9 of this bibliography.

Delton, Judy. *The Twenty-nine Most Common Writing Mistakes and How to Avoid Them.* Cincinnati: Writer's Digest Books, 1991.
Although this book is aimed at all writers, it is of particular benefit to those who write nonfiction articles and/or books. Delton urges writers to communicate rather than indulge in the luxury of self-expression; not to overpunctuate; to communicate with strong verbs and nouns, rather than depend on the words that modify them; and to be ruthless in editing their manuscripts.

Drewry, John E. *Writing Book Reviews.* Boston: The Writer, Inc., 1966.
This is one of the most thorough books available on its subject. It discusses reviewing in different fields (biography, history, fiction, poetry, and children's books), and contains a valuable chapter (4) on techniques of reviewing. Chapter 16 has thirteen reviews for analysis, by such reviewers as Clifton Fadiman, Orville Prescott, Max Lerner, and Stanley Walker.

Dutwin, Phyllis. *Writing the Easy Way.* New York: Barron's, 1985.
Essentially aimed at college students, this book offers direction to other writers as well. It is clearly and simply expressed, with ample examples. Chapter 7, on writing strong sentences, is excellent and leads gracefully into chapter 8, on developing powerful paragraphs.

Edelstein, Scott. *The Writer's Book of Checklists.* Cincinnati: Writer's Digest Books, 1991.
Edelstein, a much-published author himself, begins by discussing writers' attitudes, then goes on in chapters with such titles as "The Ten Biggest Writing Fears and How to Get Over Them" and "Ten Reasons to Be Persistent and Patient." He then focuses on the writer's craft, on publishing opportunities, and on the business end of publishing as it affects writers. For additional comments about this book, see chapter 10 of this bibliography.

Fitz-Randolph, Jane. *Writing for the Juvenile and Teenage Market.* New York: Funk and Wagnalls, 1969.
Chapter 21 deals with writing both fiction and nonfiction for juveniles. The author emphasizes that authors in this field must always keep in the forefront of their minds the psychology of the audiences to whom they are writing. For additional comments about this book, refer to chapters 4, 6, and 7 of this bibliography.

Fredette, Jean M. *Writer's Digest Handbook of Magazine Article Writing.* Cincinnati: Writer's Digest Books, 1990.
In her more than thirty-five chapters, Fredette suggests an amazing array of outlets to which nonfiction writers can send their writing. Fredette keeps her eye on remuneration and suggests ways in which one's articles can command maximal pay. For additional remarks about this book, see chapters 9 and 10 of this bibliography.

Freedman, Helen Rosengren, and Karen Krieger. *The Writer's Guide to Magazine Markets: Non-fiction.* New York: New American Library, 1983.
The first twenty-six pages of this book give information on how to market manuscripts. The next 329 pages give an overview of some 125 magazines, from *Penthouse* to *Prevention*, from *Health* to *Hustler*, and from *American Baby* to *Young Miss*. The address of the editorial offices of each magazine is given (although some have changed since 1983). Information is also given about each magazine's pay scale and about the number of manuscripts it typically receives and the number accepted for publication. This information is extremely valuable, because it reveals how competitive a market one is entering. See also chapter 9 of this bibliography.

Gabriel, H. W. *How to Write for Money.* Englewood Cliffs, N.J.: Prentice-Hall, 1965.
Gabriel suggests markets that few writers would identify on their own. His chapter 3, on picking a field to write about, is cogent. Chapter 6 deals with ghostwriting. Chapter 12 is entitled "How to Get Money Making Assignments" and offers the most astute advice in the book.

Gilbert, Nan. *See Yourself in Print: A Handbook for Young Writers.* New York: Hawthorne Books, 1968.
Gilbert suggests ways for young writers to find topics, to research them and write about them, and to find markets for their work. The emphasis is on nonfiction, although some fiction is covered as well.

Goulart, Frances Sheridan. *How to Write a Cookbook and Sell It.* Port Washington, N.Y.: Ashley Books, 1980.

Among the most durable books on many publishers' booklists are cookbooks and books on gardening. Goulart, herself the author of cookbooks, suggests ways that writers can tap this market. She presents in chapter 2 a history of cookbooks, an interesting social history. In part 2, Goulart discusses in depth Ruth Ann and Bill Manners' cookbook, *The Quick and Easy Vegetarian Cookbook*. She discusses how to prepare a proposal and manuscript, whether or not to use an agent, how to find a publisher, and how to promote a cookbook once it has been published (chapters 4 to 7 inclusive). For further comments on this source, refer to chapter 10 of this bibliography.

Gunther, Max. *Writing the Modern Magazine Article*. Boston: The Writer, Inc., 1968.
Although this book is now badly dated, it is still worth consulting for its case histories of articles in *True*, *Playboy*, and *The Saturday Evening Post*. Writers of short fiction and nonfiction can productively use the method Gunther suggests to review current magazines in such a way that they will be able better to understand what such outlets generally publish and what they are looking for. Gunther also discusses, in part 2, chapter 5, ways of doing research by mail, an asset to writers who live in remote areas where research facilities are limited.

Hayes, Helen, Ellen Rolfes, et al. *How to Write and Publish a Classic Cookbook*. Illustrated by Michelle Dent. New York: New American Library, 1986.
Although chapter 1 deals with such matters as theme development, recipes, and design, this book is primarily concerned with marketing cookbook manuscripts. From chapter 2 to the end, it addresses such matters as finding a publisher, preparing the manuscript, negotiating a contract, trying self-publishing, starting a publishing business, marketing, and approaching voluntary organizations that might wish to publish cookbooks compiled by their members. For further comments about this book, see chapter 10 of this bibliography.

Jacobi, Peter. *The Magazine Article: How to Think It, Plan It, Write It*. Cincinnati: Writer's Digest Books, 1991.
Jacobi walks his readers through an approach to writing articles by first analyzing successful ones. The approach is essentially one of imitating examples, but it goes far beyond that and is an imaginative and realistic book. For additional comments about this book, refer to chapter 9 of this bibliography.

Kammerman, Sylvia E., ed. *Book Reviewing*. Boston: The Writer, Inc., 1977.
A decade more recent than Drewry's book (see above), this one offers composite advice from a number of regular reviewers of books. The material on children's books, especially that found in chapters 6, 17, and 20, is extensive and solid. Chapter 20 tells how to review a children's book, basing its information on material from the Children's Services Division of the Santiago (California)

Library System. For additional comments about this book, see chapter 7 of this bibliography.

Kelley, Jerome E. *Magazine Writing Today.* Cincinnati: Writer's Digest Books, 1978.
This item gives a good overview of markets, which, although slightly dated, is still serviceable. It also goes into such matters as interviewing (chapter 6) and dealing with the middles of articles to keep them from sagging (chapter 9). Clearcut appendices deal with proofreaders' symbols and the rights of writers. For additional comments about this book, refer to "General Studies" in chapter 9 of this bibliography.

Kevles, Barbara. *Basic Magazine Writing.* Cincinnati: Writer's Digest Books, 1983.
Of particular use to the writer of nonfiction will be Kevles' suggestions about interviewing. The techniques she suggests work well and result in the kinds of searching interviews that are at the heart of much solid nonfiction writing. She urges interviewers to stick to one issue per interview; when interviewers branch off into topics other than the central one, they lose focus, and usually the material they obtain is not enough to address sufficiently any of the issues covered. For additional comments on this book, refer to chapter 9 of this bibliography.

Konner, Linda. *How to Be Successfully Published in Magazines.* New York: St. Martin's Press, 1990.
Konner provides strategies that should help would-be freelance writers produce materials that periodicals can use. Chapter 3 deals with writer-editor etiquette. Chapter 4 is concerned with what writers must know about the magazines they plan to write for if they are to be successful in placing articles with those magazines. Extremely valuable is chapter 6, in which Konner presents interviews with twenty-eight editors about what they are looking for and about what makes them feel favorably disposed toward those who submit material to them. Chapter 7 presents similar interviews with ten authors.

Mager, N. H., S. K. Mager, and P. S. Mager. *Power Writing, Power Speaking: Two Hundred Ways to Make Your Words Count.* New York: William Morrow, 1978.
Although this book is directed more toward public speakers than writers, the analysis of what makes certain phrases memorable is directly applicable to those writing both fiction and nonfiction. Chapters 4, "Figures of Sound and Sight," and 9, "Figures of Emotion and Fallacy," speak most directly to writers.

Maloney, Martin, and Paul Max Rubenstein. *Writing for the Media.* Englewood Cliffs, N.J.: Prentice-Hall, 1980.
Chapter 1 discusses the business aspects of writing for the media. Chapter 2 is

devoted to writing the nonfiction script. Chapter 12, which suggests the opportunities in writing advertising copy, can help writers to find a means of surviving if their other work is not making its mark. The advice about getting writing assignments (chapter 3) is useful. For further comments about this source, refer to chapter 6 of this bibliography.

Marston, Doris Ricker. *A Guide to Writing History*. Cincinnati: Writer's Digest Books, 1976.
This book addresses well the needs of history writers whose emphasis is fiction, nonfiction, or poetry. The first and second chapters are concerned with identifying the audience and finding ideas. The next chapters focus on research, including the interview (chapter 7). Chapter 10 provides examples of ten opening paragraphs, with comments about each. The following chapter categorizes the kinds of articles one can write that have historical bases. Chapter 17 is concerned directly with the writing of nonfiction with a historical base. For additional comments on this source, refer to chapters 1, 2, 5, and 7 of this bibliography.

Martindale, David. *How to Be a Freelance Writer: A Guide to Building a Full-Time Career*. New York: Crown, 1982.
Although he goes into many aspects of freelance writing, Martindale devotes more attention to the nonfiction article than to other forms of this activity. He gives solid information on the mechanics of producing freelance pieces and on marketing them. He addresses the question of the financial arrangements that freelance writers can expect, and this information, although it becomes quickly dated, provides some general direction. For additional comments on this book, refer to chapter 9 of this bibliography.

Mau, Ernest E. *The Free-Lance Writer's Survival Manual*. Chicago: Contemporary Books, 1981.
Although Mau's approach may seem a bit crass to some readers, he succeeds in providing sound information and advice about how to approach editors and about what kinds of financial arrangements to expect and to negotiate. He offers generally accurate information about contracts with publishers and about tax considerations of which freelance writers need to be aware. For further comments on this book, refer to chapters 9 and 10 of this bibliography.

Morris, Terry, ed. *Prose by Professionals: The Inside Story of the Magazine Article Writer's Cost*. New York: Doubleday, 1961.
In this collection, one finds chapters by Donald Murray on getting started as a freelance writer, by Betty Friedan on finding and developing ideas, by Robert J. Levin and Beatrice Schapper on interviewing and research, by Donald G. Cooley on working in media, and by David Lester on writing about ordinary people. Most of the suggestions pertain directly to nonfiction writing. The tone

is upbeat and the writing informed. For additional comments about this source, see chapter 9 of this bibliography.

Newcomb, Duane. *A Complete Guide to Marketing Magazine Articles.* Cincinnati: Writer's Digest Books, 1975.
Although some of the specific information in this book is dated, chapter 10, "How to Use the Interest of Your Writing—Not the Principal," chapter 11, "How to Turn Out Writing in Volume," and chapter 15, "How to Resell Your Material Profitably," have important information for nonfiction writers. The book has been superseded by later such volumes, but this was one of the best in its time, and it remains a valuable resource if it is used judiciously. For additional comments on this book, refer to chapter 9 of this bibliography.

_____. *How to Sell and Re-sell Your Writing.* Cincinnati: Writer's Digest Books, 1987.
Many writers address the matter of how to sell one's writing, but Newcombe shows ways in which writers can make their writing pay two or three times without violating any legal or ethical codes. This book should pay for itself with the first resale of a piece of nonfiction. For further comments on this book, refer to chapter 10 of this bibliography.

Peterson, Franklynn, and Judi Kesselman-Turkel. *The Magazine Writer's Handbook.* Englewood Cliffs, N.J.: Prentice-Hall, 1982.
Although this book may seem on the surface to be *pro forma*, it will be helpful to nonfiction writers who wish to crack the magazine field. The authors offer ten standard article formats, one, certainly, to cover any sort of article; four elements of a good article; three standard writing techniques; and five pieces of advice that no professional writer should forget. For additional comments about this book, see chapter 9.

Piotrowski, Maryanne V. *Re: Writing: Strategies and Suggestions.* New York: Harper & Row, 1989.
Aimed essentially at business people, this book nevertheless speaks directly to some of the concerns of nonfiction writers who are producing work for publication. The sections on gaining control of one's audience, on beginnings, and on conclusions are all well thought through and ably presented. Part 4, on paragraphs and sentences, also has considerable general application to all nonfiction writers.

Poynter, Dan, and Mindy Bingham. *Is There a Book Inside You? How to Successfully Author a Book Alone or Through Collaboration.* Cincinnati: Writer's Digest Books, 1985.
Although this book deals with all forms of book publishing, it will be of primary

interest to those who wish to write nonfiction. The authors contend that writers can publish books if they learn how to pick their topics sensibly, break down the topic into its component parts, and do the research necessary to enhance their material, following a step-by-step process that makes writing easy, evaluating publishing options realistically, and developing an individualized, workable plan. The book also suggests ways to find collaborators, ghostwriters, contract writers, editors, researchers, and clerical support. This book is aimed more at the desperate than at the dedicated writer, but its suggested methods will probably result in publication.

Rees, Clair F. *Profitable Part-Time/Full-Time Freelancing*. Cincinnati: Writer's Digest Books, 1980.
Chapter 2 discusses how to begin as a part-time freelance writer, while chapter 10 focuses on full-time freelancing. Chapter 5 is interesting. It discusses specialization versus versatility. It points out that specialization will lead to repeat sales but that it severely limits one's scope. Chapter 4 suggests ways to build repeat sales short of specializing. Chapter 9 discusses moving from writing short pieces to writing one's first book. For further comments on this book, refer to chapters 2 and 9 of this bibliography.

Rehmehl, Judy. *So, You Want to Write a Cookbook*. Louisville, Ky.: Marathon International Publishing, 1984.
Rehmehl begins with selected specific recipes that show potential cookbook writers how to start. She then goes into how to organize the cookbook community, assuming that many people want to produce cookbooks that are collections of recipes from a region, a town, or from members of organizations. In part 2, she discusses apportioning the workload among those who are involved. Her information on format (part 3) and composition and layout (part 4) is realistic. For additional comments about this book, refer to chapter 10.

Reynolds, Paul R. *The Non-Fiction Book: How to Write and Sell It*. New York: William Morrow, 1970.
The most interesting chapter in this book is 14, "One Book's Earnings for Author and Publisher," in which Reynolds shows exactly how much Margery Allingham's *The Mind Readers* (New York: William Morrow, 1965) made for the parties involved. Although the figures are dated, the percentages are approximately those one can expect today. Also contains chapters on research, the working outline, revision, and other topics. For additional comments about this book, see chapter 9 of this bibliography.

Rockwell, F. A. *How to Write Nonfiction That Sells*. Chicago: Henry Regnery, 1975.
Rockwell's classification of types of articles is helpful. He deals with such types

as the interview, biography, the survey article, the exposé, travel writing, and in chapter 11 urges writers to "Cash in on the Historical Revival." For further comments about this book, see chapter 10 of this bibliography.

Scully, Celia G., and Thomas J. Scully. *How to Make Money Writing About Fitness and Health*. Cincinnati: Writer's Digest Books, 1986.
This is a highly reputable book whose appendix B, on the American Medical Writers' Association Code of Ethics, clearly indicates the ethical orientation of its authors. They begin by surveying the current medical scene regarding health and fitness. They then suggest starting points and freelance opportunities. Chapter 5 addresses the topic of basic research. Chapter 11, on personal experience, is in many ways the most useful chapter in this excellent book, which receives further attention in chapter 10 of this bibliography.

Townsend, Doris McFerran. *The Way to Write and Publish a Cookbook*. New York: St. Martin's Press, 1985.
Townsend does a fine job of getting into the matter of how to write recipes, to which she devotes chapter 3. Chapter 4 deals with the writing of nonrecipe material. The remainder of the book has to do with marketing and promotion, except for chapter 9, which considers food photography, an important topic not always found in books of this sort. For further comments about this source, see chapter 10 of this bibliography.

Vachon, Brian. *Writing for Regional Publications*. Cincinnati: Writer's Digest Books, 1979.
Although many fictional works have regional settings, this book is concerned chiefly with nonfiction that is written for regional markets such as city magazines, newspapers' weekly regional sections, and guide books to dining or shopping or sightseeing in a city or area. Chapter 1 emphasizes the need to develop a sense of place to engage in such writing; this is a thriving market, into which many inexperienced writers break. Vachon devotes chapter 3 to examining things that alienate editors and chapter 4 to suggesting ways to entice editors. For additional comments on this source, see chapter 9 of this bibliography.

The Writing Business: A Poets and Writers Handbook. Edited jointly by the editors of *Coda: A Poets and Writers Newsletter*. New York: Poets and Writers, 1985.
Part 6 of this comprehensive book lists fourteen major magazines with an indication of what sorts of work they are seeking and what they pay their authors. The guide to reference books for writers is helpful, as is the list of publishers' addresses, which, although minimal, is accurate. The information early in the book, on overcoming writer's block and on how to revise effectively, is of general interest. For further comments about this source, see chapters 1, 2, 5, 9, and 10 of this bibliography.

Yolen, Jane. *Writing Books for Children*. Boston: The Writer, Inc., 1973.
Chapter 6 of this excellent resource suggests imaginative approaches to writing nonfiction pieces for children. The information Yolen provides for marketing children's books, both fiction and nonfiction, is also relevant, although somewhat outdated. For further comments about this book, refer to chapters 7 and 10 of this bibliography.

Zinsser, William. *On Writing Well: An Informal Guide to Writing Nonfiction*. 4th ed. New York: Harper & Row, 1990.
This is perhaps one of the three or four most useful books ever produced on the subject of writing. Zinsser's comments on how to avoid clutter, on expressing ideas clearly, crisply, and directly, make a lasting impression. He also addresses such matters as writing the lead and the ending, writing travel material, writing about science and sports, and writing humorous pieces. Actually, any of the four editions of the book will serve readers admirably, although the later editions contain information about writing with a word processor that is not found in the earlier editions. It is comforting to read a book about writing by someone who writes extraordinarily well himself. The much-published Zinsser is a consummate practitioner of the writing craft.

_____, ed. *Spiritual Quests: The Art and Craft of Religious Writing*. Boston: Houghton Mifflin, 1988.
In this collection, Zinsser, along with those who participated in the Book-of-the-Month Club talks at the New York Public Library in 1987, suggests how to tap an extremely broad market that extends to both commercial and specialized presses. The contributors to the volume are Mary Gordon, David Bradley, Jaroslav Pelikan, Frederick Buechner, Hugh Nissenson, and Allen Ginsberg. Writing in this field is often historical, sometimes academically philosophical, and often inspirational. The field demands books that are both broadly religious and more narrowly, sectarianly religious. Many organized religions run their own presses and welcome submissions from people who have not published previously.

Zobel, Louise Purwin. *The Travel Writer's Handbook*. Cincinnati: Writer's Digest Books, 1980.
Zobel explores what it takes to be a travel writer, suggesting in chapter 3 that the first trip is to the library to get background material for any subsequent traveling. She suggests studying the marketplace before setting out so that the kinds of writing one will do and the audience one anticipates will be clearly defined early. Chapter 8, on having empathy with the reader, is sound. Chapter 11 suggests that potential travel writers should try to sell the article(s) or book before they leave on the trip. Perhaps the most valuable chapter in the book is chapter 12, which suggests the most popular article ideas in the field of travel.

Chapter 4
WRITING PLAYS

Austell, Jan. *What's in a Play?* New York: Harcourt, Brace and World, 1968.
The main body of this book analyzes intelligently such plays as Thornton Wilder's *Our Town* and Tennessee Williams' *The Glass Menagerie*. The book's appendices are of exceptional importance to playwrights. They deal with such matters as play direction, floor plans of plays as they are staged, and lighting. This is a practical book with information of lasting value.

Cartmell, Van H., ed. *Plot Outlines of One Hundred Famous Plays*. New York: Barnes & Noble Books, 1945.
Written essentially as a study guide for students of drama, this book is of interest because in reading through it one begins to make generalizations about what has constituted the successful writing of plot through several centuries. The book provides outlines for plays as disparate as Aristophanes' *Lysistrata*, Christopher Marlowe's *Tamburlaine the Great*, and Robert Sherwood's *The Petrified Forest*.

Davis, Eugene C. *Amateur Theater Handbook: A Complete Guide to Successful Play Production*. New York: Greenberg Publishers, 1945.
Although this book is not directly about playwriting, potential playwrights will gain from it insights into technical matters of theater of which all playwrights need to be aware if their plays are to be stageworthy. Chapter 1, on the theater plant, and chapter 2, on the production staff, are essential reading for people who wish to write plays, as are chapter 9, which discusses the unit set, and chapter 10, which focuses on stage lighting. This book will succeed in making playwrights aware of the physical limitations of the genre within which they are writing. The book's age is not a significant problem, although some recent developments in the mechanics of the stage permit more flexibility than was available to playwrights in the 1940's.

Egri, Lajos. *The Art of Dramatic Writing: Its Basis in the Creative Interpretation of Human Motives*. Rev. ed. New York: Simon & Schuster, 1960.
The revised edition of this standard book in the field of playwriting (originally published in 1946) begins with a discussion of the basic premise of a play. It then discusses in depth the creation of character, the development and uses of conflict, and such general matters as the obligatory scene, exposition, dialogue, experimentation, the important matter of entrances and exits, and writing for television. In four appendices, the author analyzes a number of plays, tells how best to market plays, reviews analytically plays that have made money, assesses the reasons for their commercial success, and suggests ways to write for films. Much of the practical information is still useful, although the book is generally dated

in its discussions of marketing and of writing for television and films, as well as the genre of plays it discusses.

Fergusson, Francis. *The Idea of a Theatre: The Art of Drama in a Changing Perspective*. Princeton, N.J.: Princeton University Press, 1949.
Fergusson's book has, through the years, assumed the position of a classic. It is comprehensive, considering theater theory from Aristotle and Plato to T. S. Eliot and Tennessee Williams. Fergusson's discussions of such matters as the scapegoat theme, the uses of ritual in drama, and dramaturgy are without equal, lucid and accessible to readers lacking a specialized background in drama. The appendices on technical concepts, plot and action, form and purpose as related to plot, and mimetic perception of action are exceptionally rich in their insights. Perhaps the most memorable material in the book occurs as part of chapter 5 and has to do with the tragic rhythm of a small figure.

Finch, Robert. *How to Write a Play*. New York: Greenberg Publishers, 1948.
This book is still of value because of its first chapter, "The One-Act Play." The suggestions given for writing a one-act play are especially relevant to the beginning playwright, who likely will start with short plays rather than with fully developed two- or three-act dramas. The following chapter, on mechanical matters, is as significant today as it was when it first appeared. It contains good suggestions about how to move actors around on the stage and on how to plot their entrances and exits gracefully. Less successful is Finch's brief analysis (chapter 6) of one of his own plays, *Old What's-His-Name*. Obviously, his list of Broadway producers, managers, and agents, once eminently useful, is now completely outdated.

Fitz-Randolph, Jane. *Writing for the Juvenile and Teenage Market*. New York: Funk and Wagnalls, 1969.
Fitz-Randolph devotes chapter 22 of this book to drama for the juvenile market. This outlet provides a reasonable beginning for many novice playwrights and has been a fertile field for some noted ones. For additional comments about this book, refer to chapters 3, 6, and 7 of this bibliography.

Freytag, Gustav. *Freytag's Technique of the Drama: An Exposition of Dramatic Composition and Art*. 2d ed. Translated by Elias J. MacEwen. Chicago: S. C. Griggs, 1896.
This book is primarily of historical interest and is based largely on concepts of classical rather than modern theater. Under the heading "Dramatic Action," it addresses such matters as the basic idea of a play (form and structure), what constitutes the dramatic, unity, probability, importance and magnitude, movement and ascent, and the idea of tragedy. The chapters on the construction of drama, the construction of scenes, the characters, and verse and color delve into matters

of less concern to recent playwrights than they were when the book was written. The final chapter, "The Poet and His Work," is of particular historical interest and reflects the situation in American theater in the years before Eugene O'Neill began its transformation.

Grebanier, Bernard. *Playwriting*. New York: Thomas Y. Crowell, 1961.
Grebanier's book is intimately evocative in its approach. One feels that the author is there, giving encouraging nudges to the reader. The questions considered are how a play is written, where playwrights begin, how they develop their plots, how they create characters and convincing dialogue, and how they identify the elements that will bring the play to its climax. Grebanier discusses the essential elements of comedy, tragedy, melodrama, and farce. Chapter 8 is concerned with the one-act television play, in which Grebanier shows how to achieve characterization through dialogue and action.

Griffiths, Stuart. *How Plays Are Made: The Fundamental Elements of Play Construction*. Englewood Cliffs, N.J.: Prentice-Hall, 1982.
The heart of this book is chapter 7, which deals in four compact but fruitful pages with the matter of complication in drama. Certainly it is out of complication that all conflict grows, and without conflict, a drama is quite undramatic. Chapter 11, "Words and Silence," is a sensitively recorded chapter. The chapters on action (2), dramatic tension and suspense (3), exposition (4), and emphasis and contrast (6) are sound if not profound. The information given about characterization in chapter 9 and dialogue in chapter 10 is worthwhile.

Hatten, Theodore W. *Orientation to the Theater*. 4th ed. Englewood Cliffs, N.J.: Prentice-Hall, 1987.
This textbook, first published in 1972 and frequently revised and reissued since then, is especially valuable for its second chapter, "The Play and Its Parts," whose forty pages give an extensive orientation to the theater. It provides excellent insights into plot, characterization, diction, music, and spectacle in drama. Chapters 7, "Theatricalism and the New Theater," and 12, which focuses on the audience and what it expects and demands, are splendid. Practical advice is given in chapter 8, which explains the role of directors; chapter 9, which explains the role of actors; and chapter 10, which focuses on scene design. Chapter 11 considers theater architecture, without a knowledge of which no playwright can succeed. The glossary, index, and extensive bibliography enhance the book's usefulness.

Hull, Raymond. *How to Write a Play*. Cincinnati: Writer's Digest Books, 1983.
Hull, who was coauthor with Laurence J. Peter of *The Peter Principle*, begins by discussing the playwright's business, focusing sharply upon audience expectations. Chapter 2 deals with the history and conventions of the theater. Hull then

treats such topics as dramatic structure, conflict, characterization, dialogue, action, complications, crises, catastrophes, and the physical limitations of the stage. His chapter on special forms (farce, melodrama, comedy, tragedy, and so forth) is sound. The last chapter contains a comprehensive glossary of theatrical terms. For further comments about this source, see chapter 10 of this bibliography.

Krook, Dorothea. *Elements of Tragedy*. New Haven, Conn.: Yale University Press, 1969.
Krook identifies four elements that are fundamental to most serious and lasting drama: (1) act or situation, (2) shame or horror, (3) human suffering that grows out of shame or horror, and (4) a deeper knowledge of the human condition. The thesis is thoughtfully developed and substantially buttressed by appropriate examples from major plays of Sophocles, William Shakespeare, Henrik Ibsen, and Anton Chekhov. Those who wish to write drama that will endure, particularly tragedy, will benefit mightily from reading this excellent study.

Lawson, John Howard. *Theory and Technique of Playwriting and Screenwriting*. New York: G. P. Putnam's Sons, 1936, 1949.
Book 1 of this volume is devoted to writing plays. It begins with a history of dramatic thought, then moves to a discussion of the theater of today. Chapter 3, on dramatic structure, and chapter 4, on dramatic composition, are particularly useful, discussing such subjects as the obligatory scene, the progression of a play, the climax of a script, and characterization. For additional comments about this book, see chapter 6 of this bibliography.

Mathieu, Aron M., ed. *The Creative Writer*. Cincinnati: Writer's Digest Books, 1961.
A. L. Fierst's "A Few Choice Seats Still Available" and John Van Druten's "Playwright at Work" both address the writing and marketing of drama intelligently and from the standpoint of insiders in theater. For additional comments about this book, see below and also refer to chapters 1, 4, and 7 of this bibliography.

Mueller, Lavonne. "The S-N-A-P-P-E-R Test for Playwrights." In *The Writer's Handbook, 1987*, edited by Sylvia K. Burack. Boston: The Writer, Inc., 1987.
The letters in Mueller's test stand for Secret, Names, Action, Props, Plot, Ending, and Relatives. She contends that these universal ingredients help drama to succeed. Some of these items are self-evident; others are not. For example, Mueller recommends selecting names carefully—Tennessee Williams' Big Daddy is perfectly named, as are the "no-necked Monsters," his noisy, performance-oriented grandchildren. By endings, Mueller really means exit lines: Give characters memorable lines to use as they leave the stage, something to keep them in the audience's mind. The advice here is practical and easily applied.

Muth, Marcia. *Writing and $elling: Poetry, Fiction, Articles, Plays, and Local History.* Santa Fe, N.Mex.: Sunstone Press, 1985.

If one can see beyond Muth's dollar sign, the information she provides about writing drama is worthwhile. Certainly beginning with short plays is a good idea, and the information about writing with the technicalities of the stage in mind is sound. The marketing aspects of the chapter are not particularly valid in all cases, but the chapter overall is worth a quick read. For additional comments on this book, see chapters 1, 5, 9, and 10 of this bibliography.

Niggli, Josefina. *New Pointers on Playwriting.* Boston: The Writer, Inc., 1967.

This book proceeds from chapter 1, which deals with priorities— through chapters on laws of design, story line, crisis and climax, character development, and scene— to a final chapter on how to market plays. Chapter 10, "What Is Plot?," is of unique value. Niggli's recommendations have remained useful through the years and are still of general interest to playwrights. For additional comments on this source, see chapter 10 of this bibliography.

Packard, William. *The Art of Playwriting: Creating the Magic of the Theatre.* New York: Paragon House, 1987.

Packard demonstrates the dimensions of expression this genre makes available to writers. He differentiates between drama and other genres, especially screenwriting, on which he has also produced a valuable book (see chapters 6 and 10 of this bibliography). Packard understands well the underlying unities that make drama work, paying careful attention to the Aristotelian unities of time and place.

Peacock, Ronald. *The Art of Drama.* London: Routledge & Kegan Paul, 1957.

Among this book's twelve chapters are those on words and images (chapter 5), art and experience (chapter 7), music and poetry (chapter 9), and the art of drama (chapter 10). The book's most compelling chapter, chapter 8, which deals with the principle of the characteristic intertexture of poetry, is also one of its most difficult. The book is well documented and has a comprehensive index.

_____. *The Poet in the Theatre.* London: Routledge, 1946.

This book is, broadly speaking, a critical study. It has chapters on such poet-playwrights as T. S. Eliot, Henry James, Franz Grillparzer, Friedrich Hebbel, Henrik Ibsen, George Bernard Shaw, John Millington Synge, William Butler Yeats, and Hugo von Hoffmansthal. The book's final chapter, on tragedy, comedy, and civilization, raises interesting issues about the social functions of drama. This is not a how-to-write-a-play book. Rather, it is a thoughtful scholarly study that will cause readers to think through some of the fundamental issues that serious playwrights face in their writing.

Pike, Frank, and Thomas G. Dunn. *The Playwright's Handbook*. New York: New American Library, 1985.
The first three chapters of this book deal with the workshop approach to playwriting—one chapter devoted to beginning, one to intermediate, and one to advanced. Chapter 4 suggests a way of getting unproduced plays into the right hands for a reading. Chapter 6, on entering contests, is useful. The authors' examples are excellent, drawn from a broad variety of plays and playwrights. For further comments about this book, see chapter 10 of this bibliography.

Polking, Kirk, ed. *A Beginner's Guide to Getting Published*. Cincinnati: Writer's Digest Books, 1987.
Peg Kehret's short chapter "Opportunities for New Playwrights" is indispensable for anyone trying to break into the highly competitive field of playwriting. Kehret's suggestions on how to get plays produced in small theaters and other out-of-the-way places provide valuable ideas. For additional comments about this book, look under "General Studies" in chapters 1, 5, and 7.

Polking, Kirk, Jean Chimsky, and Rose Adkins, eds. *The Beginning Writer's Answer Book*. 2d ed. Cincinnati: Writer's Digest Books, 1978.
Chapter 26 of this serviceable book (cited also in chapters 2 and 6) addresses the questions of how to write dramatic dialogue and how to time a play. The information is eminently practical and should be of direct use to novice playwrights.

Polti, Georges. *The Thirty-six Dramatic Situations*. Boston: The Writer, Inc., 1988.
Polti's remarkable analysis of what constitutes plot has been of great help to many playwrights and novelists. Polti narrows the types of dramatic situations down to thirty-six basic plots upon which he contends all plays and novels are based. The book is not formulaic, but it is thought-provoking and provides a fine stimulus to the creative imagination. Polti's extensive knowledge of dramatic literature and of prose fiction makes it possible for him to arrive at significant generalizations about the nature of literature and of the creative process.

Raphaelson, Samson. *The Human Nature of Playwriting*. New York: Macmillan, 1941.
In this unique study, Raphaelson presents a verbatim chronological account of how he and thirty of his students delved into their memories to find dramatic material in their own past lives. The book deals essentially with ways of unlocking the unconscious mind and using its revelations to generate dramatic material of the sort that playwrights can use effectively in their art.

Rowe, Kenneth Thorpe. *A Theater in Your Head: Analyzing a Play and Visualizing Its Production*. New York: Funk and Wagnalls, 1960.
Rowe, once professor of playwriting at the University of Michigan, presents

several helpful chapters before (in part 3 of this book) he analyzes in depth the play *Our Lan'*, by Theodore Ward. Rowe's earlier sections deal with experiencing the play, understanding it, and evaluating it. He considers the functions of the producers, directors, designers, and actors in any production. In part 2, he discusses structure and meaning, modes of drama—farces, melodrama, tragedy, comedy, and social drama, among others—and modern theatrical movements, such as naturalism, realism, surrealism, expressionism, dada, and theatricalism.

_____. *Write That Play*. New York: Funk and Wagnalls, 1939, 1968.
The heart of this enduring study is found in chapter 5, an analysis of John Millington Synge's *Riders to the Sea*. Besides this perceptive reading of a single play, the book deals with the elements that are fundamental to playwriting: character, dialogue, and revision. The book also provides an analysis of a longer play, Henrik Ibsen's *A Doll's House*, which is informative, although Rowe's analysis of the short Synge play is much better focused (largely because of the nature of the two plays involved). An appendix on marketing plays is useful, although obviously dated. For further comments on this source, see chapter 10 of this bibliography.

Scholes, Robert, and Carl H. Klaus. *Elements of Drama*. New York: Oxford University Press, 1971.
Although its intended audience is not the playwright, three major sections of this book, "Contexts of Drama," "Modes of Drama," and "Elements of Drama," address matters of considerable importance to those who write plays. The last of these sections gives particularly strong analyses of dialogue, plot, and characterization. The coverage is extensive, ranging from classical drama to some of the absurdist plays of the 1960's. The analysis of Samuel Beckett's *Endgame* is particularly insightful and should suggest writing tactics to those who would create for the modern theater. It is interesting to read Scholes at this early stage in his critical career.

Smiley, Sam. *Playwriting: The Structure of Action*. Englewood Cliffs, N.J.: Prentice-Hall, 1971.
Despite its age, this book speaks directly to the concerns of many modern playwrights. Smiley begins with a chapter on the writer's vision, followed by a practical one on the process of playwriting. The ensuing chapters on dramatic structure, character, thought, diction, sounds, and spectacle cover most of the salient elements of composing plays. The final chapters are on the practical problems of play production and on how playwrights can address living audiences. Chapter 11, on marketing scripts, is badly dated, although the information it contains on copyright and submitting manuscripts is still relevant.

Straczynski, J. Michael. *The Complete Book of Scriptwriting*. Cincinnati: Writer's Digest Books, 1987.

Straczynski suggests tactics, particularly relating to dialogue, that will help writers in all forms of drama, although his main interest is obviously in helping film and television authors use the possibilities of those two visual media to their best effect. Nevertheless, the section on the stage play is valuable and offers good advice about marketing scripts in that genre. For further comments on this book, see chapter 6 of this bibliography.

Styan, J. L. *The Dramatic Experience*. Cambridge, England: Cambridge University Press, 1965.
In this book, a master of dramatic art shows how to bring drama to life. Chapter 2 emphasizes that the stage is alive and that plays that grace it must seethe with intensity and authenticity. The emphasis is on classical British drama, which Styan knew best, but chapter 7 discusses a broad range of other applications for drama. For additional comments about this book, see chapter 6 of this bibliography.

Weber, Olga S., and Stephen J. Calvert, eds. *Literary and Library Prizes*. 10th ed. New York: R. R. Bowker, 1980.
This frequently published volume lists international, American, British, and Canadian literary and library prizes. It gives the years and the names of the prizes and the names of winners. This edition devotes eight pages to prizes for drama. For additional comments about this book, see chapters 1 and 7 of this bibliography.

Chapter 5
WRITING POEMS

Aiken, Joan. *The Way to Write for Children.* New York: St. Martin's Press, 1982.
Chapter 7 of this book contains valuable information about writing poetry for young readers. Aiken's book, which goes into the stages of child development and which discusses such important topics as taboos in children's literature, also has a chapter on myth and fantasy (chapter 8) that contains information useful to poets wishing to produce work for children or young people. The book is uneven but has much to recommend it. For further comments about it, look under "General Studies" in chapter 7 of this bibliography.

Andrews, C. E. *The Writing and Reading of Verse.* New York: D. Appleton, 1918.
Despite its age, much of the advice in this volume remains relevant today. Part 1 focuses on such technical matters as meter, stress, scansion, accent, verse pattern, rhyme, and melody, or what the writer designates "tone color." This latter chapter is perhaps the most valuable one in part 1. Part 2 addresses the question of special verse forms and is of historical interest to the serious poet, who can read in it about stanzaic forms, the tetrameter couplet, the pentameter line, the heroic couplet, blank verse, the sonnet and ode as poetic forms, and a variety of foreign forms such as the ballade, the rondel, the rondeau, the triolet, the villanelle, and the sestina. The final, very brief chapter on blank verse was considered daring in its time.

Aristotle. *On the Art of Poetry.* Edited by Lane Cooper. Ithaca, N.Y.: Cornell University Press, 1962.
Aristotle's work about the creative arts has endured the ages and is still essential reading for those who write. Aristotle used the word usually translated *poetry* in a much broader sense than it is usually used today. He included under its heading many forms of creative expression, including but not restricted to what is now commonly called poetry. Cooper's is a particularly strong edition of Aristotle's important work; his six-page introduction is well informed, discussing epic poetry and problems in criticism. It also defines *tragedy* in the Greek sense of the word.

Barr, June. *Writing and Selling Greeting Card Verse.* Boston: The Writer, Inc., 1966.
Few who aspire to careers in poetry think of it in terms of writing greeting-card verse. Nevertheless, greeting cards provide one of the most voluminous outlets for verse, if not great poetry. This book is rich in examples. Its list of twenty-seven publishers who welcome unsolicited contributions was useful in its day but now is only generally useful, given changes in the greeting-card business; of

equal help was the list of publishers that were not looking for such verse. For additional comments about this source, see chapter 10 of this bibliography.

Barry, Elaine. *Robert Frost on Writing.* New Brunswick, N.J.: Rutgers University Press, 1977.
The information Barry has drawn from Frost's letters, lectures, introductions, and interviews reveals a great deal about the poetic process as Frost conceived of it. Of particular interest are Frost's comments on vocal reality (addressed to John Freeman), his remarks about verbal exactness (to George Browne), and his thoughts on variety (to F. S. Flint). Of even greater interest are his observations about the influence of talk on writing expressed in a letter to Lewis N. Chase. He writes to John Bartlett on sentences and on the "sound of sense."

Behn, Harry. *Chrysalis: Concerning Children and Poetry.* New York: Harcourt, Brace and World, 1949.
This book has been so popular that it was reissued ten times in the first twenty years of its existence. Although its focus is on helping children to write poetry as a learning device, the basic information can be applied to poets of any age. Of special interest to many older poets will be the section entitled "The Source of Images," as well as a later section that considers haiku as a poetic form and suggests ways to produce it. For additional comments, see chapter 7 of this bibliography.

Buchler, Justus. *The Main of Light: On the Concept of Poetry.* New York: Oxford University Press, 1974.
This book focuses on defining poetry. Chapter 3, "The Idea of Concreteness," is of some relevance, as are the sections of chapter 5 that deal with poetic query. Although it is thoughtful and is based upon a broad knowledge of poetry, this book essentially is stodgy, at times overwritten and pompous. It is essentially of philosophical rather than directly practical value.

Cane, Melville. *Making a Poet: An Inquiry into the Creative Process.* New York: Harcourt, Brace, 1962.
Melville Cane attempts to help readers understand the creative steps of forging poems by taking them through the process with some of his own poems. The approach is fruitful. Despite the age of this book, the material it contains has a ring of truth to it; Cane's analyses are thoughtful and psychologically sound. For additional comments about this book, refer to chapter 8 of this bibliography.

Carey, Michael A. *Poetry Starting from Scratch: How to Teach and Write Poetry.* Urbana, Ill.: National Council of Teachers of English, 1989.
Carey is more concerned with process than with product, and his advice is sound. He shows how writers can use their senses and their sensibilities to create verse,

capturing images, mood, thoughts, and colors through following the suggestions made in the book. The writing here is excellent and the insights into how poets create is good. Although the book is aimed at youngsters in grades three through seven, seasoned poets can profit from reading this book.

Caws, Mary Anne. *A Metapoetics of the Passage: Architextures in Surrealism and After*. Hanover, N.H.: University Press of New England, 1981.
Caws, a professor of English at New York City's Hunter College, has produced a well-researched and carefully considered study that deals with such topics as "Interruption and Traversal," "Surrealism and Its Architexture: Reading Backwards," and "Metapoetic Moderns." Perhaps the most interesting consideration is "Rites of a Flowing Element: From Surrealism to [Octavio] Paz and [James] Merrill." The index is comprehensive and serviceable. This book is definitely for sophisticated readers.

Ciardi, John. "Everyone Wants to Be Published, But. . . ." In *The Writer's Handbook, 1987*, edited by Sylvia K. Burack. Boston: The Writer, Inc., 1987.
This essay is encouraging but hard-nosed. Ciardi insists that too many unsuccessful poets are unsuccessful because they do not study their medium sufficiently before they begin to write. He notes the careful word choice, particularly of verbs, that characterizes excellent poetry, which may be deceptively simple at first glance. He contends that genuinely good poets *are* acknowledged, although the road to recognition may be discouraging and winding. He notes how poets have to search for markets, realizing that American magazines publish 98 percent nonfiction, less than 1 percent poetry. He places heavy emphasis on the effective use of metaphor.

Colley, Ann C., and Judith K. Moore. *Starting with Poetry*. New York: Harcourt Brace Jovanovich, 1973.
This volume is a textbook aimed essentially at helping students to develop a sensitivity to poetry. It has some excellent information on the sounds of language (section 2), on the rhythms of language (section 3), and on details, including sights, smells, and textures (section 4). The latter information is so well presented that it will make would-be poets rethink some of the ways in which they perceive things around them.

Cook, Albert. *Figural Choice in Poetry and Art*. Hanover, N.H.: University Press of New England, 1985.
This book is scholarly but accessible to moderately sophisticated readers. Among its chapters are "The Range of Image" (chapter 2), "Surrealism and Surrealisms" (chapter 5), "William Carlos Williams: Ideas and Things" (chapter 6), "Maximizing Minimalism" (chapter 7), and "Expressionism Not Wholly Abstract" (chapter

8). The author is imaginative and well informed. His facts are accurate, his speculations well thought out and balanced.

Creeley, Robert. *The Uncollected Essays of Robert Creeley*. Berkeley: University of California Press, 1989.
American poetry changed drastically with the publication of T. S. Eliot's *The Waste Land* in 1922, but those who followed in his footsteps—poets such as Ezra Pound, Marianne Moore, and William Carlos Williams—did not have an easy time getting their poetry before the public. Creeley, a close friend of Pound, began in the early 1950's to chronicle these difficulties in essays that appeared in small magazines and journals and that are now collected in this volume. They are instructive in showing how public taste and poetic excellence are frequently at loggerheads. Creeley understands well the realities of what poets face as they try to move in new, experimental directions.

Dessner, Lawrence Jay. *How to Write a Poem*. New York: Washington Mews Books, 1979.
Chapters 2 and 3, on how to motivate writing, will be helpful to fledgling poets who are not quite finding their way. The best chapter in the book, however, is chapter 5, "Leaving Things Out," which deals with subtlety and verbal economy in poetry. Many writers have discussed this topic, but none with quite the practicality and specificity of Dessner. For additional comments on this source, see chapter 7 of this bibliography.

Drury, John. *Creating Poetry*. Cincinnati: Writer's Digest Books, 1991.
Drury is at his best when he discusses how those who work with words can experiment with unique poetic forms. Each of the book's chapters is complete and whole unto itself, so that one can use the book in a variety of ways. The exercises are challenging but rewarding. Drury's observations about imagery and measured verse seem particularly apt. The reading list toward the end of the book and the information about how and where to submit poetry are sound and current.

Esbensen, Barbara Juster. *A Celebration of Bees: Helping Children Write Poetry*. Minneapolis: Winston Press, 1975.
This book is discussed fully in chapter 7 of this bibliography.

Eliot, T. S. *On Poetry and Poets*. New York: Farrar, Straus, and Cudahy, 1957.
This collection of essays by the 1948 Nobel Prize laureate in literature contains seven essays on poetry and nine on various poets, including two on John Milton and one each on Vergil, Sir John Davies, Samuel Johnson, Lord Byron, Johann Wolfgang von Goethe, Rudyard Kipling, and William Butler Yeats. The essays on poetry try to get at the essence of poetry and are deeply philosophical. Because Eliot is one of the most important originators of modern poetry, serious poets will benefit from reading the essays in this compact volume.

Fehrman, Carl. *Poetic Creation*. Translated by Karin Petherick. Minneapolis: University of Minnesota Press, 1980.
Poetic Creation is a translation from the Swedish of Fehrman's *Diktaren Och Doden*, which was published in Sweden in 1953. It begins with a section on documentation and experimentation in poetry and is especially valuable in what it has to say about experimentation. The next portion is on improvisation, rite, and myth. This is followed by carefully considered critical essays on the poetry of Samuel Taylor Coleridge, Edgar Allan Poe, Paul Valéry, and Henrik Ibsen, each engrossing and intelligent. The book is well documented and has a serviceable index.

Fulton, Len, ed. *The International Directory of Little Magazines and Small Presses*. 26th ed. Paradise, Calif.: Dustbooks, 1990.
This book, earlier editions of which have served writers for many years, provides an alphabetical listing of little magazines and small presses throughout the United States, giving addresses, names of editors, and significant details about each. At 939 pages, the volume is comprehensive and its information is accurate and reliable. Toward the end of the text is a helpful geographical cross-referencing of the entries, which will be of particular use to those who write about regional topics. For further comments on this entry, refer to "General Studies" in chapter 1 of this bibliography.

Gibbons, Reginald, ed. *The Poet's Work: Twenty-nine Masters on Twentieth Century Poetry, the Origins and Practice of Their Art*. Boston: Houghton Mifflin, 1977.
Because they focus directly on the creative process in their writing of poetry, the statements of these twenty-nine poets are uniquely valuable to those who write poetry. Among the poets included in this sampling are Boris Pasternak, Federico García Lorca, Wallace Stevens, Delmore Schwartz, Karl Shapiro, Hugh MacDiarmid, Marianne Moore, Paul Valéry, Hart Crane, William Carlos Williams, Denise Levertov, Gary Snyder, Randall Jarrell, and Dylan Thomas. The variety of approaches to writing poetry manifested in these essays is particularly challenging.

Hamilton, Anne. *How to Revise Your Own Poems*. Boston: The Writer, Inc., 1945.
Hamilton uses a question-answer format in this book, which deals with matters of rhythm (chapter 3), connotation (chapter 9), and bad poetry (chapter 17), along with the usual conventions of writing poetry. The chapter on bad poetry will likely be, for today's readers, the best in the book. Hamilton clearly helps poets develop one of the most precious resources they can possess: self-criticism based on an understanding of what makes poetry strong.

Harrower, Molly. *The Therapy of Poetry*. Springfield, Ill.: Charles C. Thomas, 1972.

Four chapters of this book show ways in which poets can use their pasts to inform their writing. Chapter 7, on "you-directed" poems, and chapter 9, "The Self-Sustaining Poems," are of lasting value. The title is slightly misleading. For additional comments on this source, refer to chapter 8 of this bibliography.

Higginson, William J., with Penny Harter. *The Haiku Handbook: How to Write, Share, and Teach Haiku.* New York: McGraw-Hill, 1985.
Part 1 of this book presents information about the haiku old and new, including early haiku writing in the West. It also treats the haiku movement in England and around the world. Part 2 deals in chapter 6 with the art of the haiku, in chapter 7 with its nature, in chapter 8 with its form, and in chapter 9 with its craft. Three extremely useful appendices provide a season-word list and index, a glossary, and a list of resources. For additional comments about this book, see chapter 7 of this bibliography.

Hill, Archibald A. *Constituent and Pattern in Poetry.* Austin: University of Texas Press, 1976.
This book has become something of a classic. University of Texas professor of linguistics Archibald Hill presents some extremely demanding material, but the lucidity of his prose and of his examples makes the book rewarding to read. He discusses such topics as types of meaning and imagery; principles for interpreting meaning; the use of analogies, icons, and images; the locus of the literary work; and the poem as cryptogram and as an example of deviant grammar. His discussion of John Keats's *Ode on a Grecian Urn* (chapter 10) and his analyses of two Emily Dickinson poems (chapter 12) are exceptionally clear and crisp.

Hillyer, Robert. *First Principles of Verse.* Boston: The Writer, Inc., 1938.
The book, drawn from Hillyer's essays published in *The Writer* during his years of teaching at Harvard, is designed as a practical guide for people who want to write poetry and for those who would critique it. Hillyer discusses the usual elements addressed in books of this sort—diction, rhyme, meter, basic metrical forms, and foreign forms. He is at his best, however, in discussing what he calls "the magic of language." This book has been reprinted quite often and is easily found in libraries or for second-hand purchase. The writing is spirited and vibrant. The final essay, based on an address Hillyer delivered at Wheaton College, discusses some of the roots of English poetry and is of historical interest.

Hochman, Sandra. *Streams: Life-Secrets for Writing Poems and Songs.* Englewood Cliffs, N.J.: Prentice-Hall, 1978.
Hochman intersperses the text with valuable exercises relating to what is being discussed. The first chapter, which has to do with opening the mind, is vigorous and interesting. Chapter 2 deals with words and their impact and is not particu-

larly novel. In chapter 3, however, which focuses on choosing the subjects for poems, Hochman succeeds admirably. Chapter 4 emphasizes the writing of songs, which is certainly a good approach to poetry among those who play musical instruments.

Holmes, John. *Writing Poetry*. Boston: The Writer, Inc., 1960.
This book remains interesting for the nine essays between pages 79 and 142, by such poets as Marianne Moore, Robert Frost, Richard Eberhart, William Carlos Williams, W. H. Auden, Wallace Stevens, and Richard Wilbur, on how they produce their poetry. Chapter 4, which essentially discusses the genesis of five poems, is also worthwhile.

Hood, Thomas. *The Rules of Rhyme: A Guide to English Versification*. New York: D. Appleton, 1882.
This standard work by Thomas Hood (1799-1845) has been issued and reissued. Poets still find Hood's advice on versification cogent, although modern poetic forms have moved beyond many of the strictures Hood imposes. The book considers elements of classical verse, guides and handbooks available in Hood's time on writing verse, and such metrical matters as poetic feet and the caesura. The section on comic and burlesque verse is illuminating, but the book's initial appeal—and some of its present appeal—rests in the 85-page dictionary of rhymes that Hood includes. The final essay on versification is also much alluded to.

Houseman, A. E. "The Name and Nature of Poetry." In *The Writer's Craft*, edited by John Hersey. New York: Alfred A. Knopf, 1974.
Houseman works from the premise that poetry is more physical than intellectual. He stresses the need for careful observation and crisp, direct presentation of concrete detail if poems are to succeed. This is a refreshing essay by one of the most controlled poets of the twentieth century. Houseman's own work resonates with specifics from which he builds atmosphere. In this essay, he suggests how poets can accomplish what he has so successfully achieved in his own work. For further comments about this collection, see other entries in this chapter as well as in chapters 1 and 2.

Jarrell, Randall. *Poetry and the Age*. New York: Alfred A. Knopf, 1953.
This is a comfortable book in which one of the major poets in the United States discusses his impressions and interpretations of a hodgepodge of poets such as Robert Frost (on whom Jarrell has written two essays), John Crowe Ransom, Walt Whitman, Wallace Stevens, Walter de la Mare, Alex Comfort, Tristan Corbière, Muriel Rukeyser, and R. P. Blackmur. The last chapter, on the situation of the poet, provides insights into a part of the past that produced some of the country's best poets.

Jerome, Judson. *The Poet's Handbook.* Cincinnati: Writer's Digest Books, 1980. This perennial best-seller is comprehensive and readable. Jerome, himself a poet of note, begins by discussing language as a medium. In chapter 2, he moves from that to a discussion of diction, followed in chapter 3 by a consideration of line division and meter. Subsequent chapters deal with such matters as accentual meter, alliteration, end rhymes, fixed forms, blank verse, free verse, imagery, and finding an audience.

_____, ed. *The Poet and the Poem.* Cincinnati: Writer's Digest Books, 1963. Jerome's later books are currently more relevant than this one. It is, however, interesting to see this early work. In part 2, Jerome deals with making poems, touching on such topics as diction, meter, line units, rhyme, figurative language, sound texture, tone, and meaning. Part 3 is entitled "Inside the Workshop." It deals with steps to take when one is beginning to write, then goes on to discuss revision and publication and marketing.

Kirby, David. *Writing Poetry: Where Poems Come from and How to Write Them.* Boston: The Writer, Inc., 1989.
Kirby's book is exceptionally reader-friendly and sequential. It begins by asking, "What is poetry?" It addresses the question but also goes into what poetry is not. Kirby looks at poems as journeys, discoveries, explorations. Part 2 considers how to write a poem, and suggests such strategies as keeping lists, reporting on reversals, excerpting material from speeches, prayers, letters, and other common sources. Part 3, "The Poet's Toolbox," expands on the material in part 2.

Koch, Kenneth. *I Never Told Anybody: Teaching Poetry in a Nursing Home.* New York: Random House, 1977.
The first 58 pages of this book are concerned with how to get nursing-home residents to write, how to jog their memories and get them to tap their pasts by asking evocative questions and creating a supportive and nonthreatening atmosphere. The final 170 pages of the book constitute an anthology of work produced in the poetry workshops that Koch conducted in nursing homes.

Kreutzer, Jame R. *Elements of Poetry.* New York: Macmillan, 1955.
Despite its age, this widely distributed book remains useful for its considerations of diction (chapter 2), metrics (chapter 3), rhyme and other sound effects (chapter 4), images (chapter 7), and irony, paradox, and ambiguity (chapter 8). More philosophical is chapter 9, "The Nature of Poetry." Chapter 10 discusses the major types of poetry (ballad, ode, and so forth) and the verse forms available to poets. This is a particularly practical chapter, and it is understandable, although somewhat specialized.

Kumin, Maxine. *To Make a Prairie: Essays on Poets, Poetry, and Country Living.* Ann Arbor: University of Michigan Press, 1979.

Something of a hodgepodge, by one of the leading contemporary writers in the United States, *To Make a Prairie* makes its most valuable contribution in its interviews with Virginia Elson, Beverlee Hughes, Joan Norris, Martha George Meek, and Karla Hammond. Part 3, "Three Lectures on Poetry," is searching and intelligent. Especially relevant is the section entitled "Four Kinds of I," which addresses poets' relation to their work and how important background is to the kind of poetry one writes.

Kunitz, Stanley. *A Kind of Order, a Kind of Folly: Essays and Conversations.* Boston: Little, Brown, 1975.

This is a collection of desultory essays that Kunitz through the years has written on such matters as poetry, the translating of poetry, and such poets as Theodore Roethke, Mark Rothko, Rainer Maria Rilke, H. D., and E. E. Cummings. The book's greatest contribution, perhaps, is in its five essays on relatively unknown young poets: Hugh Seidman, Peter Klappert, Michael Casey, Robert Haas, and Michael Ryan. In writing about these poets, Kunitz offers some keen insights into the poetic process that will be of value to those interested in writing poetry.

Lanier, Sidney. *The Science of English Verse.* New York: Charles Scribner's Sons, 1911.

In this classic study by one of America's leading writers, sound is addressed as the artistic material of which verse is made. Lanier attempts analytically to understand and exemplify all of the rhythms of verse in the English language, to approach the subject with the scientific objectivity suggested in his title. He focuses on secondary rhythms in speech, as well as on rhythms that he designates as 3-, 4-, and 5-rhythm speech. He speaks of the colors of verse, meaning presumably its rhyme. He pays special attention to vowel and consonant distribution, as well as to alliteration and assonance as poetic devices. It is interesting to compare Lanier's ideas with those of modern critics, particularly the deconstructionists.

Lewisohn, Ludwig. *The Magic Word: Studies in the Nature of Poetry.* New York: Farrar, Straus, 1950.

The title essay, which appears first in the volume, is worth reading. It is imaginative and perceptive. The subsequent essays on Homer, William Shakespeare, Johann Wolfgang von Goethe, and contemporary poetry reflect a mode of literary criticism that has long since been superseded.

Livingston, Myra Cohn. *When You Are Alone/It Keeps You Capone: An Approach to Writing with Children.* New York: Atheneum, 1973.

This imaginative approach to teasing writing out of children deals in its initial pages with sharing, then goes on to focus essentially on the writing of poetry. Chapter 5 discusses form versus no form in writing poetry. Chapter 7 shows how collective poems can be generated by groups of children. Chapter 10, on rhyme, is nicely balanced and not dogmatic. Chapter 11, on the haiku, is practical, and chapter 16, on generating ideas, offers valuable suggestions. For additional comments on this source, see chapter 7 of this bibliography.

Marston, Doris Ricker. *A Guide to Writing History*. Cincinnati: Writer's Digest Books, 1976.
This book covers a broad range of writing. It begins with information about audience and choosing topics to write about. It then devotes a few chapters to research. Chapter 12, "Historical Poetry and Short Fiction," is directly relevant to poets and is especially valuable for its three-page list of magazines that publish historical poetry. The list is slightly dated, but a remarkable number of the sources listed in it are still viable outlets for this genre. For further comments about this book, see chapters 1, 2, 3, and 7 of this bibliography.

Morton, William C. *The Harmony of Verse*. Toronto: University of Toronto Press, 1967.
Morton, a British physician, became interested in the rhythm and autometer of speech. He classifies meter into basic, major, and minor, and identifies metrical series, metrical linkages, pauses, metrical syllables, accent and tempo, phonetic melody, tone and pitch, and norms and progressions in speech and in verse. This is a technical approach, but one that raises many fundamental questions about how poetry communicates and about how some of the things that poets do unconsciously can be categorized and considered in broad, universal terms. The section on appeal and response raises interesting aesthetic questions that serious poets need to consider.

Muth, Marcia. *Writing and $elling: Poetry, Fiction, Articles, Plays, and Local History*. Santa Fe, N.Mex.: Sunstone Press, 1985.
Chapter 1 of this book discusses the writing and marketing of poetry. The approach is somewhat crass, although the chapters are organized well, each one having sections on how to proceed, how and where to market one's work, and other such information that is of some practical value. See additional comments about this source in chapters 1, 4, 9, and 10 of this bibliography.

Osgood, Charles Grosvenor. *Poetry as a Means of Grace*. Princeton, N.J.: Princeton University Press, 1941.
This is a very scholarly book and is not easy reading. The first chapter, on the nature of poetry, is nevertheless of considerable relevance for those seriously interested in poetry and willing to put forth the effort to understand the complex arguments the chapter contains. Subsequent chapters deal with such individual

poets as Dante, Edmund Spenser, John Milton, and Samuel Johnson. The approach to their work seems extremely dated.

Osmond, T. S. *A Study of Metre*. London: Alexander Moring, 1920.

This classic study of meter considers it in most of its forms, including duple, triple, and quadruple meter, metrical elements that have been given little attention in recent years. Osmond presumes more conventionally structured forms than those that have characterized most modern poetry. His book is of interest because it was written at a time when modernism was being born, two years before the publication of T. S. Eliot's *The Waste Land*, the single poem that helped to turn the tide away from conventional forms into more experimental ones. Some recent poets have begun trying to revive poetic forms of the past and to apply them in modified forms to the modern writing of verse.

Packard, William. *The Poet's Dictionary: A Handbook of Prosody and Poetic Devices*. New York: Harper & Row, 1989.

Pages 1-212 of this book consist of an alphabetical listing and discussion of terms, from *accent* to *zeugma*, that have to do with poetry, touching on such words and expressions as *assonance, palindrome, macaronics, idyll*, and *Ubi Sunt*. The appendix that deals with how to prepare and submit poetic manuscripts is of considerable practical value and should give poets insight into how best they can market their work successfully. For additional comments about this book, see chapter 10 of this bibliography.

Paz, Octavio. *The Bow and the Lyre*. Translated by Ruth L. C. Simms. Austin: University of Texas Press, 1973.

This book, first published in Spanish under the title *El arco y la lira* in 1956, has major sections on the poem, on the poetic revelation, and on poetry and history. The appendices are entitled "Poetry, Society, State," "Poetry and Respiration," and "Whitman, Poet of America." Although this is not a how-to-write-poetry book, it offers insights into the creative process that poets will find informative and intelligently suggestive. The political dimensions of poetry are emphasized, a quality that makes the book appropriate for contemporary poets.

Percy, Bernard. *The Power of Creative Writing: A Handbook of Insights, Activities, and Information to Get Your Students Involved*. Englewood Cliffs, N.J.: Prentice-Hall, 1981.

This book, discussed also in chapter 1 of this bibliography, gives solid general advice in its first two chapters. Chapter 6 is concerned with the writing of poetry, and its fifteen pages contain valuable insights into what motivates such writing and into strategies for success in such writing. Chapter 4 focuses on the criticism and evaluation of writing and is valuable to the poet because from it can be gleaned information that will make poets intelligently critical of their own writing.

Poe, Edgar Allan. "The Philosophy of Composition." In *The Writer's Craft*, edited by John Hersey. New York: Alfred A. Knopf, 1974.

Poe is much concerned with a writer's identifying the effect or impression to be conveyed and with how to capture that effect or impression. In discussing poetry, he addresses and emphasizes the matter of tone and of the effective use of such poetic devices as the refrain, which he used extensively in his own writing. He is also fully aware of the fact that language, even when it is read silently, has sound and that the sound is what makes poetry succeed or fail. For additional comments about Poe's essay, refer to chapter 1 under "General Studies."

Polking, Kirk, ed. *A Beginner's Guide to Getting Published*. Cincinnati: Writer's Digest Books, 1987.

The advice offered by John D. Engle, Jr. in his chapter "Poet's Primer" is sound and practical. Engle is more concerned with how to publish poetry than with how to write it, and his suggestions should enable fledgling poets to see some of their work in print if it is of reasonable quality. For additional comments about this book, see chapters 1, 4, and 7 of this bibliography under "General Studies."

Pound, Ezra. *ABC of Reading*. New Haven, Conn.: Yale University Press, 1934. Reprint. New York: New Directions, 1960.

In this book, which was really intended to be a textbook, the famous author of the *Cantos* addresses matters of metrics, explaining their use in some early poetry such as *Beowulf* and "The Seafarer." He also discusses sound and metrics in the music of Claude Debussy and Maurice Ravel. The book is pedagogical, containing useful exercises throughout. The prefatory material on how to study poetry, although it is only three pages long, is incisive and intelligent.

Preminger, Alex, ed. *Princeton Encyclopedia of Poetry and Poetics*. Enlarged ed. Princeton, N.J.: Princeton University Press, 1974.

This compendious book, which runs to 992 tightly packed pages, is essentially an alphabetical listing of terms that relate to poetry and poetics. The explanations are generally clear and accurate. The entries range from *Abecedarius* to *Zulu Poetry*, with an incredibly comprehensive list of entries between the first and last.

Press, John. *The Chequere'd Shade: Reflections on Obscurity in Poetry*. London: Oxford University Press, 1958.

Press demonstrates convincingly that obscurity in writing poetry is not limited to modern poets and goes on to substantiate his claim with an amazing array of examples from the broad range of poetry through the centuries. He quotes John Ruskin as saying, "The right of being obscure is not to be lightly claimed; it can only be founded upon long effort to be intelligible." The chapters on common readers (chapter 4) and on public worlds (chapter 6) are illuminating. Chapter 9, on the nature of poetry, is well conceived and thought-provoking.

Riccio, Ottone M. *The Intimate Art of Writing Poetry.* Englewood Cliffs, N.J.: Prentice-Hall, 1980.

Were this book to be purchased only for its three appendices, it would be worth the cost. Appendix 1 has a list of one hundred books, journals, and quarterlies relating to or publishing poetry. Appendix 2 lists a variety of markets. Appendix 3 identifies poetry workshops that are open to those who write in this genre. Fortunately, the rest of the book is also quite worthwhile, particularly chapter 2, "Brain and Heart," which delves into the conscious and unconscious minds, considers the use of memories and dreams in writing, and shows how emotions and experiences mold what poets write. Chapter 9 focuses on how to develop the discipline to write seriously and has great practical value. Overall, this book is excellent, although portions of it are now somewhat dated.

Rilke, Rainer Maria. *Letters to a Young Poet.* Translated with a foreword by Stephen Mitchell. New York: Random House, 1984. Reprint. New York: Vintage Books, 1986.

In this slim volume are reproduced some of the famous Austrian poet's letters to Franz Xaver Kappus, a student at the Military Academy at Wiener Neustadt with whom Rilke sustained a correspondence. Kappus was first put into touch with Rilke when the chaplain of the school, Professor Horaček, found the cadet reading a volume of Rilke's poetry. Horaček had been chaplain at the Lower Military School at Sankt-Pölen fifteen years earlier, when Rilke was a student there, and he urged Kappus to write to the poet. In his letters, Rilke reveals much about his creative process.

Rosen, Michael. *Did I Hear You Write?* London: Andre Deutsch, 1989.

Although this book is aimed at helping children to write, it has many good suggestions for writers of all ages. Its major aim is to stimulate the imagination in order to move children from speech to writing. Chapter 2, "Writing and the Written Mode," and chapter 3, "Starting Points for Oral Writing," will be of interest to writers of either poetry or prose. See chapter 1 of this bibliography under "General Studies" for additional comments on this entry.

Rosenthal, M. L. *Poetry and the Common Life.* New York: Oxford University Press, 1974.

The virtue of this well-written book is that it heightens the awareness of its readers to everything that surrounds them in the world with which they are in daily contact. Rosenthal finds sources of poetry in common speech, objects, and events. Good poets, he contends, have a special awareness of their surroundings and share their acute sensibilities with readers who, through them, are brought to new sensibilities themselves. Valuable examples are drawn from poets ranging from W. H. Auden to William Butler Yeats and touching on most of the major poets in Western literature.

_____. *The Poet's Art*. New York: W. W. Norton, 1987.

Chapter 2, "Growing into Poetry," suggests an approach that anyone can use to attempt writing in this medium. Chapter 5 deals extensively with musical form, which Rosenthal calls "the poem's musical body." The following chapter evaluates poems meaningfully and skillfully, providing a critical context that writers in this field can apply productively to their own work and the writing of others.

Stein, Gertrude. "Poetry and Grammar." In *The Writer's Craft*, edited by John Hersey. New York: Alfred A. Knopf, 1974.

Ever concerned with pattern and rhythm in poetry, Gertrude Stein, in this essay from her "Lectures in America," philosophizes about language and about the relationship of grammatical structures to the writing of poetry. Her style demonstrates how Stein pushes language and linguistic structures to new extremes. She poses and answers, often whimsically, such questions as "What is poetry"? "What is prose?" and "What does a comma do?" Her answers are not straightforward but rather cause readers to pose their own questions. The approach is absurdist but, when considered carefully, deadly serious. For further comments about this book, see chapters 1 and 2 of this bibliography.

Steward, Joyce S., and Mary K. Croft. *The Leisure Pen: A Book for Elderwriters*. Plover, Wis.: Keepsake Publishers, 1988.

Chapter 10 of this book concentrates on the poetry that older people write and encourages them to analyze their poems for specific detail, because it is this detail that makes their poems appealing and, sometimes, acceptable for publication. The approach is gentle, the advice sensible. For additional comments about this book, see chapters 1 and 8 of this bibliography.

Tarliskaja, Marina. *English Verse: Theory and History*. The Hague, Netherlands: Mouton, 1976.

Although this book is rather ponderous, it is well researched, and some of the extensive information it gives about word stress and phrasal stress has exceptional pertinence to one who approaches the writing of poetry seriously. The chapter on nondramatic iambic pentameter is also useful, although at times esoteric. Far too esoteric for most readers will be chapter 5, "A Typology of English Four-Ictic Verse." Chapter 8, the final one, is entitled "The Transition from Iambics to Syllables," and while quite specialized, is extremely thought-provoking in its discussions of the metrical thresholds of iambic pentameter and of the verse structure of the unknown meter. This book is definitely not for the beginner, but rather for the reader who seeks an intellectual challenge.

Tempest, Norton R. *The Rhythm of English Prose: A Manual for Students*. Cambridge, England: Cambridge University Press, 1930.

This work is of more historical than practical interest. It was greatly revered by some would-be poets of the 1930's, but its approach now seems quite remote. The author, a Fellow at the University of Liverpool when he wrote the book, discusses—in almost too much detail—rhythm, prose rhythm, and cadence, then uses his last chapter to apply and illustrate what he has said. The glossary following the main body of the book is also of historical interest. Many of the terms in it are not heard much in poetic circles today, but they are a mirror to a past from which modern poetry was springing—often more as a reaction against this sort of approach than as a direct result of it.

Tsujimoto, Joseph I. *Teaching Poetry Writing to Adolescents*. Urbana, Ill.: National Council of Teachers of English, 1988.
Although Tsujimoto wrote essentially with teachers in mind, the strategies through which he leads his readers are sequential, interesting, and good fun. Anyone who wants to write poetry will benefit from looking into this well-conceived and well-executed book. Samples of students' poems and the eighteen poetry assignments that are the heart of the book will increase one's fluency in that medium. For further comments about this book, refer to chapter 7 of this bibliography.

Untermeyer, Jean Starr. *Private Collection*. New York: Alfred A. Knopf, 1965.
This is a book of recollections by a woman who was herself an established poet. She reminisces about many of the poets she knew during her life, including Edna St. Vincent Millay, Sara Teasdale, Amy Lowell, Vachel Lindsay, and Robert Frost. The book is sensitively written and provides excellent insights into the creative process that results in the writing of poetry.

Untermeyer, Louis. *The Pursuit of Poetry*. New York: Simon & Schuster, 1969.
Untermeyer, well known as an anthologist and poet himself, divides his book into two portions, "The Craft of Poetry" (pages 1-138) and "The Anatomy of Poetry" (pages 139-304). The latter section is essentially a dictionary of poetic terms. Untermeyer demonstrates a broad understanding and firm grip on the matter of how poetry is wrought and of what succeeds and does not succeed in poetry. The book is readable and informative.

Welsh, Andrew. *Roots of Lyric: Primitive Poetry and Modern Poetics*. Princeton, N.J.: Princeton University Press, 1978.
Welsh shows convincingly how recent poets have used the poetic conventions of the earliest poetry and how they have built on them and modified them to meet the demands of new poetry. He considers such forms as riddles, emblem poetry, the ideogram, the charm, and chants. Chapter 8 is on rhythm and is quite useful to those interested in prosody. Chapter 9, on melopoeia, is less lucid than some of the other chapters in the book. It deals with a difficult topic, dividing the topic into the song melos, the charm melos, and the speech melos. Overall, the book

is excellent, if quite demanding. Not for the uninitiated or for those with a limited sense of history.

Whallon, William. *Formula, Character, and Context: Studies in Homeric, Old English, and Old Testament Poetry.* Washington, D.C.: Center for Hellenic Studies, 1969.
The six chapters of this book are concerned largely with verbal formulas and how they relate to characterization and context in ancient poetry. Although the book is quite specialized, it has much to offer modern poets who are willing to exert themselves to the utmost to understand what Whallon is saying. Heroic poetry, once the chief means of conveying history, is far from dead among American and British poets, although it has been drastically modified to meet the demands of modern readers.

Williams, Miller, ed. *Patterns of Poetry: An Encyclopedia of Forms.* Baton Rouge: Louisiana State University Press, 1986.
This volume considers every conceivable form of poetry. Chapter 3 deals with stanza patterns in traditional forms of set length, such as the rondel, triolet, and haiku. Chapter 4 considers stanzaic patterns in forms of indefinite length. Chapter 6 deals with variations on typical stanzas, and chapter 7 focuses on variations on poems, such as rime royal, sestina, and blank verse. The book is extensive and accurate.

Wilson, Robert N. *Man Made Plain: The Poet in Contemporary Society.* Cleveland: Howard Allen, 1979.
A volume in the Anthropology and Sociology series, this book explores such topics as "Literature, Society, and Personality" (chapter 1), "The Language of Poetry" (chapter 2), "Creativity: The Self as Vocation" (chapter 3), and "Views of the Self as Poet" (chapter 5). Chapter 6 focuses on Ezra Pound. The consideration of subjective concerns in the writing of poetry as addressed in chapters 3 and 5 is stimulating and provocative.

The Writing Business: A Poets and Writers Handbook. Edited jointly by the editors of *Coda: A Poets and Writers Newsletter.* New York: Poets and Writers, 1985.
Part 4 of this useful book deals directly with poetry, suggesting ways for young poets to get started by submitting their work not only to poetry magazines and literary journals but also for possible inclusion in poetry anthologies that appear regularly. The editors also suggest that poets arrange to give public readings of their work and that they try to get employment by teaching in poetry workshops. The book contains a writer's guide to reference books, a checklist for giving readings, and a list of publishers' addresses, which is minimal but is at least a beginning. For additional comments about this source, see chapters 1, 2, 3, 9, and 10 of this bibliography.

York, R. A. *The Poem as Utterance*. New York: Methuen, 1986.
The most interesting portion of this thirteen-chapter book for practicing poets will likely be the second chapter, "Pragmatics and Style." More specialized are the analytically critical chapters on William Butler Yeats, T. S. Eliot, W. H. Auden, Paul Verlaine, Rainer Maria Rilke, Stéphane Mallarmé, Salvatore Quasimodo, and Charles Baudelaire. This well-documented study has a useful index and is lucid, though not easy to read. Definitely for the seasoned reader.

Chapter 6
WRITING FOR FILM AND TELEVISION

Blackner, Irwin R. *The Elements of Screenwriting: A Guide for Film and Television Writers.* New York: Macmillan, 1986.
This book, which considers such matters as conflict, structure, character, and exposition in its early chapters, is strongest in chapter 8, which focuses on matters of production. It is also strong for its appendices, the first of which enumerates the functions and services of the Writers' Guild of America, and the second of which presents the Writers' Guild Agency list. The material on dialogue (chapter 6) and the look at a professional script (chapter 7) are of significance to those who write in these media.

Brady, Ben, and Lance Lee. *The Understructure of Writing for Film and Television.* Austin: University of Texas Press, 1988.
Brady and Lee apply many techniques of recent critical and rhetorical theory to their astute analysis of what underlies much film and television writing. They actually strip these media of their flesh and get to the bone, the essential structure of what constitutes successful writing in the two media they consider here. The book, although it is not easy reading, rewards readers by providing penetrating insights into the theoretical side of writing drama for film and television. Part 2, which addresses questions of developing character and achieving conflict—including crises and climaxes—is particularly helpful.

Brenner, Alfred. *The TV Scriptwriter's Handbook.* Cincinnati: Writer's Digest Books, 1985.
Brenner knows his way around in the competitive world of television writing. His handbook is direct and specific. It emphasizes making the most of the visual effects this medium makes possible. One of the fundamental elements of television writing is motion, and Brenner understands broadly and deeply how to make this element work effectively for writers. His two chapters on the script conference are particularly useful. He suggests ways in which writers can sharpen their visual sensitivity and use it to shape their scripts into marketable properties. Chapter 19, on situation comedies and soap operas, offers some good advice, although the book in general has become dated.

Bretnor, Reginald, ed. *The Craft of Science Fiction.* New York: Harper & Row, 1976.
Bretnor's essay "SF: The Challenge to the Writer" both defines the market and suggests its difficulties. Harlan Ellison, in his essay "With the Eyes of the Demon: Seeing the Fantastic as a Video Image," writes knowledgeably about the topic and is specifically relevant. Frank Herbert's essay "Men on Other Planets" is also useful. For further comments about this book, see chapters 1 and 2.

Catron, Louis E. "Guidelines for the Beginning Playwright." In *The Writer's Handbook, 1987*, edited by Sylvia K. Burack. Boston: The Writer, Inc., 1987.
Catron's unlucky thirteen guidelines for playwrights could turn out to be very lucky for the people who follow them. Among these, the author urges people to begin with one-act plays because they are easier to control than full-length dramas. People must write about something they care passionately about, and they must know how to incorporate conflict into their plays. Playwrights are advised to be realistic in their writing and to allow emotion its full range in the play. Limit the number of characters, keep their speeches short, and keep them on stage as long as possible. Aim for a unity of time and try at first to fit it within a play that runs about thirty minutes. Capitalize on the protagonist/ antagonist relationship.

Clareson, Thomas D., ed. *SF: The Other Side of Realism—Essays on Modern Fantasy and Science Fiction*. Bowling Green, Ohio: Bowling Green University Press, 1971.
Several contributions to this book have to do with science-fiction films. Among these is Richard Hodgens' "A Short and Tragical History of the Science Fiction Film," whose in-depth consideration of *When Worlds Collide* is extremely interesting, pointing out the technical problems and technical faults found in the film. Morris Beja, Robert Plank, and Alex Eisenstein's joint contribution, "Three Perspectives of a Film," considers *2001: A Space Odyssey* from three vastly differing points of view. For further comments about this source, see chapter 2 of this bibliography under the heading "Science Fiction."

Coe, Michelle E. *How to Write for Television*. New York: Crown, 1980.
Chapter 30, which treats interviewing, is well done, as is the following chapter on narrative. Essential to anyone who writes in this field is chapter 28, on timing. Coe offers considerable advice for those who wish to write commercials for television. For further comments about this book, see chapter 10.

Ephron, Henry. *We Thought We Could Do Anything: The Life of Screenwriters Phoebe and Henry Ephron*. New York: W. W. Norton, 1977.
This lighthearted book, replete with excellent pictures, provides an inside look at the creative activities of the pair who wrote the screenscripts for *Carousel, There's No Business Like Show Business*, and *The Jackpot*. This is a warm book that permits an informal approach to understanding how creative energy culminates in screenplays.

Fitz-Randolph, Jane. *Writing for the Juvenile and Teenage Market*. New York: Funk and Wagnalls, 1969.
Chapter 23 deals specifically with writing juvenile material for film and television. Some of this material is dated, but in general outline it is still of value.

For additional comments about this book, refer to chapters 3, 4, and 7 of this bibliography.

Frong, William. *The Screenwriter Looks at the Screenwriter: Twelve Top Screenwriters Talk About Their Craft, Their Techniques, and Their Role in Shaping a Film.* New York: Macmillan, 1972.
Despite its lugubrious title, Frong's book is worthwhile for its extensive interviews with Lewis John Carlino, William Bowers, Walter Brown Newman, Jonathan Axelrod, Ring Lardner, Jr., I. A. L. Diamond, Buck Henry, David Giles, Nunnally Johnson, Edward Anhalt, Stirling Silliphant, and Fay Kanin. This is an impressive list of some of the most successful screenwriters of several decades, and their insights into their art and into the profession are extremely candid, searching, and useful to those who wish to write in this high-paying medium.

Garvey, Daniel E., and William L. Rivers. *Broadcast Writing.* New York: Longman, 1982.
Garvey and Rivers write about both television and radio scripts and have realistic suggestions for writing in both fields. They discuss quite fruitfully writing television dramas and comedies, but in chapter 5 they also broach the subject of writing television commercials and public service announcements. Chapter 9 addresses the matter of television news writing. Chapter 7 deals with writing radio commercials and chapter 8 with radio news writing. Chapter 10, on writing semi-scripted programs, is especially valuable and unique among the popular books in the field.

Giustino, Rolando. *The Filmscript: A Writer's Guide.* Englewood Cliffs, N.J.: Prentice-Hall, 1980.
Giustino traces the development of a shooting script, *Night Flight*, from conception to final production. Particularly useful are chapter 4, "The Screenplay," which presents sample master scenes from *Night Flight*, and chapter 5, "The Shooting Script," which gives well-chosen samples from the shooting script. Giustino definitely is an insider who knows his subject intimately.

Herman, Lewis. *A Practical Manual of Screen Playwriting for Theater and Television Films.* New York: The World Publishing, 1966.
This book, which has been reissued several times through the years, is an exhaustive study of the tools of filmmaking. The first section considers dramaturgy and has a useful discussion of studio procedures. It also identifies several plot patterns: the love pattern, the Cinderella pattern, the triangle pattern, and others. The second section goes into technical matters, among them the full shot, the long shot, the medium shot, the close-up, the tilt shot, and the dolly shot.

The third and last major section goes into the actual writing of a shooting script and deals with matters such as image size and angle, dialogue cutaways, tempo, and rhythm. The material on sound and music is particularly solid, and the material on the "subjective camera" is thought-provoking.

Hill, Wycliffe A. *Ten Million Photoplay Plots: The Master Key to All Dramatic Plots.* Los Angeles: The Feature Photodrama, 1919.
The title of this book badly overstates what the text delivers, but it is of interest to read this guide to writing for silent films; the first talkie was not released until a decade after this book was published. The contribution it makes to modern readers is in its identifying thirty-seven basic dramatic situations from which photoplays could be made. These are broken down into such subdivisions as happy situations, pathetic situations, inspiring situations, disastrous situations precipitated without criminal intent, and the same situations precipitated with criminal intent. It is also interesting to read the author's comments on censorship regulations of his day and on twelve reasons that scripts do not sell. His suggestion for building stories backward from their climaxes is also enticing and has contemporary possibilities.

Lawson, John Howard. *Theory and Technique of Playwriting and Screenwriting.* New York: G. P. Putnam's Sons, 1936, 1949.
Book 2 of this volume is devoted to screenwriting. It parallels closely book 1, which is devoted to playwriting, but it takes fully into account the fluidity that motion pictures make possible. Lawson discusses many of the same matters he talks about in book 1—progression, the obligatory scene, climax, and characterization—but he deals with these topics quite differently in his discussions of screenwriting from the way he approaches them in his discussions of writing plays. For further comments about this book, see chapter 4 of this bibliography.

McGivern, William P. "Writing for Television and Movies." In *The Mystery Writer's Handbook*, edited by Lawrence Treat. Cincinnati: Writer's Digest Books, rev. ed. 1984.
McGivern, who has written some sixty television scripts and twelve film scripts, gives practical advice about writing and marketing mysteries for these media. He gives savvy advice about taboos that will kill a script. He recommends that if one writes a script with a particular actor or actress in mind, it is reasonable to send the script directly to that actor or actress. Although this is a rather brash and risky thing to do, it sometimes yields results that could be obtained in no other way. The author's philosophy is "nothing ventured, nothing gained."

Maloney, Martin, and Paul Max Rubenstein. *Writing for the Media.* Englewood Cliffs, N.J.: Prentice-Hall, 1980.
Chapter 1 discusses the business aspects of writing for the media. Much of the

rest of the book focuses on writing specific types of material for the media. Chapter 12, for example, suggests the opportunities in writing advertising copy, which can help writers to survive if their other work is not making its mark. Chapter 5, which is concerned with deciding on the treatment a script should get, also remains informative and practical. The advice about getting writing assignments (chapter 3) is useful. For further comments about this source, refer to chapter 3 of this bibliography.

Manvell, Roger. *Theater and Film: A Comparative Study of the Two Forms of Dramatic Art, and of the Problems of Adaptation of Stage Plays into Films.* Rutherford, N.J.: Fairleigh Dickinson University Press, 1979.
This scholarly study initially establishes the principles of theater and of film, differentiating the two media from each other in considerable detail. The book's second section, which is the heart of the text, discusses specific stage plays that have been made into films and is at its best in its discussions of Eugene O'Neill's *Long Day's Journey into Night*, Tennessee Williams' *A Streetcar Named Desire*, Harold Pinter's *The Caretaker*, Edward Albee's *Who's Afraid of Virginia Woolf?*, and Anton Chekhov's *Three Sisters*. All told, Manvell discusses fifteen plays, including five by William Shakespeare, that have been adapted to film. He also offers a twenty-page list of dramatists whose plays have been adapted to films.

Packard, William. *The Art of Screenwriting: Story, Script, and Markets.* New York: Paragon House, 1987.
Packard zeroes in on the elements of screenwriting that differentiate it from writing in other genres, including drama, which has fewer possibilities because of the space limitations of the stage. Packard shows the flexibility of the screenplay, which is constantly rewritten to meet the needs that arise as the film is being shot. For further comments about this book, see chapter 10 of this bibliography.

Parsons, Louella O. *How to Write for the "Movies."* Chicago: A. C. McClurg, 1915.
It is historically interesting to read this book by a woman who was shortly to become one of Hollywood's leading gossip columnists. Written before she went to California to launch the career for which she is best remembered, Parsons drew material for this book from her experience as editor of the *Essay Companion* and from letters she exchanged with photoplaywrights during her tenure as a columnist for the *Chicago Herald*. Of the thirty-three chapters the book contains, chapter 8, on the continuity of scenes, and chapter 9, on scenic action, hold most for modern readers. Chapters 19 and 20, on plot, and chapter 24, on the "punch," are also of interest.

Polking, Kirk, Jean Chimsky, and Rose Adkins, eds. *The Beginning Writer's Answer Book*. 2d ed. Cincinnati: Writer's Digest Books, 1978.

Cited also in chapters 2 and 4 of this bibliography, this book, in chapters 27 and 28, addresses writing for television and for motion pictures. The chapters are effective in illustrating the differences in point of view and in handling the passage of time that exist in these two media and that differentiate them from other forms of literary expression.

Rilla, Wolf. *The Writer and the Screen: On Writing for Film and Television*. New York: William Morrow, 1974.

Part 1, on the image, the word, and the writer, is competent but quite conventional. Part 2, which focuses on the screenplay—although it considers the usual elements of plot, language, character, dialogue and *mise-en-scène*—has considerable originality and is filled with valuable, fresh insights, as is the following section, which focuses on the documentary film and on writing for television. Rilla considers filmscripts from *Battleship Potemkin* to *Midnight Cowboy*, filmwriters from Orson Welles to Andy Warhol. This section also has material on marketing scripts, much of which has been superseded by more recent books. For further comments about this book, see chapter 10 of this bibliography.

Roberts, Edward Barry. *Television Writing and Selling*. Boston: The Writer, Inc., 1954.

This book's eighteen chapters provide a prodigiously comprehensive approach to writing for television, although some of its suggestions are a bit dated. Despite this, chapter 4, which discusses camera directions, and 5, which considers problems of time in writing for television, remain on the whole extraordinarily useful. There are chapters on the half-hour live teleplay (chapter 9), the half-hour taped teleplay (chapter 10), the fifteen-minute teleplay (chapter 11), and the hour-long teleplay (chapter 12). The information on special effects (chapter 3) is still essentially cogent, although computerized effects have altered that field considerably.

Rouverol, Jean. *Writing for the Soaps*. Cincinnati: Writer's Digest Books, 1984.

Rouverol obviously knows the specialized field of her book intimately. She discusses knowledgeably the history of soaps in the first chapter, then discusses the assembly-line approach to writing. In chapter 3, she discusses the head writer and the story conference. Chapter 4 considers time, place, and money limitations within which writers in this industry must work. In chapter 5, Rouvenol analyzes a single episode of a soap. She goes on in later chapters to discuss means of maintaining tension and how to write hour-long and half-hour scripts, with examples. Chapter 14 deals with agencies, ratings, and pay. The material on marketing scripts is informed and realistic. For additional comments about this book, see chapter 10 of this bibliography.

Sargeant, Epes Winthrop. *Technique of the Photoplay*. 2d ed. New York: The Moving Picture World, 1913.

Sargeant's book, because of its age, is mostly of historical interest, but it is remarkable that a book of this sort existed in 1913. Particularly amazing is that chapter 21 is devoted to the talking picture, which at that time was more a dream than a reality. Chapter 5, which focuses on the form of the photoplay, and chapter 6, which focuses on the plot of action in photoplays, have some remarkably modern ideas in them. It is extremely interesting to see how prescient Sargeant was in speculating about a medium that in his day was relatively new.

Seldes, Gilbert. *Writing for Television*. New York: Greenwood Press, 1968.

This book is a reprint of the 1952 edition and, despite its age, has some interesting comments to make about such matters as writing with the director in mind (chapter 5), writing the serial (chapter 12), and writing the full-length play (chapter 14). Chapter 4, "Working with—and Against—Time," is essential. Chapter 18 gives good advice about writing for local markets. For additional comments about this book, refer to chapter 7 of this bibliography.

Straczynski, J. Michael. *The Complete Book of Scriptwriting*. Cincinnati: Writer's Digest Books, 1987.

Straczynski suggests tactics, particularly relating to dialogue, that will help writers in all forms of drama, although his main interest is obviously in helping film and television authors to put the possibilities of those two visual media to their best use. Chapter 1 focuses on writing television scripts, chapter 2 on writing radio scripts, chapter 3 on writing screenplays, and chapter 4 on writing stage plays. Each section covers the history of writing in the genre under discussion, the art of that genre, the craft of the genre, and marketing scripts in that genre. For further comments on this book, see chapter 4 of this bibliography.

Styan, J. L. *The Dramatic Experience*. Cambridge, England: Cambridge University Press, 1965.

Styan focuses on classical British drama in this book, but in chapter 7, he has some uniquely penetrating things to say about cinema, radio drama, and the television play. These observations are fresh and valuable. For additional comments about this book, see chapter 4 of this bibliography.

Van Nostran, William. *The Nonbroadcast Television Writer's Handbook*. White Plains, N.Y.: Knowledge Industry Publications, 1983.

In this one-of-a-kind book, Van Nostran considers the broad area of television filming that is not intended for commercial or educational television stations but is aimed at training sessions for corporations and educational organizations, for government agencies, and for the medical profession. Discussed are such areas as "Research Techniques: Getting to the Sources" (chapter 3), "Writing for the

Eye" (chapter 7), "Writing Unscripted Formats" (chapter 9), and "Writing for Interactive Video" (chapter 11). The list of professional organizations in appendix B is useful.

Wolff, Jurgen, and Kerry Cox. *Successful Scriptwriting*. Cincinnati: Writer's Digest Books, 1988.
Wolff and Cox productively address the relationship between characterization and dialogue and show how dialogue drives drama. They are also well aware of the visual effects that are available to scriptwriters for film and television that are not available—or at least easily available—to the more conventional playwright or dramatist. The amount of dialogue in scripts written for film and television is sometimes substantially less than that in the traditional drama because the camera can articulate details without using words. The book is stronger in discussing the theoretical aspects of scriptwriting than it is in suggesting markets for scripts but is, nevertheless, a practical and useful reference for writers.

Wylie, Max. *Writing for Television*. New York: Cowles Book Company, 1970.
Although this volume is a bit dated, Wylie's comments about audience in part 1 are still quite valid. The material in part 3 on comedy, in part 4 on drama, and in part 5 on soap operas is of passing interest. Chapter 14 of part 6, on plotting drama, is well worth reading. Wylie presents appropriate examples for all of the categories of television writing he discusses, and his comments are generally perceptive. For additional comments about this book, refer to chapter 7 of this bibliography.

Chapter 7
WRITING FOR, WITH, AND ABOUT JUVENILES

Aiken, Joan. *The Way to Write for Children.* New York: St. Martin's Press, 1982.
Although its title suggests a quite dogmatic approach, the author essentially is not dogmatic. She suggests that authors first differentiate between writing *for* children and writing *about* children. She identifies taboo subjects that writers for children should avoid. She also divides the children's audience into three basic groups determined largely by age. She then discusses what is appropriate to each group. Chapter 7, on picture books, poetry, and teenage novels, is strong. Less satisfactory is chapter 9, on the important topic of taboos. In this chapter, Aiken sometimes seems insensitive to language and its nuances. For further remarks about this book, see chapter 5 of this bibliography.

Arbuthnot, May Hill. *Children and Books.* 3d ed. Chicago: Scott, Foresman, 1964.
A staple of children's literature courses, this large (688-page) textbook is so comprehensive in its approach that it makes a good starting point for those who want to learn as much as they can about the field quickly. Among its twenty-one chapters, chapter 6, "Poetry and the Child's World," chapter 7, "Growing Up with Poetry," and chapter 8, "Using Poetry with Children," are particularly well expressed and valuable. Chapter 14, "Animal Stories," and chapter 17, "Biography," are also important and provide sound direction for those who would write in these areas.

Ashley, L. F. *Children's Reading and the 1970's.* Toronto: McClelland and Stewart, 1972.
Eight of this book's nine chapters have their own appendices, which contain interesting examples and comments. Of special pertinence are chapters 2 and 3, respectively covering children's preferences and dislikes in reading. Chapter 4 touches on a topic not found in many books of this sort: likes and dislikes concerning the format of children's books. The book's first chapter, concerned with children's reading and society, raises interesting social and political questions, as does chapter 5, which deals with children's reading and television.

Asimov, Janet, and Isaac Asimov. *How to Enjoy Writing: A Book of Aid and Comfort.* New York: Walker, 1987.
Chapter 12 of this lighthearted book, which is appropriately illustrated with cartoons, focuses on writing children's books. Although the chapter is brief—only six pages—it provides useful insights and conveys a positive attitude toward writing that should help writers to revivify their spirits when they are lagging. This entry is also mentioned in chapter 2 of this bibliography.

Avery, Gillian. *Childhood's Pattern: A Study of Heroes and Heroines of Children's Fiction, 1790-1950*. London: Hodder and Stoughton, 1975.

Much of this scholarly volume is devoted to background material that may be of limited value to those who write for children. Chapter 8, "The Manly Boys from 1800 to 1914," and chapter 9, "'Modern Girls' and Schoolgirls, 1880-1940," however, provide indispensable information for writers pursuing this genre. Chapter 10, "The Child's Hero," is also interesting, because it traces (as do the two preceding chapters) changes and progressions in tastes and enthusiasms. These changes and progressions are presently occurring at an accelerated pace, but it is useful to writers to know about their course in the past.

Baker, Augusta, and Ellin Greene. *Storytelling: Art and Technique*. New York: R. R. Bowker, 1987.

Although the major thrust of this book is oral storytelling, it is from such stories that many children's books grow, making this book valuable to those who wish to write for children. The authors consider what makes stories tellable and how children learn from stories. Of great value to writers in this field is the thirty-four-page appendix 2, which is a tightly packed list of resources for storytellers. Many of these sources are equally appropriate for those who write or wish to write in this genre.

Behn, Harry. *Chrysalis: Concerning Children and Poetry*. New York: Harcourt, Brace and World, 1949.

Behn knows how children think and has devised strategies for helping them to write poetry as a means of learning. Especially useful are the sections on the sources of images and on haiku. The section concerning words is fresh and lively. The final section of the book on myth and poetry has a pleasing philosophical/historical tone yet is easily accessible to readers. For additional comments about this book, see also chapter 5 of this bibliography.

Bicknell, Treld Pelkey, and Felicity Trotman, eds. *How to Write and Illustrate Children's Books*. Cincinnati: Writer's Digest Books, 1988.

Bicknell and Trotman's book will be of greatest interest to those who are writing for young children, preschool through age eight or nine. The editors suggest topics of interest to children at different age levels and note that details must be accurate but not so complex and convoluted as to require a great deal of time to develop well. Young children respond best to stories that move rapidly toward their climaxes and end with little falling action. Children should not be talked down to. It is all right to use some demanding vocabulary *if* unfamiliar words and terms are defined intertextually. Writers should pay special attention to the sound of what they are writing, because much of it will be read aloud. Parents usually respond best to books that have some didactic elements and are more willing to spend their money on such books than on those that do not teach overtly.

Brady, John, and Jean M. Fredette, eds. *Fiction Writer's Market*. Cincinnati: Writer's Digest Books, 1981.
Lee Wyndham's essay, "How to Organize a Book for Children and Young Adults," gets to the heart of how books for juveniles are put together. Wyndham knows a great deal about attention span, taboo topics, and the kinds of endings that young people anticipate in the books they like best to read. This essay, short though it is, is crammed with valuable insights as relevant today as when the essay was written. Also of value is Brian Garfield's essay on juvenile and young adult novels. For further discussion of this collection, see chapters 1, 2, and 10 of this bibliography.

Bratton, J. S. *The Impact of Victorian Children's Literature*. London: Croom Helm, 1981.
Bratton's study, while essentially scholarly, offers information that will be of immediate practical use to many writers who contribute to the juvenile market. Chapter 2 provides a useful and interesting historical background to the field, considering juvenile and children's publishing in England from 1800 to 1850. Chapter 4 considers books for boys and the following chapter addresses books for girls. What appealed to each in the period under consideration is not drastically different from what appeals to boys and girls at present. An understanding of this difference is essential to anyone trying to break into this market. Strong documentation and comprehensive index.

Burgett, Gordon. *Query Letters/Cover Letters*. Carpenteria, Calif.: Communication Unlimited, 1985.
Narrow in focus, this small book has valuable information for illustrators of children's books as well as for their authors. Chapter 2 specifically addresses the topic of query letters about artwork for books; it provides useful samples to cover several types of situations. Chapter 3, which treats query letters about books, and chapter 4, treating cover letters, are both clear and direct. Both chapters contain sample letters.

Carpenter, Lisa. *1991 Children's Writer's and Illustrator's Market*. Cincinnati: Writer's Digest Books, 1991.
Despite its somewhat burdensome title, this book moves beyond its hyperapostrophizing and offers valuable information about current markets for juvenile literature, covering both book and magazine outlets. The information on how writers can illustrate their own books is fresh and upbeat.

Carr, Jo, comp. *Beyond Fact: Nonfiction for Children and Young People*. Chicago: American Library Association, 1982.
For those interested in the rapidly growing field of nonfiction for young readers, this book offers considerable guidance. It contains useful sections on nonfiction

writing, on the excitement of discovery (largely focusing on science), history, biography, and controversial social and political matters. Sections are provided by an impressive array of experts in their fields. Carr has organized the book well and chosen the topics to be covered in it with an obvious understanding of this field of study.

Collins, James L., ed. *The Western Writer's Handbook.* Boulder, Colo.: Johnson Books, 1987.
Chapter 5 of this collection, "Writing the Young Adult Western" by G. Clifton Wisler, is excellent. It gives a fine overview of the field, citing such westerns as *Shane* and showing how stories about the west can be well wrought and are extremely appropriate to young adults, who are receptive to them. For additional comments about this book, see chapter 2 of this bibliography.

Dessner, Lawrence Jay. *How to Write a Poem.* New York: Washington Mews Books, 1979.
Midway through this twelve-chapter book is chapter 7, which focuses on authors and heroes. It is particularly relevant to those who wish to write poetry for children because the creation of heroes is an important ingredient of children's literature generally, and certainly of children's poetry. The material early in the book on motivating writing is also useful. For additional comments on this title, see chapter 5 of this bibliography.

Duncan, Lois. *How to Write and Sell Your Personal Experiences.* Cincinnati: Writer's Digest Books, 1979.
Chapters 14 and 15 focus on writing for young people, showing how writers can draw on the memories of their childhood experiences to write stories that appeal to young readers. The book also identifies markets and suggests how to shape query letters and to prepare manuscripts for submission. The emphasis here is on using one's own background experience to shape fiction. For additional comments on this book, see chapters 1 and 8 of this bibliography.

Eidenier, Connie, ed. *1990 Children's Writer's and Illustrator's Market.* Cincinnati: Writer's Digest Books, 1990.
This frequently updated and reissued guide offers comprehensive information about markets for literature aimed at the juvenile market and has valuable contributions by writers of children's books on how to approach such writing, including information about what appeals to children in certain age groups. Sound is emphasized as a vital ingredient in children's literature. The material for illustrators is particularly useful in suggesting the preparation and submission of illustrations, including how to package such items in ways that will prevent their being damaged in transit. Certainly one of the most comprehensive guides in the field, this book touches on every significant matter affecting the writers of books aimed at the juvenile market.

Esbensen, Barbara Juster. *A Celebration of Bees: Helping Children Write Poetry*. Minneapolis: Winston Press, 1975.

In this imaginative book, Esbensen, whose chapters are unnumbered, discusses words and their uses, the cinquain and haiku as poetic forms appropriate to children, and subjects to write about. She also has an interesting section entitled "Animating the Inanimate," which is among the most useful in the book. Esbensen also provides extensive samples of poems written by students from ages seven to eighteen. This book has many good suggestions that go beyond the age range of the intended audience. Anyone who wants to write poetry can learn from this book.

Fitz-Randolph, Jane. *Writing for the Juvenile and Teenage Market*. New York: Funk and Wagnalls, 1969.

Fitz-Randolph's categories of stories—the incident story (chapter 5), the story of purpose achieved (chapter 6), the wish-fulfillment story (chapter 7), and others—are useful. Chapter 17, "What's Different About Teenagers?," is psychologically sound. Chapters 19 and 20 consider writing articles for various outlets that serve the juvenile market. For additional comments about this book, refer to chapters 3, 4, and 6 of this bibliography.

Frey, Charles, and John Griffith. *The Literary Heritage of Childhood*. New York: Greenwood Press, 1987.

Even though this is not a how-to-write-for-juveniles book, those who write children's fiction will benefit from reading the thoughtful analyses the authors have provided of such books as the Grimm brothers' fairy tales (chapter 4), Hans Christian Andersen's fairy tales (chapter 5), Edward Lear's *Nonsense Poems* and *Laughable Lyrics* (chapter 8), Charles Dickens' *A Christmas Carol* (chapter 9), Louisa May Alcott's *Little Women* (chapter 16), James Barrie's *Peter Pan* (chapter 23), and E. B. White's *Charlotte's Web* (chapter 28). The book is well written, and the bibliography and index are both useful.

Gallo, Donald R. *Speaking for Ourselves: Autobiographical Sketches by Notable Authors of Books for Young Adults*. Urbana, Ill.: National Council of Teachers of English, 1990.

In this book, authors for juveniles—Judy Blume, S. E. Hinton, Paul Zindel, and eighty-four others—reveal insights into how autobiographical details have informed their writing for young people. They discuss how significant events in their lives have been transformed into the fiction for which they are well known and regarded. For additional comments about this book, see chapter 8 of this bibliography.

Giblin, James Cross. *Writing Books for Young People*. Boston: The Writer, Inc., 1990.
Giblin, an editor and publisher for more than two decades, has written several award-winning nonfiction books for young children. This helpful guide gives practical advice for writing both fiction and nonfiction for young people ranging in age from preschool to adolescence. Gilbin's advice on marketing is clear and direct. Chapter 6, on common failings in juvenile fiction, will help authors in this field avoid some major problems. The book covers all aspects of juvenile writing, including picture books for very young children. Gilbin obviously understands the stages of development through which children pass and applies this knowledge to the suggestions he makes for writing that will appeal to children of various ages. For further comments on this book, refer to chapter 2 of this bibliography under the heading "Science Fiction."

Gilbert, Nan. *See Yourself in Print: A Handbook for Young Writers*. Illustrated by Jacqueline Tomes. New York: Hawthorne Books, 1968.
After discussing basic markets, Gilbert suggests how young people can get writing ideas from such mundane pursuits as babysitting. Chapter 20 deals with stories for the very young. Chapter 22 is devoted to "plotting the tiny tot," chapter 23 to sports stories for juniors, chapter 24 to regional history for juniors, and chapter 25 to teenage stories. The next two chapters are on teen holiday stories and other stories for teenagers. Gilbert offers some good marketing ideas. For more comments on this book, see chapter 10 of this bibliography.

Higginson, William J., with Penny Harter. *The Haiku Handbook: How to Write, Share, and Teach Haiku*. New York: McGraw-Hill, 1985.
Chapter 11 of this book concerns getting youngsters to write haiku. It is both workable and delightful for its highly positive and realistic approach. Three extremely useful appendices provide a season-word list and index, a glossary, and a list of resources. For additional comments about this book, see chapter 5 of this bibliography.

Hildick, Wallace. *Children and Fiction*. New York: World Publishing, 1981.
This book is something of a classic for those who want to approach the writing of children's literature realistically. Chapter 2, on the likes and dislikes of young readers, explodes some long-held myths. The following chapter considers timing as a significant component in writing for young people and offers valuable examples. Chapter 4 recommends using extensive detail, and chapter 5 suggests variations that must be adjusted to the age of the readers. First published in the United Kingdom, this book has been well received by American writers.

Hinds, Marjorie M. *How to Write for the Juvenile Market*. New York: Frederick Fell, 1966.

Not all of the psychological insights in this book are valid for today's juveniles, although what is said was valid at the time this book was published. However, the information in chapters 4, "What to Write About," and 5, "Where to Get Ideas," remains pertinent. The advice given in chapter 6, "Writing for Tiny Tots," is less dated than the material in the three subsequent chapters about writing for juniors, intermediates, and teenagers. For additional comments about this book, refer to chapter 10 of this bibliography.

Hunter, Mollie. *Talent Is Not Enough: On Writing for Children*. New York: Harper & Row, 1976.
This collection of essays by a noted Scottish writer for children includes the essay from which the volume derives its title, her May Hill Arbuthnot Honor Lecture at the University of Pennsylvania in 1975. She has additional essays on one world, the other world, and the limits of language. She discusses ways of using history, fantasy, and folklore as bases for writing directed to young readers. The essays are lively and well informed. Although they deal broadly with their topics, they never lose sight of practical considerations that writers need to keep in mind as they write.

Irwin, Hadley, and Jeannete Eyerly. *Writing Young Adult Novels*. Cincinnati: Writer's Digest Books, 1988.
This popular guide to writing for adolescents is especially strong in identifying markets and in suggesting topics that can be used as the subjects of novels in this genre. Perhaps the most valuable advice it gives is to beware of thoughtless stereotypes. In chapter 6, the authors caution writers about making sure that the styles they depict in their writing are really authentic for their times. Chapter 14, on hidden messages, is also excellent.

Johnson, Audrey P. "The Teenage Formula." In *How to Write a Romance and Get It Published*, edited by Kathryn Falk. New York: Crown, 1983.
In this essay, Johnson, herself a successful author of teen romances, analyzes what makes such romances work. She goes into the matter of taboo subjects. She also points out that although teen readers do not demand—or even want—all happy endings, they do demand satisfactory solutions to the dilemmas posed in the story. Johnson obviously knows her way around in this medium. Her advice is sound and practical. For additional comments about Falk's book, look under Falk in chapter 2 of this bibliography.

Kammerman, Sylvia E., ed. *Book Reviewing*. Boston: The Writer, Inc., 1977.
The material on children's books in this collection of essays by a number of regular book reviewers, especially that found in chapters 6, 17, and 20, is extensive and solid. Chapter 20 tells how to review a children's book, basing its information on material from the Children's Services Division of the Santiago

(California) Library System. For additional comments about this book, see chapter 3 of this bibliography.

Koontz, Dean R. *How to Write Best-Selling Fiction.* Cincinnati: Writer's Digest Books, 1981.
Chapters 6, "Heroes and Heroines," and 8, "Achieving Plausibility Through Character Motivation," are most relevant to those who write juvenile literature, much of which succeeds by producing memorable heroes and heroines who must come across as plausible even though they are usually larger than life. For additional comments about this book, see chapters 2 and 10 of this bibliography.

Lewis, Claudia. *Writing for Young Children.* Garden City, N.Y.: Anchor Press/Doubleday, 1981.
Claudia Lewis of the Bank Street College of Education knows and understands young children. Her first chapter, on the language of sensory perception, amply demonstrates this. Subsequent chapters on rhythm, sound, form, and content reaffirm her competence. Chapter 6, which discusses common pitfalls encountered by those who produce children's literature, is the capstone of this perceptive book.

Lindbergh, Anne. "Thoughts in the Rabbit Hole." In *The Writer's Handbook, 1987*, edited by Sylvia K. Burack. Boston: The Writer, Inc., 1987.
In a delightfully informal essay, Lindbergh captures the way children interpret words. She captures the magic of their misunderstandings when they misinterpret homonyms and shows how this tendency can lead to wonderful wordplay in writing for young people. She makes a point of how necessary surprise and suspense are to writing for young people, as, of course, they are to most literature. What she has to say about fantasy and how to create it in writing is insightful and valuable for any writer, but especially for those who write for juveniles.

Livingston, Myra Cohn. *When You Are Alone/It Keeps You Capone: An Approach to Writing with Children.* New York: Atheneum, 1973.
This imaginative approach to teasing writing out of children deals in its initial pages with sharing, then goes on to focus essentially on the writing of poetry. Chapter 5 discusses form versus no form in writing poetry. Chapter 7 shows how collective poems can be generated by groups of children. Chapter 10, on rhyme, is nicely balanced and not dogmatic. Chapter 11, on the haiku, is practical, and chapter 16, on generating ideas, offers valuable suggestions. For additional comments on this source, see chapter 5 of this bibliography.

Lowrey, Marilyn M. *How to Write Romance Novels That Sell.* New York: Rawson Associates, 1983.
Lowrey devotes chapter 18 of this comprehensive book to writing the young adult

romance. She goes into such matters as getting a realistic view of one's audience and of recognizing certain taboos prescribed by this audience. She emphasizes that romance and explicit sex are not synonymous and warns that explicit sex scenes will severely limit the commercial possibilities of a young adult romance. For further comments, see chapter 2 of this bibliography.

McLarn, Jack Clinton. *Writing Part-Time for Fun and Money*. Wilmington, Del.: Enterprise Publishing, 1978.
McLarn's treatment of writing juvenile fiction is informed and competent. In chapter 7, McLarn addresses the writing of children's stories, but appendix 3, on the juvenile story, is even more relevant. Chapter 9, which deals generally with writing fiction, and chapter 11, which treats the writing of light verse, are also of general interest. For additional comments about this book, see chapters 1, 2, 9, and 10 of this bibliography.

Marston, Doris Ricker. *A Guide to Writing History*. Cincinnati: Writer's Digest Books, 1976.
With discussions of audience, motivation, and research in its early chapters, this book goes on in chapter 18 to discuss writing history for young readers. The market for work in this field is promising in an age when youngsters are urged to learn about, and from, real-life heroes and heroines. The flood of books about women and members of racial minorities reflects changes in the population of the United States that will continue, so the market is unlikely to diminish in the foreseeable future. Marston is concerned with how authors can write relevantly for modern youth. Her suggestions are apt and penetrating. For further comments on this source, refer to chapters 1, 2, 3, and 5 of this bibliography.

Mathieu, Aron M., ed. *The Creative Writer*. Cincinnati: Writer's Digest Books, 1961.
This collection contains two valuable contributions that will speak directly to those who write for juveniles. Claudia Lewis contributes "Writing for Young Children," and Miriam M. Mason writes about "Big Ideas from Little Words." For additional comments about this book, refer to chapters 1, 2, and 4 of this bibliography.

May, Jill, ed. *Children and Their Literature: A Readings Book*. West Lafayette, Ind.: CHLA Publishers, 1983.
Used selectively, this textbook will be of use to potential writers of books for children for its brief but cogent introduction and for a few of its selections. Among these is Jack Zipes's "The Use and Abuse of Folk and Fairy Tales with Children," which offers interesting criticism of Bruno Bettelheim's *The Uses of Enchantment*. Chapter 3 is on award-winning books and films for children.

Chapter 5 concentrates on poetry for children, while chapter 6 focuses on literary criticism as it pertains to children's literature.

Pianka, Phyllis Taylor. *How to Write Romances*. Cincinnati: Writer's Digest Books, 1988.
Romances represent an incredibly brisk market in prose fiction and account for a major percentage of the book sales in United States. Pianka goes into the economic as well as the artistic sides of writing romances, many of which bring lump-sum payments rather than the continuing royalties that most novels command. In chapter 12, Pianka specifically addresses writing romances for the young adult market. Chapter 10, "Sensuality vs. Sexuality," is also relevant. Chapter 15, which enumerates fifty-three reasons a book may be rejected, is of immense practical value. For additional comments about this source, refer to chapters 2 and 10 of this bibliography.

Polking, Kirk, ed. *A Beginner's Guide to Getting Published*. Cincinnati: Writer's Digest Books, 1987.
Donna Anders' chapter entitled "Writing the Juvenile Mystery" is brief but valuable for its directness and specificity. Anders understands the differences between adult mysteries and juvenile mysteries, demonstrating clearly her penetration of the juvenile psychological makeup. For other discussions of this book, see chapters 1, 4, and 5 of this bibliography.

Roberts, Ellen E. M. *The Children's Picture Book: How to Write It, How to Sell It*. Cincinnati: Writer's Digest Books, 1981, 1987.
Among the principles Roberts articulates is that of using pictures to enrich but not to complicate the story. Chapter 4, on picture-book people, is delightful. Pictures, Roberts warns, should not be so frightening as to cause nightmares, but they can be frightening enough to heighten tension and implant images in the memory. Roberts' guidance in marketing children's picture books, including preparing the manuscript and mailing pictures in ways that will protect them, is sound. For additional comments about this book, refer to chapter 10 of this bibliography.

Seldes, Gilbert. *Writing for Television*. New York: Greenwood Press, 1968.
This book is a reprint of the 1952 edition. Despite its age, in chapter 19 it makes interesting comments about writing for juvenile markets. Some of what is said in this chapter is dated, but the advice about taboos, characterization, and level of language is still worth consideration. For additional comments about this book, refer to chapter 6 of this bibliography.

Shreve, Susan. "Writing for Children vs. Writing for Adults." In *Novel and Short Story Writer's Market*, edited by Laurie Henry. Cincinnati: Writer's Digest Books, 1989.

Shreve surveys quite optimistically the burgeoning field of literature for young people, noting some of the differences authors must take into account when they choose to write in this field. She mentions the variety of age ranges and maturity levels within the broad area of literature for young people and gives sage advice about adapting one's writing to this market. She notes the need for clearly defined heroes and heroines, who become role models for some young readers.

Shulevitz, Uri. *Writing with Pictures: How to Write and Illustrate Children's Books.* New York: Watson-Guptill, 1985.

This remarkably handsome volume, rich in illustrations, consists of four parts: telling the story, planning the book, creating the pictures, and preparing pictures for reproduction. Shulevitz leaves little unsaid about how to work in this area. His knowledge of it is comprehensive, and he communicates both by word and by example.

Tsujimoto, Joseph I. *Teaching Poetry Writing to Adolescents.* Urbana, Ill.: National Council of Teachers of English, 1988.

Tsujimoto presents eighteen different writing assignments designed to be used in schools with adolescents. He also reproduces some of the poetry students have written in his workshops. Although the book has a specific focus, anyone who writes poetry can benefit from reading it and from doing its assignments. For further comments about this book, refer to chapter 5 of this bibliography.

Weber, Olga S., and Stephen J. Calvert, eds. *Literary and Library Prizes.* 10th ed. New York: R. R. Bowker, 1980.

This frequently published volume lists international, American, British, and Canadian literary and library prizes. It gives the year and the names of the prizes and the names of winners. In this edition of the book, forty-six pages are devoted to prizes for juvenile literature. For additional comments about this book, see chapters 1 and 4 of this bibliography.

Whitney, Phyllis A. *Writing Juvenile Stories and Novels.* Boston, Mass.: The Writer, Inc., 1978.

This book has reached the status of a classic among those who write for juvenile markets. Some of it is now outdated, especially the material on taboos in literature for young people. Many of the taboos of the 1970's have ceased to be taboo in more recent years. The chapter on specialization lists the major topics about which most juvenile literature is written. Whitney tells would-be juvenile authors where to look for ideas and how to proceed once having formulated the idea of what the book or short story will be. Her notions of keeping notebooks for work-in-progress as well as for projected work is specific and valuable. The material on marketing manuscripts is generally sound, although some of its details need updating from more recent sources.

Wilbur, L. Perry. *How to Write Books That Sell*. Chicago: Contemporary Books, 1979.
Chapter 17 of Wilbur's book, "Children's Books You Can Sell for Years," treats the juvenile market. It shows what an enduring market this one is and how the life of a children's book often exceeds that of a typical novel. The information on marketing and on literary agents is worth reading. For further comments about this book, see chapters 2 and 10 of this bibliography.

Willis, Meredith Sue. *Personal Fiction Writing: A Guide to Writing from Real Life for Teachers, Students, and Writers*. Urbana, Ill.: National Council of Teachers of English, 1985.
Willis is particularly interested in showing ways in which juveniles can learn how to write, but the advice is of significant value to a much broader audience. The use of details from one's daily life is stressed, and the suggestions for putting such information to work are well presented. For additional comments about this book, see chapters 1 and 8 of this bibliography.

Wylie, Max. *Writing for Television*. New York: Cowles Book Company, 1970.
Although the book is a bit dated, Wylie's comments about audience in part 1 are still quite valid. Part 2 emphasizes writing television scripts that will appeal to children and teenagers. Wylie presents appropriate examples for all of the categories of television writing he discusses, and his comments are generally perceptive. For additional comments about this book, refer to chapter 6 of this bibliography.

_____. *Writing for Children and Teen-Agers*. Rev. ed. Cincinnati: Writer's Digest Books, 1972.
Wyndham covers such matters as developing efficient work habits, plotting stories, creating dialogue, establishing atmosphere, and projecting emotion in books for young people. Of considerable use is a listing of categories of children's books. Also helpful is the material on children's magazines in chapter 2, although the material in this chapter is now quite dated. For additional comments on this source, refer to chapter 9 of this bibliography.

Wyndham, Lee. *Writing for Children and Teenagers*. 3d ed. Revised by Arnold Madison. Cincinnati: Writer's Digest Books, 1989.
This volume has been one of the best-selling books about writing for the juvenile market and, in its revised third edition, it is up-to-date in the information it provides about markets and subsidiary rights. The book demonstrates the writer's accurate understanding of the stages of development that people go through in the process of growing up. Wyndham has excellent advice about how to decide upon topics, how to research them, and how to maintain a consistent point of

view, which is one of the hardest things for adult writers to do when they are writing for and about young people.

Yolen, Jane. *Guide to Writing for Children*. Boston: The Writer, Inc., 1989.
This comprehensive guide by the author of more than one hundred children's books—prose and poetry, fiction and nonfiction—traces the entire creative process for writing children's books, from the initial inspiration through the perspiration (the actual writing) to preparing professional manuscripts and marketing them. The scope is broad, offering suggestions on how to produce picture books, fairy tales, animal stories, science fiction, novels, and nonfiction, leading readers to an understanding of the fundamental techniques required for such writing.

_____. "Storytelling: The Oldest and Newest Art." In *The Writer's Handbook, 1987*, edited by Sylvia K. Burack. Boston: The Writer, Inc., 1987.
Although Yolen focuses on juvenile literature in this piece, it has relevance for writers of any kind of fiction. The emphasis is on the art of storytelling, and Yolen considers the beginning, the *incipit*, as she terms it, fundamental to any worthwhile story because readers who are not quickly engaged are generally lost totally. From the incipit, Yolen goes on to the story's middle, the great bulk of most stories, saying that the middle must be well controlled and muscular; it cannot afford to be flabby or wandering. All stories worth their salt have meaning, metaphor, and human emotion. Without these fundamental elements, no story can succeed, especially stories for young people, who are demanding readers.

_____. *Writing Books for Children*. Boston: The Writer, Inc., 1973.
Although this book has been superseded by Yolen's *Guide to Writing for Children* (see above), it offers some excellent advice. The book discusses types and genres of children's books. Chapter 5, "There Would Be Unicorns," which focuses on fantasy, is particularly beguiling. For further comments about this book, refer to chapters 3 and 10 of this bibliography.

Zinsser, William, ed. *Worlds of Childhood: The Art and Craft of Writing for Children*. Boston: Houghton Mifflin, 1990.
This collection, in which Jean Fritz, Maurice Sendak, Jill Krementz, Jack Prelutsky, Rosemary Wells, and Katherine Paterson are represented, is balanced and informative. A major emphasis is on storytelling and how it leads to writing for children. The contributors quite generally accept the premise that a fundamental ingredient for success in writing for children is that of capturing the freshness and orality of tales that essentially are meant to be told and retold.

Zuckerman, Suzanne. "Turning Teen Age Fantasies into Fiction." In *How to Write a Romance and Get It Published*, edited by Kathryn Falk. New York: Crown, 1983.

Zuckerman identifies the market as average, middle-class girls between nine and fourteen years old. The typical novel in this genre is short—between thirty thousand and fifty thousand words. It should contain no explicit sex and should avoid profanity. It should also avoid slang, because most slang expressions are ephemeral. On page 277, Zuckerman provides a summary of tips that will be helpful to those who wish to write in this area. For additional comments about the book from which Zuckerman's essay comes, look above under Johnson, as well as in chapter 2 of this bibliography.

Chapter 8
WRITING AUTOBIOGRAPHY, BIOGRAPHY, AND FAMILY HISTORY

Autobiography

Block, Lawrence. *Write Your Life*. Cincinnati: Writer's Digest Books, 1986.
Block suggest strategies for assessing the elements from one's own life that have possibilities as the raw material for writing. Essentially, 95 percent of all creative writing, regardless of genre, has an autobiographical base and strong autobiographical overtones. Block leads writers to the kind of self-discovery that can result in developing story lines and in sharpening characterization. The approach suggested here will be valuable to writers who want specifically to write autobiographically, but it also has significant carryover value for those who are writing in other genres, helping to make them more aware of and sensitive to the nuances of their own internalized experience.

Cane, Melville. *Making a Poet: An Inquiry into the Creative Process*. New York: Harcourt, Brace, 1962.
Melville Cane is well aware of how autobiographical much poetry is, even if it is not overtly so. This book provides readers with an inside view of what goes into making poems by leading them through the process by which a number of its author's poems came into being. Cane's analyses are psychologically sound and generally perceptive. For additional comments about this book, refer to chapter 5 of this bibliography.

Cockshut, A. O. J. *The Art of Autobiography in Nineteenth and Twentieth Century England*. New Haven, Conn.: Yale University Press, 1984.
Cockshut places great emphasis on the importance of childhood in autobiographical writing. He considers the autobiographical works of many writers: Edwin Muir, W. H. Hudson, Forrest Reid, Victor Gollancz, Stephen Spender, John Ruskin, Edmund Gosse, H. G. Wells, Bertrand Russell, Thomas De Quincey, and others. This book is quite scholarly and not always eminently readable, but the information it contains is worth the effort put forth to understand it.

Colwell, C. Carter, and James H. Knox. *What's the Usage? The Writer's Guide to English Grammar and Rhetoric*. Reston, Va.: Reston Publishing Company, 1973.
What's the Usage? is much like many typical grammar/rhetoric books, but it is worth mentioning for it first chapter, entitled "How to Make a Theme of Yourself." The authors show how fundamental autobiographical information is to most writing and suggest concrete methods by which writers can tap this rich resource in ways that will enhance their writing. The book also has good information about

assessing a writer's audience. In an appendix, it gives forty nonstandard expressions for review and revision.

Duncan, Lois. *How to Write and Sell Your Personal Experiences*. Cincinnati: Writer's Digest Books, 1979.
Duncan demonstrates ably how one can mold autobiography into fiction. This book considers the most appropriate outlets for writing of this sort and ways of accommodating the marketplace. Chapter 6, on rewriting, is useful. Chapters 7 and 8 consider religious markets and confessions respectively. Chapters 14 and 15 are devoted to writing personal-experience fiction for young readers. For additional comments about this book, refer to chapters 1 and 7 of this bibliography.

Gallo, Donald R. *Speaking for Ourselves: Autobiographical Sketches by Notable Authors of Books for Young Adults*. Urbana, Ill.: National Council of Teachers of English, 1990.
The eighty-seven authors of juvenile fiction covered in this book show clearly how significant events in their own lives have shaped the fiction they write for juveniles. Among the authors represented are Judy Blume, S. E. Hinton, and Paul Zindel. For additional comments on this book, see chapter 7 of this bibliography.

Godwin, Gail. "The Uses of Autobiography." In *The Writer's Handbook, 1987*, edited by Sylvia K. Burack. Boston: The Writer, Inc., 1987.
Godwin, herself an accomplished novelist, contends that most of what people write has autobiographical roots, even though the actual facts may be distorted for artistic reasons. She shows how sensitivity to the commonplace realities of people's own lives heightens their ability to shape characters and situations that succeed in all kinds of writing, particularly in the writing of imaginative fiction. Godwin says categorically that when a piece of fiction she has labored over does not come to fruition, it is nearly always because the piece "did not belong to me in the first place." That is, the piece lacked the verisimilitude that writing based in autobiography usually has.

Harrower, Molly. *The Therapy of Poetry*. Springfield, Ill.: Charles C Thomas, 1972.
Four chapters of this book show ways in which poets can use their pasts to inform their writing. Chapter 2 deals with the emerging self, chapter 3 with reflections on one's childhood, chapter 4 with the poet-self discovered, and chapter 10 with the search again for the poet-self. The title is slightly misleading. For additional comments on this source, refer to chapter 5 of this bibliography.

Maugham, W. Somerset. *Strictly Personal*. Garden City, N.Y.: Doubleday, Doran, 1941. Reprint. New York: Arno Press, 1977.

This autobiography reports largely on Maugham's reactions to the first two years of World War II, a period that he spent first in France and later, after a harrowing trip, in Britain. Maugham shows the effects that social and political dislocation have on writers and, by intimation, how they weave these traumatic events into the fabric of their later writing. For additional comments on this book, see chapter 2 of this bibliography.

———————. *The Summing Up*. Garden City, N.Y.: Doubleday, Doran, 1938. Reprint. New York: Penguin, 1978.
Maugham's early, thoroughgoing autobiography gives insights into the problems that face young writers in writing and marketing their work. Maugham, a physician, tells in chapter 43 about his early work, including his first novel, *Lisa of Lambeth* (1897). Chapters 62, 63, and 64 are especially relevant to novelists. In them, Maugham asks about the value of what one has written and suggests how to evaluate one's own work. Chapter 64 focuses particularly on the interconnections between philosophy and literature in writing. For further comments about this source, see chapter 2 of this bibliography.

Milios, Rita. "Writing Articles from Personal Experience." In *The Writer's Handbook, 1987*, edited by Sylvia K. Burack. Boston: The Writer, Inc., 1987.
Milios, who writes frequently for such magazines as *Reader's Digest*, *McCall's*, and *Woman's World*, emphasizes that magazines are looking for writing that has emotion to it, that reflects real life from a human point of view. Milios suggests that writers start articles at some dramatic point to arouse reader interest and then convey their thoughts and emotions as honestly and directly as they can. Good articles contain experiences with which readers can identify personally. They establish a relationship with their readers, sharing with them their insights and their reactions to events in their stories. Once the article is finished, the writer should scan market listings looking for such phrases as "seeking meaningful stories of personal experience" or "wants personal narratives."

Morris, Wright. *A Cloak of Light: Writing My Life*. New York: Harper & Row, 1985.
The virtue of this book is that it shows quite clearly how writers turn autobiography into fiction. The comments Wright Morris makes about two of his novels in particular, *The Field of Vision* and *Man and Boy*, show the ways in which the whole of a writer's life impinges upon his or her writing indelibly. Morris, an accomplished photographer, uses many of his photographic techniques in his own writing. He understands well the debt he owes to his own experience and background as he crafts his fiction.

Nin, Anaïs. *The Novel of the Future*. New York: Macmillan, 1968.
The title chapter of this book is chapter 7 and does not fully represent what the

book is about. Most of the book gives knowledgeable advice to novelists. Focusing particularly on the uses of autobiographical detail in the writing of novels are chapters 4, 5, and 6, which deal, respectively, with the genesis of a story idea, the genesis of a writer's diary, and diary versus fiction. Nin clearly understands the autobiographical nature of much writing in this field, and these three chapters take that tendency into full account. For further comments about this source, see chapter 2 of this bibliography.

Paris Review. *Writers at Work: The Paris Review Interviews*. New York: Viking Press, published periodically.
This series of books, edited by such renowned literary figures as Van Wyck Brooks, George Plimpton, and Malcolm Cowley, appears annually and has, through the years, published searching, lengthy interviews with such major authors as Harold Pinter, Edward Albee, Ernest Hemingway, Arthur Miller, T. S. Eliot, Joyce Carol Oates, and others. Through reading these interviews, one can glean the extent to which autobiographical detail enters into the writing processes and outcomes of significant writers.

Price, Reynolds. *Clear Pictures: First Loves, First Guides*. New York: Atheneum, 1989.
Clear Pictures is an incredible study in how autobiographical details inform the fiction of a much-published novelist. Price was reintroduced to his earliest past, seemingly long forgotten, when hypnosis undertaken to help him control pain after spinal surgery brought forth a flood of memory beginning with his infantile experiences. Because of his hypnosis, Price embarked on writing this autobiography, which reveals to those who know his novels the way in which he transformed autobiographical information into fiction without being either confessional or indiscreet. This book is warm and interesting, and it provides valuable information about artistic creation. For additional comments about this source, refer to chapter 2 of this bibliography.

Sandburg, Carl. *Always the Young Strangers*. New York: Harcourt, Brace, 1953.
Sandburg's thoroughgoing autobiography was certainly informed by the kind of research he did for his far-ranging biography of Abraham Lincoln. It is perhaps because of this research that he was able to write about himself in a detached and analytical way. It is clear that Sandburg's writing continually drew on the stories he heard as a child, on the legends that have become a part of his writing. His political awareness also came to be a highly significant element in his writing, and this autobiography traces the development of his social conscience.

_____. *Ever the Winds of Change*. Edited by Margaret Sandburg and George Hendrick. Urbana: University of Illinois Press, 1983.

Although Sandburg had not completed this memoir when he died in 1967, his daughter and George Hendrick pieced together the papers they had and filled in the missing parts as well as they could, doing a sensitive job of editing and enhancing the text. The memoir presents interesting and insightful reflections on Sandburg's early days, particularly on his career at Lombard College in Illinois, where he wrote for the college newspaper. He also was a frequent contributor to the Illinois paper the *Galesburg Mail*. The memoir shows how Sandburg reshaped personal experience into poetry.

Simons, George F. *Keeping Your Personal Journal*. New York: Paulist Press, 1978.
Simons realizes the relationship between autobiography and much writing, both fiction and nonfiction. His suggestions about keeping and sharing a journal acknowledge this relationship. The information on starting a journal is rather *pro forma*, but the advice about how to maintain one is excellent. For additional comments about this source, refer to chapter 1 of this bibliography.

Thomas, Frank P. *How to Write the Story of Your Life*. Cincinnati: Writer's Digest Books, 1990.
The greatest service Thomas renders in this book is to show the novice writer how to extract from the full range of life and memory those experiences that will represent the subject of an autobiography fairly and accurately. He devotes chapter 6 to helping writers find ways to jog their memories. He discusses how much should be told and what should be held back. To what extent must the writer protect living people? How can living people be protected without weakening the autobiography? What is the best way to handle the chronology of an autobiography? Sometimes the straight chronological approach works, but sometimes it results in a boring narrative. If one violates the time order in any way, the gaps must be filled. Thomas shows ways in which this can be done. He also demonstrates that all lives are interesting if one knows how to extract from them those universals that make them interesting.

Williams, Nan Schram. *Confess for Profit: Writing and Selling the Personal Story—A Comprehensive Guide*. Los Angeles: Douglas-West Publishers, 1973.
Williams discusses various methods of planning, plotting, and writing stories as first-person narratives. She understands well the uses of autobiographical detail, although she is not so naïve as to suggest that confessions need to be (or should be) directly autobiographical. Her guide to book publishers and magazines, useful in its day, is now dated. For more information about this book, see chapters 2 and 10.

Willis, Meredith Sue. *Personal Fiction Writing: A Guide to Writing from Real Life for Teachers, Students, and Writers*. Urbana, Ill.: National Council of Teachers of English, 1985.

The author has a keen sense of how autobiography is a part of any writing. In this book, readers are shown how to draw from the commonplace and turn it into interesting fiction that has some universal appeal. For additional comments about this book, see chapters 1 and 7 of this bibliography.

Zinsser, William, ed. *Inventing the Truth: The Art and Craft of Memoir.* Boston: Houghton Mifflin, 1987.
This book is a collection of lectures given in a lecture series produced by the Book-of-the-Month Club at the New York Public Library in 1986 and 1987. Among the lecturers were Russell Baker, Annie Dillard, Alfred Kazin, Toni Morrison, and Lewis Thomas. Of particular interest to those interested in writing autobiography is Russell Baker's contribution, "Life with Mother," in which Baker tells of having to rewrite entirely his memoir, *Growing Up*, when he discovered that he had left out of it two salient elements that gave it its veracity. Writers must constantly be aware of how their unconscious minds work both to bring forth details from their pasts and to suppress similar details.

Biography

Benedict, Helen. *Portraits in Print: A Collection of Profiles and the Stories Behind Them.* New York: Columbia University Press, 1990.
In this book that contains profiles of such people as Isaac Bashevis Singer, Beverly Sills, Jessica Mitford, and Joseph Brodsky, Helen Benedict follows each profile with an essay in which she tells in detail the circumstances of the profile. Benedict shows clearly how one can write profiles and goes into useful detail about marketing them. Anyone aspiring to write biographies will learn much from this book. For further comments, see chapters 3 and 10 of this bibliography.

Bowen, Catherine Drinker. *Adventures of a Biographer.* Boston: Little, Brown, 1959.
In this enticing book, Bowen reminisces about going to Moscow and Leningrad in the mid-1930's to research *Beloved Friend*, the story of Peter Ilich Tchaikovsky and Nadejda von Meck. She talks about the structure of such a biography and about the balance the biographer of two figures of this sort must struggle to achieve if each is to be treated fairly and fully. An extraordinarily well-written book, *Adventures of a Biographer* offers much of practical value.

_____. *Biography: A Craft and a Calling.* Boston: Little, Brown, 1968.
This book, by the author of *Yankee from Olympus* and *John Adams and the American Revolution*, both landmark biographies, is generally considered the best in the field. Bowen goes step by step through the elements of successful biography, giving excellent advice on how to organize and arrange the diffuse sources

from which any significant biography must grow. Bowen knows fully what a biographer's responsibilities are. She manages to convey the balance between these responsibilities and demands from readers and publishers. She stresses the important of the opening and closing scenes of a biography and pays close attention to biographers' relationship to their subjects. She is especially helpful in chapter 8, which has to do with capturing the past; chapter 9, which pays close attention to how people actually looked at various times in history; and chapter 10, on how people spoke. She also offers valuable advice on how to deal with the passage of time.

Caro, Robert A., David McCullough, Paul C. Nagel, Richard B. Sewell, Ronald Steel, and Jean Strouse. *Extraordinary Lives: The Art and Craft of American Biography.* New York: American Heritage, 1986.
This book consists of a series of lectures about writing biography that grew out of a lecture series produced by the Book-of-the-Month Club and held at the New York City Public Library in 1985 and 1986. Each of the contributors has had considerable experience in writing biography and gives helpful information about what some of the pitfalls are and how to avoid them. The book is varied and filled with the kinds of specific information that will save potential biographers considerable energy while helping them to focus on the topic and to organize it realistically in ways that readers will appreciate.

Clifford, James L. *From Puzzles to Portraits: Problems of a Literary Biographer.* Chapel Hill: University of North Carolina Press, 1970.
Part 1 is entitled "Finding the Evidence" and has to do with basic biographical research and detective work. Part 2, "Putting the Pieces Together," shows how to bring order to the disparate elements of one's research. Clifford addresses the thorny ethical issue of how much a biographer should reveal. In chapter 6, he suggests excellent methods of testing material for authenticity.

Edel, Leon. *Writing Lives: Principia Biographica.* New York: W. W. Norton, 1984.
This renowned biographer of Henry James and others divides his book into two parts, the first of which considers the "new biography," including typical dilemmas biographers face, choosing and relating to one's subject, the psychoanalytical approach to biographical writing, myth, and narratives. The second, more practical, part of the book provides what Edel calls a personal workshop. In it, under the title "The Genesis of a Chapter," he painstakingly shows specifically and in detail how he converts his research material into a coherent chapter that is eminently readable. He both discusses and demonstrates the importance of nuance in fleshing out a chapter.

Gittings, Robert. *The Nature of Biography.* Seattle: University of Washington Press, 1978.

Writing Autobiography, Biography, and Family History 115

This volume contains the Jessie and John Danz Lectures for 1977, delivered at the University of Washington in June of that year. The first lecture is on history, the second on present practices in biography, and the final on paths of progress. This book is interesting because Gittings understands that writing biography is a progression and that it changes in focus and method as time goes on.

Lomask, Milton. *The Biographer's Craft*. New York: Harper & Row, 1986.

Lomask covers the usual material about research in chapters 3 and 4, but then goes on to discuss in the following chapter such techniques as writing in clusters. Chapter 6 considers form as beginning, middle, and end. Chapter 9, on discovering the hero, is astute, as is the following chapter, on revealing the hero. Chapter 13, on psychobiography, is extremely pertinent for contemporary biographers. Less theoretical but equally useful is chapter 14, on how to handle quotations and the uses of paraphrase.

Schumacher, Michael. *Creative Conversations: The Writer's Complete Guide to Conducting Interviews*. Cincinnati: Writer's Digest Books, 1990.

Although this book has implications for all writers, it will be of special value to people writing biographies, particularly those of contemporary or quite recent subjects. The physical elements of an interview must be well planned in advance. If a tape recorder is to be used—the most effective method—the machine should be inconspicuous and the interviewer should make sure how it works (and that it works) long before the interview occurs. The interviewer also should take a sufficient supply of recording cassettes to ensure that the interview can continue for as long as it must in order to succeed. Interviewers must learn not to talk too much, but to direct conversation when such direction is necessary.

Schwartz, Ted. *The Complete Guide to Writing Biographies*. Cincinnati: Writer's Digest Books, 1990.

Schwartz does one of the best jobs in print of identifying markets for biography. A biographer himself, Schwartz is knowledgeable about the legal hazards involved in writing unauthorized biographies. He discusses in depth both researching and writing authorized and unauthorized biographies, as well as the writing of biographies for juvenile markets. Perhaps the most useful information provided in this book's 208 pages, all of them filled with practical advice, is the information about how to structure and conduct effective interviews, certainly a *sine qua non* of writing contemporary biography. Much of the information in this book will help the writer interested in ghostwriting autobiographies for public figures.

Shelston, Alan. *Biography*. London: Methuen, 1977.

Although portions of this book lapse into stuffiness, chapter 4, "Public Legends: Private Lives," is fascinating and valid. Chapter 5, "The Truth of Fact and the Truth of Fiction," is also thought-provoking. The writer addresses some interesting problems in the use of anecdote in chapter 2. A somewhat dated book, but some of the material remains fresh.

Zinsser, William, ed. *Extraordinary Lives: The Art and Craft of American Biography*. New York: American Heritage, 1986.
In this book, Zinsser has gathered interviews with six writers of biography—David McCullough, Richard B. Sewall, Paul C. Nagel, Ronald Steel, Jean Strouse, and Robert Caro—who share with him the techniques they use in writing in this genre. Although the adjective "American" appears in the title, the book has something to say to biographers of any nationality writing about subjects of any nationality. Zinsser has edited this book well, making it tight and fast-moving.

Family History

Boyer, Carl, III. *How to Publish and Market Your Family History*, 3d ed. Newhall, Calif.: Author, 1987.
The first and second editions of this popular book appeared in 1982 and 1985, respectively. Any of the three editions will provide readers with specific information about how to begin genealogical research. The third, however, has been updated and is superior to the two earlier ones. The book, whose chapters are not numbered, is well indexed. It discusses how to research both ancestors and living relations. Boyer shows how to write a draft and how to use a systematic approach to scheduling and completing the writing. He provides a sample preface and sample genealogies. He also includes a list of genealogical bookstores, societies, and libraries, well updated in the later edition of the work.

Steward, Joyce S., and Mary K. Croft. *The Leisure Pen: A Book for Elderwriters*. Plover, Wis.: Keepsake Publishers, 1988.
Although chapter 8 of this book focuses on family history, chapter 9, which addresses writing about the lives of others, and chapters 6 and 7, which deal with writing about seemingly minor incidents and with writing memoirs, are also relevant. This is an important resource for older people who wish to write and to capture in a permanent form some of their valuable memories. For additional comments on this book, refer to chapters 1 and 5 of this bibliography.

Stillman, Peter R. *Families Writing*. Cincinnati: Writer's Digest Books, 1989.
Stillman urges families to write what they know best: their families. The result is, of course, family history. Much of it will not be publishable or, indeed, intended for publication. Some writers who begin this way, however, will ultimately pursue their efforts to publishable levels.

Chapter 9
WRITING FOR MAGAZINES AND JOURNALS

Biagi, Shirley. *How to Write and Sell Magazine Articles.* Englewood Cliffs, N.J.: Prentice-Hall, 1981.

Biagi suggests how to approach the physical task of writing, how to organize both one's thoughts and one's time so that the writing process will become a regular part of one's daily routine, as it must for serious writers. Biagi makes it clear that the best way to write effectively is to practice writing regularly, preferably on a daily basis, preferably at the same time each day no matter how busy one is. See also chapter 3 of this bibliography.

Boggess, Louise. *How to Write Fillers and Short Features That Sell.* 2d ed. New York: Harper & Row, 1981.

Many writers keep themselves afloat financially by writing the kinds of short pieces and fillers that are part of most newspapers and popular magazines. Boggess offers practical advice about how to identify needs and about how to achieve the tone that such material demands. Such contributions range in length usually from 100 to 350 words. Once writers break into this market, which requires formulaic writing, it is easy to keep scoring successes in it if one knows how to anticipate needs. Among the types of fillers Boggess addresses are self-help articles, how-to-do-it pieces, profiles, nostalgia, personal opinion pieces, and humorous bits. Writing such items is a good starting point for many writers. See also chapter 3 of this bibliography.

Cassill, Kay. *The Complete Handbook for Freelance Writers.* Cincinnati: Writer's Digest Books, 1981.

This handbook is now dated. However, it presents useful material for writers, especially those who wish to write articles commercially. Especially useful are chapter 3, "Assessing the Markets," and chapter 12, which gives good advice about approaching agents. A glossary of writing, editing, and production terms and symbols provides an added dimension to the book. Despite its age, this information is still quite relevant. See also chapter 3 of this bibliography.

Cool, Lisa Collier. *How to Sell Every Magazine Article You Write.* Cincinnati: Writer's Digest Books, 1989.

Cool has had considerable success in teaching people how to write articles that sell, and in this book she shows not only how to write appealing articles but also how to get the best price for them. Her knowledge of the field is extensive. For additional comments about this book, refer to chapter 3 of this bibliography.

Fredette, Jean M. *Writer's Digest Handbook of Magazine Article Writing*. Cincinnati: Writer's Digest Books, 1990.
In nearly forty chapters packed with information, Fredette discusses every kind of article writing, fiction and nonfiction, specialized and general, sacred and profane. Her information on how to market articles once they are written is current and indispensable to anyone writing in this area. For additional remarks about this book, see chapters 3 and 10 of this bibliography.

Freedman, Helen Rosengren, and Karen Krieger. *The Writer's Guide to Magazine Markets: Non-fiction*. New York: New American Library, 1983.
The first 26 pages of this book give information on how to market manuscripts. The next 329 pages give an overview of some 125 magazines from *Penthouse* to *Prevention*, from *Health* to *Hustler*, and from *American Baby* to *Young Miss*. Addresses are given for each entry (although some have changed since 1983). Information is also given about each magazine's pay scale and about the number of manuscripts it typically receives and the number accepted for publication. This information is valuable because it reveals how competitive the markets of interest to individual readers are. See also chapter 3 of this bibliography.

Jacobi, Peter. *The Magazine Article: How to Think It, Plan It, Write It*. Cincinnati: Writer's Digest Books, 1991.
Jacobi uses a classroom approach to analyze hundreds of magazine articles and then to provide practical exercises that will help people to learn how to write in this medium. A professor of journalism, Jacobi brings his varied classroom experience and his experience as a journalist to bear upon this fruitful topic. For additional comments about this book, refer to chapter 3 of this bibliography.

Kelley, Jerome E. *Magazine Writing Today*. Cincinnati: Writer's Digest Books, 1978.
This book initially presents a chapter on current markets. This portion, somewhat dated, is still of some use. The author defines what an article is in chapter 2 and goes on to consider story ideas in the following chapter. Subsequent chapters are on such matters as the query letter, interviewing, research, organization of material, and writing leads that entice readers. The material on flashbacks in chapter 9 is not revolutionary, but the material on "flash-aheads" is unique and worth reading. The appendix that gives proofreaders' symbols and the appendix on the writer's rights are both useful. For further comments on this book, see chapter 3 of this bibliography.

Kevles, Barbara. *Basic Magazine Writing*. Cincinnati: Writer's Digest Books, 1983.
Of particular use to the writer of nonfiction will be Kevles' suggestions about interviewing. The techniques she suggests work well and result in the kinds of searching interviews that are at the heart of much solid nonfiction writing. She

urges interviewers to stick to one issue in doing an interview. She offers information about the service article (chapter 2), about question-and-answer techniques (chapter 4), about the "as told to" article (chapter 5), and about the celebrity interview (chapter 6). She also discusses the expository article and the multiple-viewpoint piece. For additional comments on this book, refer to chapter 3 of this bibliography.

Konner, Linda. *How to Be Successfully Published in Magazines.* New York: St. Martin's Press, 1990.
Konner offers practical suggestions for those who want to do freelance writing. Chapter 3, dealing with writer-editor etiquette, will help the novice writer avoid some pitfalls. Chapter 4 urges writers to learn something about the magazines or journals to which they want to submit their work: What is the average length of articles? What is the overall tone? What subjects seem to be best represented? Extremely valuable is chapter 6, in which Konner presents interviews with twenty-eight editors about what they are looking for and about what makes them feel favorably disposed toward those who submit material to them. Chapter 7 presents similar interviews with ten authors. See chapter 3 of this bibliography for further comments.

McLarn, Jack Clinton. *Writing Part-Time for Fun and Money.* Wilmington, Del.: Enterprise Publishing, 1978.
Especially relevant to writers for magazines and journals are chapters 5 and 6, on educational writing; chapter 11, on light verse; chapter 8, on writing about the arts; and the portion of chapter 9 that deals with writing book reviews. Appendices 1, on confessions, and 5, on book reviewing, are also of value. For additional comments about this book, see chapters 1, 2, 7, and 10 of this bibliography.

Martindale, David. *How to Be a Freelance Writer: A Guide to Building a Full-Time Career.* New York: Crown, 1982.
Martindale's advice about producing and marketing freelance pieces is sound, although similar to that found in most other books on the topic. Chapter 9, on interviewing, is a fresh, lively chapter of immense practical value. Chapter 11, which discusses author-editor relations, is also sensible and useful. The book is well written, and the information in it is relatively accurate, although the information on the finances of freelance writers is quickly becoming outdated. For further comments on this title, see chapter 3 of this bibliography.

Mau, Ernest E. *The Free-Lance Writer's Survival Manual.* Chicago: Contemporary Books, 1981.
Mau's approach has more to do with money than with art. He goes into such matters as the fees one can expect, how to negotiate fees, what tax matters

freelance writers have to consider, and what contractual arrangements they can expect. These are all basic matters, and Mau covers them in detail, although some of the information is becoming dated. Mau advocates an aggressive approach to marketing one's work. For additional comments, refer to chapters 3 and 10 of this bibliography.

Morris, Terry, ed. *Prose by Professionals: The Inside Story of the Magazine Article Writer's Cost.* New York: Doubleday, 1961.
In this collection are chapters by Donald Murray on getting started as a freelance writer, by Betty Friedan on finding and developing ideas, by Robert J. Levin and Beatrice Schapper on interviewing and research, by Donald G. Cooley on working in media, and by David Lester on writing about ordinary people. The tone is upbeat and informed. For additional comments about this source, see chapter 3 of this bibliography.

Muth, Marcia. *Writing and $elling: Poetry, Fiction, Articles, Plays, and Local History.* Santa Fe, N.Mex.: Sunstone Press, 1985.
Perhaps the best advice in this broad-ranging book is found in the chapter about writing and marketing articles. Muth obviously has had considerable experience in this area and knows what she is talking about. She also provides information about contracts and copyrights in chapter 7, and this information is sound. For additional comments about this book, refer to chapters 1, 4, 5, and 10.

Newcomb, Duane. *A Complete Guide to Marketing Magazine Articles.* Cincinnati: Writer's Digest Books, 1975.
Although some of the specific information in this book is dated, chapter 2, "How to Put the Odds in Your Favor," chapter 5 on research, "How to Get Facts and Information," and chapter 9, "How to Sell Everything You Write," still ring true in today's market. The book has been superseded by later such volumes, but this was one of the best in its time and remains a valuable resource if it is used judiciously. For additional comments on this book, refer to chapter 3 of this bibliography.

Peterson, Franklynn, and Judi Kesselman-Turkel. *The Magazine Writer's Handbook.* Englewood Cliffs, N.J.: Prentice-Hall, 1982.
This straightforward book gives ten standard formats for articles, four elements of a good article, and three standard writing techniques that writers can employ. It also presents five commandments that no professional writer ever forgets. The advice given generally is sound, although it is packaged in plastic—sort of the MacDonald's approach to writing for publication (which is not to imply that the suggestions will not work). See additional comments in chapter 3 of this bibliography.

Rees, Clair F. *Profitable Part-Time/Full-Time Freelancing.* Cincinnati: Writer's Digest Books, 1980.

The major focus of this book is on writing for magazines and journals, although chapter 9 discusses writing books. Of special relevance is the material in chapter 5 on versatility versus specialization. Chapter 3, on making the first magazine sale, offers practical advice to writers of nonfiction. For additional comments about this book, refer to chapters 2 and 3 under "General Studies."

Schapper, Beatrice, ed. *How to Make Money Writing Magazine Articles.* New York: Arco, 1974.

Extremely useful is Schapper's reproduction of a manuscript page with all the editor's markings on it. Contributions by Eve Merriam on the exposé article, by Terry Morris on a romantic biographical article about Svetlana Stalin, and by Tom Mahoney on a factual article about seatbelts demonstrate clearly the far-ranging interests of the book.

Vachon, Brian. *Writing for Regional Publications.* Cincinnati: Writer's Digest Books, 1979.

Vachon gives solid information about how to entice editors of newspapers and magazines that publish regional pieces, pointing out that experience and previous publications are less important in this market than in some others. In chapter 13, he provides ways for authors to determine whether their material warrants an article or a book. Chapter 14, on expanding one's market, is useful for all writers, not merely regional ones. For further comments about this book, refer to chapter 3 of this bibliography.

The Writing Business: A Poets and Writers Handbook. Edited jointly by the editors of *Coda: A Poets and Writers Newsletter.* New York: Poets and Writers, 1985.

This book is filled with sound advice for writers in all fields. It pays great attention to poetry and short fiction, as well as to nonfiction articles, providing a list of fourteen major magazines with indications of the kinds of writing they hope to receive and the remuneration they offer their authors. The writer's guide to reference books toward the end of the volume is invaluable. For additional comments about this source, see chapters 1, 2, 3, 5, and 10.

Wyndham, Lee. *Writing for Children and Teen-Agers.* Rev. ed. Cincinnati: Writer's Digest Books, 1972.

Although this book focuses largely on the writing of children's books, chapter 2 focuses on children's magazines and gives valuable information about writing for them. Although some of this chapter is now quite dated, its suggestions are still valid. For additional comments about this book, see chapter 7 of this bibliography.

Chapter 10
PREPARING, MARKETING, AND PROMOTING MANUSCRIPTS AND BOOKS

General Studies

Applebaum, Judith. *How to Get Happily Published*. 3d ed. New York: Harper & Row, 1988.
This durable resource (earlier editions were coauthored by Nancy Evans) has an encouraging tone. Appelbaum shows how writers can bring themselves to the attention of publishers. In addition, she discusses matters such as film and television rights, foreign rights, and paperback rights. A section on self-publishing includes many practical suggestions about marketing and promoting one's own work.

Baker, Samm Sinclair. *Writing Nonfiction That Sells*. Cincinnati: Writer's Digest Books, 1986.
Baker offers information about developing consistent work habits and preparing manuscripts. In chapter 8, he shows how writers can, by thinking like editors, enhance their chances of publication. Chapter 9 is devoted to writing proposals for artwork and chapter 10 to writing proposals on book manuscripts. Chapters 11 and 12 are devoted to marketing and promotion. The essential focus of the book is on how to market manuscripts. For additional comments on this source, see chapter 3.

Barr, June. *Writing and Selling Greeting Card Verse*. Boston: The Writer, Inc., 1966.
Greeting-card companies have a virtually insatiable need for verse, which is not to be confused with great poetry. This book identifies the market and is rich in examples. Chapter 9 is devoted to how to market verse of this sort. The book's list of twenty-seven publishers who welcome unsolicited contributions was useful in its day but now is only suggestive because of changes in the greeting-card business. Of equal help was the list of publishers that were not looking for such verse. Because this book is dated, it is useful only in general ways. For additional comments about this source, see chapter 5 of this bibliography.

Belkin, Gary S. *Getting Published: A Guide for Businesspeople and Other Professionals*. New York: John Wiley & Sons, 1984.
Although his intended audience is essentially people who specialize in business and technical writing, Belkin's advice can be applied to any kind of writing. His first chapter addresses in twenty pages opportunities for publication. Chapter 4, on how to find a publisher, is general enough that its twenty pages are useful to

all writers. In chapter 7, Belkin offers advice from professional writers and editors. In this chapter he also discusses what to look for in a publishing contract and how to get such a contract. The approach is sound, practical, and informed.

Benedict, Helen. *Portraits in Print: A Collection of Profiles and the Stories Behind Them.* New York: Columbia University Press, 1990.
Benedict shows clearly how one can write profiles and goes into useful detail about marketing them. Her profiles of notables such Jessica Mitford, Beverly Sills, Isaac Bashevis Singer, and Joseph Brodsky show by example the various forms such writing can take, and the markets she suggests are appropriate outlets for writing of this sort. For further comments, see chapters 3 and 8 of this bibliography.

Bly, Robert W. *Secrets of a Freelance Writer: How to Make $85,000 a Year.* New York: Dodd, Mead, 1988.
This book is, as the title indicates, materialistic in its approach. It is worth reading part 2, on how to get writing assignments. Bly has excellent practical suggestions for writers of advertisements, a pursuit that has helped some struggling artists to survive while they were working on more artistic writing. Bly's concern is with showing writers how to turn freelance writing into a business from which they can gain the tax and other advantages of corporations.

Brady, John, and Jean M. Fredette, eds. *Fiction Writer's Market.* Cincinnati: Writer's Digest Books, 1981.
This collection of essays by such renowned writers as André Maurois, Flannery O'Connor, and Wright Morris addresses the topic of identifying markets, but it goes far beyond this and has excellent essays in such areas as writing fiction, on being true to life, and on organizing books for children and young adults. See additional comments under "General Studies" in chapters 1, 2, and 7 of this bibliography.

Braun, Matt. *How to Write Western Novels.* Cincinnati: Writer's Digest Books, 1988.
Braun offers specific advice about marketing this genre of the novel. His advice is practical. Himself a writer of westerns, Braun has run the course and knows the pitfalls that novices can face. His tone is encouraging, his information accurate and directly presented. For additional comments about this source, see chapter 2 of this bibliography.

Burack, Sylvia K., ed. *The Writer's Handbook.* Boston: The Writer, Inc., 1990.
This annual publication is the most comprehensive book available to writers seeking direct and specific advice about writing in a variety of genres, such as television scripts, science fiction, books for young people, and nonfiction articles

for commercial publication. Especially useful is the listing of editors and agents that is updated in each year's edition. The book contains one hundred chapters written by such well-known writers as Stephen King, Ursula K. Le Guin, X. J. Kennedy, William Stafford, and Eve Bunting. It also identifies twenty-five hundred specific markets with information about how to approach them, lists of contests and prizes, and business information for writers. It gives information about the preferred length of submissions to various outlets, payment rates, general focus, and subjects for which material is currently being sought.

Coe, Michelle E. *How to Write for Television*. New York: Crown, 1980.
Coe identifies markets that might not occur to the typical writer for television. Her information on writing and marketing television commercials is extensive and should be of considerable use to writers. Chapter 4, "Radio and Television Copy Rules," and chapter 5, "The Video Page," both deal directly and accurately with the preparation of manuscripts in this field. For further comments about this book, see chapter 6.

Edelstein, Scott. *Indispensable Writer's Guide*. New York: Harper & Row, 1989.
This comprehensive book addresses many aspects of writing for publication. Its information about the physical preparation and submission of manuscripts is particularly useful. Edelstein suggests ways to impress agents and editors with the strength of a piece of writing, giving special attention to query letters and follow-up inquiries. This is one of the most complete guides and should go into many revised editions to keep its suggestions up to date.

_____. *Manuscript Submission*. Cincinnati: Writer's Digest Books, 1990.
Edelstein covers every detail of submitting manuscripts, from the letter of inquiry to the proposal to the actual submission. He goes into matters of how to package and send literary properties, what to include in the final package that contains the manuscript, and how to follow up on submissions. Everything in this book is practical and necessary to writers who want to put their best feet forward when they approach agents, publishers, and editors. Much of the material presented amounts to common sense, but authors do not always follow the best procedures when they reach the point of actually sending in their manuscripts.

_____. *The Writer's Book of Checklists*. Cincinnati: Writer's Digest Books, 1991.
Edelstein has had plenty of experience dealing with publishers, editors, and literary agents. He shares his observations about the business end of writing in the latter half of this book. His checklists are clear and direct. For additional comments about this book, see chapter 3 of this bibliography.

Fredette, Jean M. *Writer's Digest Handbook of Magazine Article Writing.* Cincinnati: Writer's Digest Books, 1990.
In her more than thirty-five chapters, Fredette suggests an amazing array of outlets to which writers can submit their work. She is at her best in her suggestions about how to market one's work. Fredette consistently keeps her eye on the bottom line and suggests ways in which one's articles can garner maximal compensation. For additional remarks about this book, see chapters 3 and 9 of this bibliography.

Gee, Robin, ed. *1992 Novel and Short Story Writer's Market.* Cincinnati: Writer's Digest Books, 1991.
This well-established spin-off of *Writer's Market* is directed exclusively to writers of fiction. The 1992 edition provides information on nineteen hundred markets, more than double the number of fiction markets covered in *Writer's Market.* Like the parent volume, this annual guide includes articles by and interviews with suggestful writers to supplement the marketing information.

Gilbert, Nan. *See Yourself in Print: A Handbook for Young Writers.* Illustrated by Jacqueline Tomes. New York: Hawthorne Books, 1968.
After discussing basic markets, Gilbert suggests how young people can get writing ideas from such mundane pursuits as babysitting. Gilbert offers sensible marketing ideas for this sort of writing. For more comments on this book, see chapter 7 of this bibliography.

Goldin, Stephen, and Kathleen Sky. *The Business of Being a Writer.* New York: Harper & Row, 1982.
The book is most valuable for its legal advice, most of which has not changed since the book was published and is, therefore, relatively current. Chapters 5 ("Rights and Copyrights"), 6 ("Legal Matters"), 7 ("Magazine Contracts and Permissions"), 8 ("Book Contracts"), and 11 ("Record Keeping") are particularly relevant. The general information about literary agents given in chapter 9 is excellent, as is the discussion of vanity publishing and self-publishing in chapter 10. Two of the three appendices, those on proofreaders' symbols and government resources, are helpful, although the appendix that gives addresses of interest is of little current use. The bibliography is also valuable, if slightly outdated.

Goulart, Frances Sheridan. *How to Write a Cookbook and Sell It.* Port Washington, N.Y.: Ashley Books, 1980.
Among the most durable books on publishers' booklists are cookbooks and books on gardening. Goulart suggest ways that writers can tap this market. She discusses how to prepare a proposal and manuscript and how to promote a cookbook once it has been published (chapters 4 and 7 respectively). For further comments on this source, refer to chapter 3 of this bibliography.

Greenfeld, Howard. *Books: From Writer to Reader.* New York: Crown, 1976.
Greenfeld considers how to market book-length manuscripts, probing into such matters as the writer's relationship with publishers and literary agents, with editors and designers and illustrators. This book does a fine job of revealing some of the inner workings of publishing houses, showing how authors can be involved with their books at various steps of their production. The glossary of terms used in publishing is extensive and accurate. It will be invaluable to writers who are proofreading galley proofs or page proofs.

Hanna, S. S. *The Gypsy Scholar: A Writer's Comic Search for a Publisher.* Ames: Iowa State University Press, 1987.
Hanna relates in a first-person narrative the problems one can face in trying to place a manuscript with a publisher. Rejected by commercial houses, university presses, and literary agents, Hanna almost gave up but was resourceful enough to turn these disappointments into a learning experience that is related here in usually amusing detail.

Hayes, Helen, Ellen Rolfes, et al. *How to Write and Publish a Classic Cookbook.* Illustrated by Michelle Dent. New York: New American Library, 1986.
This book is primarily concerned with how to market and publish a cookbook and with how to promote one's own cookbook. From chapter 2 to the end, it addresses such matters as finding a publisher, preparing the manuscript, negotiating a contract, venturing into self-publishing, starting a publishing business, marketing, and approaching voluntary organizations that might wish to publish cookbooks compiled by their members. The book has a useful appendix of proofreaders' marks, along with a list of publishing companies and their addresses. For further comments about this book, see chapter 3 of this bibliography.

Hinds, Marjorie M. *How to Write for the Juvenile Market.* New York: Frederick Fell, 1966.
Although parts of this book are dated, Hinds does a good job of identifying markets and suggesting how to meet their demands. Chapter 2, "Keys to the Craft," is still cogent and offers advice that can enhance the possibility of publishing in this field. For additional comments about this book, refer to chapter 7 of this bibliography.

Hull, Raymond. *How to Write a Play.* Cincinnati: Writer's Digest Books, 1983.
Hull addresses matters on the production and publication of plays in chapter 16, and he also has valuable comments about marketing and promoting one's work in the first chapter, "The Playwright's Business." Most of chapter 17, "How to Build a Career," is also relevant. Chapter 18 contains a comprehensive glossary of theatrical terms. For further comments about this source, see chapter 4 of this bibliography.

Jerome, Judson, ed. *1992 Poet's Market*. Cincinnati: Writer's Digest Books, 1991. This annual publication features the most comprehensive and up-to-date list of sources for publishing poetry. More than one thousand markets are listed in the 1992 edition. These annual volumes also provide information on trends in poetry, writing colonies, contests, prizes, how to prepare and submit manuscripts, organizations for poets, and publications useful to those who wish to write in this genre.

Kissling, Mark, ed. *1992 Writer's Market*. Cincinnati: Writer's Digest Books, 1991. The industry standard, this annual provides up-to-date information on markets for articles, books, fillers, greeting cards, novels, plays, scripts, and short stories. More than four thousand markets are listed in the 1992 edition, which also includes articles by and interviews with successful writers.

Koontz, Dean R. *How to Write Best-Selling Fiction*. Cincinnati: Writer's Digest Books, 1981.
Chapter 3 of this book, "The Changing Marketplace," discusses some of the dynamics of identifying new markets for one's work. Chapter 14 goes extensively into how to place manuscripts in various markets. The material provided is easy to implement and certainly will enhance one's chances of acceptance. For additional comments about this book, see chapters 2 and 7 of this bibliography.

Literary Market Place, 1991. New York: R. R. Bowker, 1991.
This annual volume is the most comprehensive directory of the book publishing industry in the United States. Information is provided for more than twenty-one hundred publishers. It is current in identifying markets and their needs, payment, reviewing procedures, and other matters pertinent to publishing. The list of literary agents is up-to-date, as is the listing of organizations that offer typing, word-processing, and editorial services. The lists of contests, prizes, writers' colonies, and writers' organizations is updated annually so that each current issue is accurate. Serious writers find this reference book among their most valuable tools when it comes to preparing their writing for publication and marketing it.

Manners, William. *Wake Up and Write: How to Write Prolifically*. 3d ed. New York: Arco Publishing Company, 1977.
First written in 1962 and regularly updated since then, this book is strongest for chapter 5, "Inside Editors, Agents, and Publishers," and chapter 6, "Where to Get Help—Emotional and Financial," both of which are concerned largely with how to market manuscripts. Chapter 5 offers a wealth of information that will get writers to think like editors and agents, an indispensable skill that many new writers have not developed.

Mau, Ernest E. *The Free-Lance Writer's Survival Manual*. Chicago: Contemporary Books, 1981.
Those interested in how to market a manuscript will benefit from reading chapter 5, "The Writer as a Salesman," and chapter 6, "Confronting a Client," in both of which an aggressive approach to selling one's work is advocated. Information is also provided about financial arrangements, contract negotiations, and tax implications that affect freelance writers. For further comments on this book, refer to chapters 3 and 9 of this bibliography.

Muth, Marcia. *Writing and $elling: Poetry, Fiction, Articles, Plays, and Local History*. Santa Fe, N.Mex.: Sunstone Press, 1985.
A major focus of this book is on how to market manuscripts. Muth's suggestions will not work for everyone, but some of them will work for most writers. The book is far-ranging and well written. Each chapter follows a similar format. For additional comments on the book, refer to the entries under "General Studies" in chapters 1, 4, 5, and 9 of this bibliography.

Newcomb, Duane. *How to Sell and Re-Sell Your Writing*. Cincinnati: Writer's Digest Books, 1987.
Newcombe shows how, without violating any laws or moral codes, writers can often make their writing do double or even triple duty. He goes specifically into how this can be done, providing useful illustrative examples. This book should pay for itself with the first resale of a piece of nonfiction. For further comments about it, refer to chapter 3 of this bibliography.

Newton, Michael. *How to Write Action/Adventure Novels*. Cincinnati: Writer's Digest Books, 1989.
Newton, himself a successful, publishing writer of adventure novels, offers good suggestions about writing the hook, defining the quest, establishing believability, and achieving clarity. His chapter on scoping markets is particularly useful to writers who write in this genre. For additional comments about this book, refer to chapter 2 of this bibliography.

Niggli, Josefina. *New Pointers on Playwriting*. Boston: The Writer, Inc., 1967.
This book, with its strong chapter 10, "What Is Plot?," is of unique value. Niggli's recommendations about how to craft plays have remained useful through the years and are still of general interest to playwrights. Her comments on how to market plays, although somewhat dated, are still valuable for their general suggestions. For additional comments about this source, see chapter 4 of this bibliography.

Packard, William. *The Art of Screenwriting: Story, Script, and Markets*. New York: Paragon House, 1987.

Over and above the sound advice Packard offers about writing for films, the material on markets and methods of marketing is outstanding. Anyone seriously interested in breaking into the business of writing screenplays will benefit directly and immediately from reading this book. For further comments about this book, see chapter 6 of this bibliography.

_____. *The Poet's Dictionary: A Handbook of Prosody and Poetic Devices.* New York: Harper & Row, 1989.
The dictionary portion of this book occupies the first 212 pages and ranges from *accent* to *zeugma*, each entry being discussed with relative fullness. An appendix addresses the matter of preparing the poetry manuscript and submitting it for publication. The suggestions are sensible and are aimed at helping readers to market their work successfully. For further comments about this book, see chapter 5 of this bibliography.

Pianka, Phyllis Taylor. *How to Write Romances.* Cincinnati: Writer's Digest Books, 1988.
Romances represent an incredibly brisk market in prose fiction and account for a major percentage of the book sales in the United States. Pianka goes into the economic as well as the artistic sides of writing romances, many of which bring lump-sum payments rather than the continuing royalties that most novels command. Chapter 14 deals directly with marketing, and chapter 12 identifies such markets as the young adult and inspirational ones. Chapter 15, which enumerates fifty-three reasons a book may be rejected, is of immense practical value. For additional comments about this source, refer to chapters 2 and 7 of this bibliography.

Pike, Frank, and Thomas G. Dunn. *The Playwright's Handbook.* New York: New American Library, 1985.
The last two chapters of this book provide excellent information about the literary marketplace for playwrights. Chapter 7, "Getting Your Play Produced," touches on the fundamentals of arranging for production if one is relatively new to the field and inexperienced. Chapter 8, "Making Ends Meet: The Financial Side of Playwriting," covers everything from alternative employment to national grants to how to use an agent effectively. For further comments about this book, see chapter 4 of this bibliography.

Preston, Elizabeth, Ingrid Monke, and Elizabeth Bickford. *Preparing Your Manuscript.* Boston: The Writer, Inc., 1990.
This small, practical book gives specific information about how to prepare manuscripts for submission to agents or publishers. It goes into the mechanical aspects of preparing manuscripts in accepted, professional form. The authors also review such fundamental matters as spelling and punctuation. Their suggestions

on copyright protection are practical and easy to follow, as is their related material about how to protect a literary property. They provide information about how to package and mail manuscripts.

Rehmehl, Judy. *So, You Want to Write a Cookbook*. Louisville, Ky.: Marathon International Publishing, 1984.
This book essentially is directed at groups of people—members of church congregations, of service clubs, or of specific communities—interested in working collectively to produce cookbooks. Part 5, focusing on marketing such books, suggests ways in which the groups producing them can market them locally or regionally. For additional comments about this book, refer to chapter 3.

Rilla, Wolf. *The Writer and the Screen: On Writing for Film and Television*. New York: William Morrow, 1974.
Part 3 of this book contains a section entitled "Film of Fact, Television, and the Market Place" in which Rilla offers some splendid insights into how to market one's work. Although some of the specifics in this section are now dated, the basic ideas are still valid and well worth considering. For further comments about this book, see chapter 6 of this bibliography.

Roberts, Ellen E. M. *The Children's Picture Book: How to Write It, How to Sell It*. Cincinnati: Writer's Digest Books, 1981, 1987.
Roberts' guidance in marketing children's picture books, including preparing the manuscript and mailing manuscripts and pictures in ways that will protect them, is sound. Chapter 10, on submitting the manuscript, is directly relevant, as is chapter 14, on promoting a book once it is in print. For additional comments about this book, refer to chapter 7 of this bibliography.

Rouverol, Jean. *Writing for the Soaps*. Cincinnati: Writer's Digest Books, 1984.
Rouverol obviously knows her field intimately. She knowledgeably discusses the history of soaps in the first chapter, then the assembly-line approach to writing. In chapter 14, Rouverol deals with agencies, ratings, and pay. The material on marketing scripts is informed and realistic. For additional comments about this book, see chapter 6 of this bibliography.

Rowe, Kenneth Thorpe. *Write That Play*. New York: Funk and Wagnalls, 1939, 1968.
This book goes into valuable and significant detail about playwriting and provides an in-depth analysis of John Millington Synge's *Riders to the Sea* and Henrik Ibsen's *A Doll's House*. Rowe's appendix on marketing plays is useful, although obviously dated. Some of the general information in it is still useful. For further comments on this source, see chapter 4 of this bibliography.

Scully, Celia G., and Thomas J. Scully. *How to Make Money Writing About Fitness and Health*. Cincinnati: Writer's Digest Books, 1986.
This excellent book suggests markets for both articles and books. Particularly relevant is chapter 13, which is concerned with proposing and promoting a book. A valuable appendix enumerates awards, honors, and prizes available to writers in this field. For more information about this book, see chapter 3 of this bibliography.

Townsend, Doris McFerran. *The Way to Write and Publish a Cookbook*. New York: St. Martin's Press, 1985.
Chapters 5 to 7 of this book have to do with the marketing and promotion of cookbooks, considering how to sell such books, what contractual arrangements to expect, and how to publicize and promote such books once they are in print. For further comments about this source, see chapter 3 of this bibliography.

Williams, Nan Schram. *Confess for Profit: Writing and Selling the Personal Story—A Comprehensive Guide*. Los Angeles: Douglas-West Publishers, 1973.
Williams discusses methods that have worked for her on how to plan, plot, and write stories as first-person narratives. Williams presents information about how to prepare and market manuscripts. She knows how to promote one's work, and her information in this area is sensible. Her guide to book publishers and magazines, useful in its day, is now dated. For more information about this book, see chapters 2 and 8.

Williamson, J. N., ed. *How to Write Tales of Horror, Fantasy, and Science Fiction*. Cincinnati: Writer's Digest Books, 1987.
Patrick Lo Brutto's essay on marketing is a useful addendum to Williamson's book. Lo Brutto has important things to say about literary agents and editors. He suggests how writers can interest them and what they can expect from them. The book itself is a well-balanced study of three overlapping forms of fiction writing. For additional comments about this book, refer to chapter 2 of this bibliography.

Yolen, Jane. *Writing Books for Children*. Boston: The Writer, Inc., 1973.
Although this book has been superseded by Yolen's *Guide to Writing for Children* (see chapter 7 of this bibliography), it offers some excellent advice. The book discusses types and genres of children's books. Chapter 10 is devoted to marketing manuscripts and to assessing markets. Although it is dated, the overall suggestions are still valid. For further comments about this book, refer to chapters 3 and 7 of this bibliography.

The Letter of Inquiry

Burgett, Gordon. *Query Letters/Cover Letters*. Carpenteria, Calif.: Communications Unlimited, 1985.
This small book from an out-of-the-way press is narrow in its focus but accomplishes admirably what it sets out to do. Especially relevant are chapter 2, which discusses and shows sample query letters for artwork related to books; chapter 3, which discusses and provides samples of query letters for book manuscripts; and chapter 4, which discusses and shows samples of cover letters to use in submitting work for possible publication.

Cool, Lisa Collier. *How to Write Irresistible Query Letters*. Cincinnati: Writer's Digest Books, 1990.
The letters Lisa Cool cites as effective contain a "hook" in the first paragraph that will make the recipient want to continue reading. The fact that publishers and editors are deluged with huge numbers of letters makes it necessary for potential writers to draft and send letters that will capture the attention of the reader immediately. Cool gives excellent examples of ineffective letters as well as examples of ones that succeed. In many cases, letters from both extremes provide almost identical information, but the letter with the "hook" will be taken seriously as a prime example of what the writer can do to arouse and maintain interest.

Rockwell, F. A. *How to Write Nonfiction That Sells*. Chicago: Henry Regnery, 1975.
Rockwell's classification of types of articles is helpful. Chapter 3 of this book deals specifically with the query letter, and the advice given is knowledgeable. For further comments about this book, see chapter 3 of this bibliography.

The Literary Agent

Cleaver, Diane. *The Literary Agent and the Writer*. Boston: The Writer, Inc., 1984.
Cleaver, herself a literary agent, gives practical suggestions to writers about when they need a literary agent and about how to find compatible and appropriate ones. She gives specific information about how to write a query to an agent about both fiction and nonfiction and discusses the customary financial arrangements as well as the agent's role in shaping an agreement with a publisher, in securing and negotiating a strong contract that will benefit the writer, in arranging for subsidiary rights, and in marketing manuscripts generally. Cleaver knows her way around in the world of publishing, and her advice, although somewhat dated, is sensible and useful to a beginner who has a manuscript to market.

Curtis, Richard. *Beyond the Bestseller: A Literary Agent Takes You Inside the Book Business.* New York: New American Library, 1989.
An experienced literary agent, Curtis in chapter 4 addresses the important matter of "What I Have Done for You Lately?," which considers the services agents can perform after they have sold the initial manuscript. Chapter 1, about turning movies into books—"novelizing" them, as he calls it—is fresh and interesting, as is its counterpart, chapter 28, which discusses turning books into movies. Chapter 13, on multibook deals, is balanced and sensible. Chapter 14 gives payout schedules. This book has considerable pertinent information for writers in all fields.

Davie, Elaine. "Close-up." In *Novel and Short Story Writer's Market*, edited by Laurie Henry. Cincinnati: Writer's Digest Books, 1989.
Elaine Davie explains what agents do and how they do it. Her brief contribution is worth reading. It is followed by a twenty-three-page list of agents with pertinent information about them. For additional comments about this source, see chapters 1 and 2 of this bibliography.

Diamant, Anita. "The 10% Solution." In *The Writer's Handbook, 1987*, edited by Sylvia K. Burack. Boston: The Writer, Inc., 1987.
Diamant, herself a literary agent, notes the difficulty that beginning authors have in getting publishing houses to read their manuscripts and acknowledges that it is equally difficult for them to be taken on by agents if they have not proved themselves. She mentions, however, several ways in which previously unpublished writers can approach literary agents, emphasizing that they should communicate in writing rather than by telephone. She also enumerates what writers can reasonably expect agents to do and what agents should not be expected to do. The agent's commission is normally 10 percent for domestic sales. One of the most important functions an agent can serve is that of fine-tuning publisher contracts before writers sign them, negotiating subsidiary rights, foreign rights, and television and movie rights.

Gee, Robin, ed. *1992 Guide to Literary Agents and Art/Photo Reps.* Cincinnati: Writer's Digest Books, 1991.
The 1992 volume is the first edition of this directory, which lists only reputable agents (both fee-charging and non-fee-charging). In addition, articles by agents provide an insider's view of the literary marketplace.

Larsen, Michael. *Literary Agents: How to Get and Work with the Right One for You.* Cincinnati: Writer's Digest Books, 1986.
The topic Larsen tackles is one of the more sensitive ones that writers have to confront. Finding an agent to represent one is not always easy, but having found one, a writer must then ask whether that person is the ideal agent for the writer's

own needs. Larsen, with shrewd psychological insight, gives commonsense advice about how to determine whether one has found the right agent, the one with whom he or she can work compatibly and productively over the long time span that often characterizes writer-agent relationships. The perfect mix will result in a more fruitful career for authors than they will experience if they attach themselves to an agent who is not right for them. This book needs updating.

Levine, Ellen. "What Every Writer Needs to Know About Literary Agents." In *The Writer's Handbook, 1987*, edited by Sylvia K. Burack. Boston: The Writer, Inc., 1987.

Using a question-answer format, Levine provides pertinent information about finding and retaining a literary agent, emphasizing that agents prefer to handle book-length manuscripts rather than articles or short stories. She gives accurate information about where to obtain up-to-date lists of literary agents and discusses such matters as whether multiple submissions are acceptable and ethical and what business arrangements an agent can help a writer make. Levine reminds her readers that because agents are in business to make money, they are unlikely to represent authors whose work, however good it might be, is too esoteric to appeal to significant numbers of readers.

MacCampbell, Donald. *Don't Step on It—It Might Be a Writer: Reminiscences of a Literary Agent*. Los Angeles: Sherbourne Press, 1972.

This book is slightly outrageous, but between the lines are some interesting observations about the relationship between writers and their agents. MacCampbell also suggests ways of approaching agents, many of whom are reluctant to take on unpublished authors. Although it is hard to agree with all of the specifics of this book, its general pronouncements are worth reading and considering.

McLarn, Jack Clinton. *Writing Part-Time for Fun and Money*. Wilmington, Del.: Enterprise Publishing, 1978.

McLarn's suggestions of markets for a significant range of genres are strong, particularly in this book's appendices. McLarn has thought of markets that are mentioned only infrequently but that present excellent possibilities. For additional comments about this book, see chapters 1, 2, 7, and 9 of this bibliography.

Reynolds, Paul R. *The Non-Fiction Book: How to Write and Sell It*. New York: William Morrow, 1970.

Reynolds, himself a literary agent, devotes chapter 15 to discussing what agents do, what they expect, and how to engage one. The information is generally accurate, although now somewhat dated. The material on finding a publisher and on negotiating a contract is also useful. For additional comments about this book, see chapter 3 of this bibliography.

Wilbur, L. Perry. *How to Write Books That Sell*. Chicago: Contemporary Books, 1979.
Chapter 11 focuses major attention on using literary agents and on how to make initial contacts with them. Information in chapter 28, "Get Thee to the ABA Convention," is also apropos because it is at this annual meeting of the American Booksellers' Association that many valuable contacts are made. For further comments about this book, see chapters 2 and 7 of this bibliography.

The Writing Business: A Poets and Writers Handbook. Edited jointly by the editors of *Coda: A Poets and Writers Newsletter*. New York: Poets and Writers, 1985.
This source is full of practical advice about placing manuscripts, both article-length and book-length, with publishers. It offers suggestions for writers of short fiction, novels, poetry, and nonfiction and includes a list of fourteen major magazines with indications of what they prefer to publish and of what they pay writers. The list of publishers' addresses is short but reasonably accurate. For further comments about this source, refer to chapters 1, 2, 3, 5, and 9 of this bibliography.

Promotion

Cassill, Kay. *The Complete Handbook for Freelance Writers*. Cincinnati: Writer's Digest Books, 1981.
Chapter 8 of this book addresses quite fully the question of promoting one's writing and oneself as a writer. Chapter 15 provides information about self-syndication, which can yield tax benefits for freelance writers as well creating a professional approach to dealing with such matters as personal appearances, talk-show interviews, and autograph parties. Much of the advice given in this chapter can help writers to become their own agents. The possibilities of self-publishing are also touched on. Such an approach can be immensely profitable if one has a winning book, although distribution and advertising problems can be daunting.

Coe, Michelle E. *How to Write for Television*. New York: Crown, 1980.
Coe devotes chapter 39 of her book to suggesting ways to promote one's writing in this area. The suggestions are realistic and should yield excellent results for those who persist. For further comments about this book, see chapter 6 and above.

Feldman, Elane. *The Writer's Guide to Self-Promotion and Publicity*. Cincinnati: Writer's Digest Books, 1990.
Feldman offers scores of practical, often commonsense, suggestions about how writers can, through their own efforts, keep their names before people in the

publishing business and before the public. By following Feldman's advice, many writers can become their own best public relations agents. The book suggests a coherent, step-by-step publicity plan that writers can put into immediate action. Feldman reveals the details of developing personal press kits. Any ambitious writer will find extremely valuable suggestions here, and the virtue of them is that they do not require vast expenditures of funds to achieve the desired results. In fact, those who follow the advice in this book should increase their incomes substantially.

Goldin, Stephen, and Kathleen Sky. *The Business of Being a Writer*. New York: Harper & Row, 1982.
Chapter 13 of this book is concerned particularly with promotion, although some of its other chapters touch on the subject as well. The authors show how writers can take the initiative in promoting their books through making presentations before clubs and other gatherings of people, by participating in autograph parties, and by participating in radio and television talk shows. Chapter 9 shows how literary agents work closely with authors to help them promote their works.

Peck, Robert Newton. *Secrets of Successful Fiction*. Cincinnati: Writer's Digest Books, 1980.
The tone of this book is so breezy that it may offend some readers. Those who do not object to a chapter title like that of chapter 2, "How to Write Good with Swell Adjectives," may find some value in this book, whose information on promotion is direct and somewhat useful. The book, however, is marginal at best. For additional comments about this book, refer to chapter 1 of this bibliography.

Chapter 11
PARTING WORDS

Writing Programs

At last count, at least three hundred community colleges, four-year colleges, and universities offered programs in creative writing that culminate in associate's or bachelor's degrees. Almost seventy universities have master's degree programs in creative writing, and seven schools offer doctorates in the field. In most cases, the traditional master's thesis or doctoral dissertation is replaced by such extended creative works as a novel, a full-length play, or a collection of short fiction. Even those higher institutions that do not offer degree programs for creative writers usually have several courses in writing from which fledgling writers can benefit.

Anyone interested in writing courses available in a given area should call or write to all the institutions of higher learning in that area. One can also find out whether the YMCA, the YWCA, the YMHA, or similar organizations have workshops in the field or whether they might consider sponsoring such workshops if a demand for them is demonstrated.

Among the more established and best-recognized degree programs in writing are the following, arranged alphabetically by state and marked **B** for those that offer bachelor's degrees, **M** for those that offer master's degrees, and **D** for those that offer doctorates.

ALABAMA
    University of Alabama at Tuscaloosa (M)

ALASKA
    University of Alaska at Anchorage (M)
    University of Alaska at Fairbanks (M)

ARIZONA
    Arizona State University (M)
    Northern Arizona University (M)
    University of Arizona (B, M)

ARKANSAS
    University of Arkansas at Fayetteville (M)

CALIFORNIA
    California State University at Fresno (M)
    California State University at Long Beach (B)
    California State University at Northridge (B)

California State University at San Francisco (B, M)
California State University at San Jose (B, M)
Chapman College (M)
Dominican College of San Rafael (B)
Mills College (B, M)
University of California at San Diego (B)
University of California at Santa Cruz (B)
University of Redlands (B)
University of San Francisco (M)
University of Southern California (B, M)

COLORADO
Colorado State University West (B)
University of Colorado at Denver (B)
University of Denver (B, M, D)

CONNECTICUT
Fairfield University (B)
Wesleyan University (B)
Western Connecticut State University (B)

DISTRICT OF COLUMBIA
American University (M)
Gallaudet University (B)

FLORIDA
Eckerd College (B)
Florida International University (B, M)
University of Miami (B, M, D)
University of Tampa (B)

GEORGIA
Agnes Scott College (B)
Emory University (B)
Georgia State University (M)

IDAHO
Boise State University (B)

ILLINOIS
Augustana College (B)
Columbia College (B, M)
Illinois State University (M)

Judson College (B)
Knox College (B)
Lake Forest College (B)
Millikan University (B)
Northwestern University (B)
Rockford College (B)
Shimer College (B)
Southern Illinois University at Carbondale (B)
University of Chicago (B)
University of Illinois at Urbana-Champaign (B)

INDIANA
Indiana State University (B, M)
Indiana University at Bloomington (B, M)
Indiana Wesleyan University (B)
Purdue University (B, M)
St. Mary's College (B)
Taylor University (B)

IOWA
Drake University (B)
Loras College (B)
Morningside College (B)
University of Iowa (M)

KANSAS
Benedictine College (B)
Wichita State University (M)

KENTUCKY
Kentucky Wesleyan College (B)
Murray State University (B)

LOUISIANA
Louisiana State and Agricultural and Mechanical College (M)
McNeese State University (M)

MAINE
University of Maine at Farmington (B)

MARYLAND
The Johns Hopkins University (B, M)
Loyola College in Maryland (B)

University of Baltimore (B)
Washington College (B)

MASSACHUSETTS
Boston University (M)
Bradford College (B)
Emerson College (B, M)
Hampshire College (B)
Harvard University (B)
Massachusetts Institute of Technology (B)
North Adams State College (B)
Radcliffe College (B)
Salem State College (M)
University of Massachusetts at Boston (Certificate)

MICHIGAN
Adrian College (B)
Alma College (B)
Central Michigan University (M)
Eastern Michigan University (B)
Northern Michigan University (M)
Olivet College (B)
University of Michigan (B, M)
Western Michigan University (M)

MINNESOTA
Bethel College (B)
Macalester College (B)
Mankato State University (B)
Southwest State University (B)

MISSOURI
St. Louis University (Certificate)
Southwest Missouri State University (B)
Tarkio College (B)
Washington University (B, M, D)
Webster College (B)
Westminster College (B)

MONTANA
Carroll College (B)
University of Montana (M)

NEBRASKA
Hastings College (B)
University of Nebraska at Omaha (B)

NEW HAMPSHIRE
Franklin Pierce College (B)
Plymouth State College (B)

NEW JERSEY
Jersey City State College (B)
Rider College (B)
Rutgers, the State University of New Jersey at Newark (M)

NEW MEXICO
College of Santa Fe (B)
University of New Mexico (B)

NEW YORK
Bard College (B, M)
Barnard College (B)
City University of New York: Baruch College (B)
City University of New York: Brooklyn College (B, M)
City University of New York: City College (B, M)
City University of New York: Queens College (B, M)
Columbia University (B, M)
Cornell University (M)
D'Youville College (B)
Eugene Lang College, New School for Social Research (B)
Friends World College (B)
Hamilton College (B)
Hofstra University (B)
Houghton College (B)
King's College (B)
Long Island University at Brooklyn (M)
Long Island University at Southampton (B)
Nazareth College of Rochester (B)
St. Lawrence College (B, M)
St. Thomas Aquinas College (B)
Sarah Lawrence College (B, M)
State University of New York at Albany (D)
State University of New York at Genesco (B)
State University of New York at New Paltz (B)
Syracuse University (M)

NORTH CAROLINA
  East Carolina University (B)
  High Point College (B)
  Methodist College (B)
  North Carolina State University (B)
  Pembroke State University (B)
  University of North Carolina at Asheville (B)
  University of North Carolina at Greensboro (M)
  Warren Wilson College (M)

OHIO
  Antioch College (B)
  Ashland University (B)
  Bowling Green State University (B, M)
  College of Wooster (B)
  Denison University (B)
  Kent State University (B)
  Miami University at Oxford (B, M)
  Oberlin College (B)
  Ohio State University at Columbus (M, D)
  Ohio University (B, M)
  Ohio Wesleyan University (B)
  Union Institute (B, D)
  Wittenberg University (B)

OKLAHOMA
  Central State University (M)
  Oklahoma Christian University of Science and Arts (B)

OREGON
  George Fox College (B)
  Linfield College (B)
  Pacific University (B)
  University of Oregon (M)

PENNSYLVANIA
  Bucknell University (B)
  California State University of Pennsylvania (B)
  Carnegie Mellon University (B, M)
  Eastern College (B)
  Gannon University (B)
  Geneva College (B)
  La Salle University (B)

Lycoming College (B)
University of Pittsburgh at Greensburg (B)
University of Pittsburgh at Johnstown (B)
University of Pittsburgh at Pittsburgh (B)

RHODE ISLAND
Brown University (B, M)
Rhode Island College (B)
Roger Williams College (B)
Salve Regina College (B)

SOUTH CAROLINA
Bob Jones University (B)
Columbia College (B)

TENNESSEE
Maryville College (B)
Memphis State University (M)
University of Tennessee at Knoxville (B)

TEXAS
McMurry College (B)
St. Edward's University (B)
Southern Methodist University (B)
University of Houston: Downtown Campus (B)
University of Houston: Main Campus (B, M, D)
University of Texas at El Paso (B, M)

UTAH
University of Utah (M)

VERMONT
Bloomington College (B, M)
Burlington College (B)
Goddard College (B, M)
Johnson State College (B)
Lyndon State College (B)
Marlboro College (B)

VIRGINIA
Averett College (B)
Emory and Henry College (B)
George Mason University (M)

Hollins College (B, M)
Old Dominion University (M)
Sweet Briar College (B)
University of Virginia (M)
Virginia Commonwealth University (M)
Virginia Intermont College (B)
Virginia Wesleyan College (B)

WASHINGTON
Eastern Washington University (B, M)
Evergreen State College (B)
Pacific Lutheran University (B)
University of Washington (B, M)
Western Washington University (B, M)
Whitworth College (B)

WEST VIRGINIA
Alderson-Broaddus College (B)
Davis and Elkins College (B)
Shepherd College (B)
West Virginia State College (B)

WISCONSIN
Beloit College (B)
Carroll College (B)
Lakeland College (B)
University of Wisconsin at Green Bay (B)

WYOMING
University of Wyoming (M)

Writers' Conferences and Workshops

The Council of Arts or its equivalent association in most states can provide information about conferences and workshops for writers in their states. A letter addressed to the executive director of such councils sent to the capital of the state in question will likely elicit a prompt response. Among the best-known writers' conferences and workshops, the following, listed by state, are the most prominent. Inquiries to them should be accompanied by a stamped, self-addressed envelope.

Parting Words 145

ALASKA
    Annual Travel Writing Conference, University of Alaska Southeast, Continuing Education, 11120-C Glacier Highway, Juneau, Alaska 99801-8682
    Sitka Summer Writers' Symposium, Box 2420, Sitka, Alaska 99835

ARIZONA
    Christian Writers' Conference, Box 443, Cornville, Arizona 86325
    Pima Writers' Workshop, Pima Community College, 2202 West Anklam Road, Tucson, Arizona 85709

ARKANSAS
    Arkansas Writers' Conference, 1115 Gillette Drive, Little Rock, Arkansas 72207
    Sense of the Wilderness: A Workshop in Environmental Perception and Nature, McCarthy via Glennallen, Arkansas 99588

CALIFORNIA
    Annual Writers' Conference in Children's Literature, Box 296, Mar Vista Station, Los Angeles, California 90066
    Bay Area Writers' Workshop, Box 620327, Woodside, California 94062
    Biola University Writers' Institute, Biola University, La Mirada, California 90639
    Book Publishing Weekends, Para Publishing, Box 4232, Santa Barbara, California 93140-4232
    Christian Writers Fellowship Writers' Conference, 2222 South Maddock, Santa Ana, California 92704
    Communication Unlimited Writing Programs, Box 6405, Santa Maria, California 93456
    Getting Ahead in the Writing Game, National Writers' Club, 1450 South Havana #620, Aurora, Colorado 80012 [conference held in California]
    Napa Valley Writers' Conference, Napa Valley College, Napa, California 94558
    San Diego State University Writers' Conference, Extended Studies, San Diego State University, San Diego, California 92182
    Selling to Hollywood, Writers' Connection, 1601 Saratoga-Sunnyvale Road #180, Cupertino, California 95014
    Sierra Writing Camp, 18293 Crystal Street, Grass Valley, California 95949
    Sonoma State University Summer Writers' Conference, Office of Extended Education, Sonoma State University, Rohnert Park, California 94928
    Summer Writing Workshops, Idyllwild School of Music and the Arts, Box 38-WD, Idyllwild, California 92349
    Valley Writers' Network, Box 458, Corcoran, California 93212
    Women's National Book Association, Los Angeles chapter, Women's National Book Association, Box 807, Burbank, California 91503-0807
    Writers' Conference in Children's Literature, Society of Children's Book Writers

Conference, Box 296, Mar Vista Station, Los Angeles, California 90066
Writing/Photography Seminars for Beginners, 9524 Guilford Drive #A, Indianapolis, Indiana 46240

COLORADO
Annual SCBW Conference, 701 Kalima Avenue, Denver, Colorado 80304
Aspen Writers' Conference, Post Office Drawer 7726-D, Aspen, Colorado 81612
Colorado Gold Writers' Conference, Rocky Mountain Fiction Writers Box 211177, Denver, Colorado 80221
Society of Children's Book Writers Annual Rocky Mountain Retreat, 807 Hercules Place, Colorado Springs, Colorado 80906
Steamboat Springs Writers' Conference, Box 771913, Steamboat Springs, Colorado 80477
Writers in the Rockies Novel Conference, 837 Fifteenth Street, Boulder, California 80302
Writing and Producing Videos: The New Wave, National Writers' Club, 1450 South Havana #620, Aurora, Colorado 80012

CONNECTICUT
Wesleyan Writers' Conference, Wesleyan University, Middletown, Connecticut 06457
Writers' Retreat Workshop, Box 139, South Lancaster, Massachusetts 01561
Writing at Yale, Yale Summer and Special Programs, Yale University, Department WD 2, Box 2145, New Haven, Connecticut 06520

DISTRICT OF COLUMBIA
Independent Writers' Conference, WIW, 730 15th Street, NW #220, Washington, District of Columbia 20005

FLORIDA
Caribbean Seminar at Sea on Creative Writing/Photo Marketing, 9524 Guilford Drive #A, Indianapolis, Indiana 46240
Florida Space Coast Writers' Conference, Box 804, Melbourne, Florida 32902
Florida State Writers' Conference, Florida Freelance Writers' Association, Box 9844-REV, Fort Lauderdale, Florida 33310
Florida Suncoast Writers' Conference, St. Petersburg Campus, University of South Florida, 140 Seventh Avenue South, St. Petersburg, Florida 33701
Key West Literary Seminar, Key West Literary Seminars/New Directions in American Theater, Box 391, Sugarloaf Shores, Florida 33044
Writers' Weekend in Florida, 3748 Harbor Heights Drive, Largo, Florida 34644

GEORGIA
Council of Authors and Journalists, Inc., 1214 Laurel Hill Drive, Decatur, Georgia 30033

Sandhills Writers' Conference, Office of Continuing Education, Augusta College, Augusta, Georgia 30910

Southeastern Writers' Conference, Route 1, Box 102, Cuthbert, Georgia 31740

ILLINOIS
Annual Christian Writers' Conference, 388 East Gundersen Drive, Wheaton, Illinois 60188

Autumn Writer's Affair, Love Designers' Writers' Club, Inc., 1507 Burnham Avenue, Calumet City, Illinois 60409

Breaking into Magazine Writing and World of Freelance Writing Seminars, 9409 Voss Road, Marengo, Illinois 60152

Freelance Writing: How To Write and Sell Fiction and Nonfiction, Division of Continuing Education, University of Toledo, Toledo, Ohio 43606-3393

Illinois Wesleyan University Writers' Conference, Illinois Wesleyan University, Box 2900, Bloomington, Illinois 61702

Mississippi Valley Writers' Conference, 3403 45th Street, Moline, Illinois 61265

Of Dark and Stormy Nights, Mystery Writers of America, Midwest chapter, Box 8, Techny, Illinois 60082

Prairie State College Writers' Conference, 202 South Halsted Street, Chicago Heights, Illinois 60411

INDIANA
Indiana University Writers' Conference, 464 Ballantine Hall, Indiana University, Bloomington, Indiana 47405

Midwest Writers' Conference, Department of Journalism, Ball State University, Muncie, Indiana 47306

IOWA
Iowa Summer Writing Program, Division of Continuing Education, University of Iowa, Iowa City, Iowa 52242

Outdoor Writers' Association of America Conference, 2017 Cato Avenue #101, State College, Pennsylvania 16801

KANSAS
National Lamplighters' Inspirational Writers' Conference, Box 415, Benton, Kansas 67017

William Inge Festival, Independence Community College, Box 708, Independence, Kansas 67301

Writers' Workshop in Science Fiction, Department of English, University of Kansas, Lawrence, Kansas 66045

KENTUCKY
Annual Appalachian Writers' Workshop, Box 844, Hindman, Kentucky 41822
Carter Caves Writers' Workshop, 11905 Lilac Way, Middletown, Kentucky 40243
Creative Writing Conference, Department of English, Eastern Kentucky University, Richmond, Kentucky 40475
Green River Writers' Retreat, 403 South Sixth, Ironton, Ohio 45638
Writing Workshop for People over 57, Donovan Scholars' Program, Ligon House, University of Kentucky, Lexington, Kentucky 40506-0442

LOUISIANA
Deep South Writers' Conference, Box 44691, University of Southwestern Louisiana, Lafayette, Louisiana 70504
New Orleans Writers' Conference, 1520 Sugar Bowl Drive, New Orleans, Louisiana 70112

MAINE
Annual Maine Writers' Workshop, Box 905, Stonington, Maine 04681
Conservatory of American Letters Writers' Conference, Box 88-TW, Thomaston, Maine 04861
In Celebration of Children's Literature, Children's Literature Conference, University of Southern Maine, 301 Bailey Hall, Gorham, Maine 04038
State of Maine Writers' Conference, Box 296, Ocean Park, Maine 04063
Stonecoast Writers' Conference, Department of English, University of Southern Maine, Portland, Maine 04103

MARYLAND
Festival of Poets and Poetry and Intensive Writing Workshop, St. Mary's College of Maryland, St. Mary's City, Maryland 20686
Mid-Atlantic Christian Writers'/Speakers' Conference, Box 11337, Bainbridge, Maryland 98110
Western Maryland Writers' Workshop in Poetry, Frostburg State University, Frostburg, Maryland 21532
Review and Herald Publishing Association Writers' Workshop, 55 West Oak Creek Drive, Hagerstown, Maryland 21740

MASSACHUSETTS
Cape Cod Writers' Conference, Cape Cod Conservatory of Music and Arts, Route 132, West Barnstable, Massachusetts 02668
Eastern Writers' Conference, Department of English, Salem State College, Salem, Massachusetts 01970
Harvard Summer Writing Program, Harvard University Summer School, Department 457, 20 Garden Street, Cambridge, Massachusetts, 02138

Parting Words

    Mount Holyoke Writers' Conference, Box 3213 Mount Holyoke College, South Hadley, Massachusetts 01075
    New England Writers' Conference, Simmons College, 300 The Fenway, Boston, Massachusetts 02115
    University of Lowell Summer Writing Program, Summer Session, University of Lowell, 1 University Avenue, Lowell, Massachusetts 01854

MICHIGAN
    Clarion Workshop of Science Fiction and Fantasy Writing, Holmes Hall E-28, Lyman Briggs School, Michigan State University, East Lansing, Michigan 48825
    Freelance Writing: How to Write and Sell Fiction and Nonfiction, Division of Continuing Education, University of Toledo, Toledo, Ohio 43606-3393
    International Christian Writers' Workshop, Andrews University, Berrien Springs, Michigan 49103
    Maranatha Christian Writers' Seminar, 4759 Lake Harbor Road, Muskegon, Michigan 49441
    Michigan Northwoods Writers' Conference, 1 Old Homestead Road, Glen Arbor, Michigan 49636
    Midland Writers' Conference, Grace A. Dow Library, 1710 West St. Andrews Road, Midland, Michigan 48640
    Western Michigan Writers' Conference, Office of Conferences and Institutes, Western Michigan University, Kalamazoo, Michigan 49008-5161

MINNESOTA
    Headwaters Writers' Conference, Office of Conferences, Bemidji State University, 1500 Birchmont Drive NE #51, Bemidji, Minnesota 56601
    Minneapolis Writers' Workshop Fiction Conference, Box 24356, Minneapolis, Minnesota 55436
    Mississippi River Creative Writing Workshop, Department of English, St. Cloud State University, St. Cloud, Minnesota 56301
    Split Rock Arts Program, 306 Westbrook Hall, University of Minnesota, 77 Pleasant Street SE, Minneapolis, Minnesota 55455
    Write to Sell Conference, Doyen Literary Services, Rural Route 1, Box 103, Newell, Iowa 50568
    Young Playwrights' Summer Conference, The Playwrights' Center, 2310 Franklin Avenue East, Minneapolis, Minnesota 55406

MISSISSIPPI
    Mississippi Writers Conference, Box 12346, Jackson, Mississippi, 39236

MISSOURI
Avila College Writers' Conference, Avila College, 11901 Wornall Road, Kansas City, Missouri 64145

Mark Twain Writers' Conference, Hannibal-LaGrange College, Hannibal, Missouri 63401

Society of Children's Book Writers Midwest Conference, 532 West Jewel, Kirkwood, Missouri 63122

MONTANA
Western Montana Writers' Conference, Office of Continuing Education, Western Montana College, Dillon, Montana 59725

Yellow Bay Writers' Workshop, Center for Continuing Education, University of Montana, Missoula, Montana 59812

NEBRASKA
Midwest Mystery and Suspense Convention, Little Professor Book Center, Baker Square, 13455 Center Road, Omaha, Nebraska 68144

NEVADA
Western Mountain Writers' Conference, Western Nevada Community College, 2201 West Nye Lane, Carson City, Nevada 89701

Write to Sell, Doyen Literary Services, Rural Route 1, Box 103, Newell, Iowa 50568

NEW HAMPSHIRE
Festival of Poetry, The Frost Place, Franconia, New Hampshire 03580

Mildred I. Reid Writers' Conference, Writers' Colony, Penacook Road, Contoocook, New Hampshire 03229

Seacoast Writers' Conference, Seacoast Writers' Association, Box 6553, Portsmouth, New Hampshire 03801

NEW JERSEY
Annual New Jersey Romance Writers' Conference, Box 646, Oldbridge, New Jersey 08857

Making a Dent: Writing to Change the World, International Women's Writing Guild, Box 810, Gracie Station, New York City, New York 10028

Metropolitan Writers' Conference, Bayley Hall, Seton Hall University, South Orange, New Jersey 07079

NEW MEXICO
Sandia Publishing Writers' Conference, 2501 San Pedro Drive NE, Albuquerque, New Mexico 87110

Santa Fe Writers' Conference, Recursos de Santa Fe, 826 Camino de Monte Rey, Santa Fe, New Mexico 87501
Southwest Christian Writers' Seminar, Box 2635, Farmington, New Mexico 87499
Southwest Writers' Conference, Box 14632, Albuquerque, New Mexico 87191
Taos Institute of Arts, Box 1389, Taos, New Mexico 87571

NEW YORK
American Society of Journalists and Authors Annual Conference, 1501 Broadway, New York City, New York 10036
Annual IWWG Women's Summer Writing Conference, International Women's Writing Guild, Box 810, Gracie Station, New York City, New York 10028
Brockport Writers' Forum, State University of New York at Buffalo, Brockport, New York 14420
Catskill Writers' Workshop, Hartwick College, Oneonta, New York 13820
Chautauqua Institution Annual Writers' Workshop, Schools Office, Chautauqua Institution, Box 1098, Chautauqua, New York 14722
Feminist Women's Writing Workshops, Inc., Box 6583, Ithaca, New York 14851
Highlights Foundation Writers' Workshop at Chautauqua, Department W, 71 Court Street, Honesdale, Pennsylvania 18431 [workshop held at Chautauqua, New York]
Hofstra's Annual Summer Writers' Conference, Hofstra Memorial Hall #232, Hofstra University, Hempstead, New York 11550
Society of Children's Book Writers New York Conference, Box 20233, Park West Finance Station, New York City, New York 10025-1511
Southampton Writer's Conference, Long Island University, Southampton Campus, Southampton, New York 11968
Vassar Institute of Publishing and Writing, Publishing Institute, Vassar College, Box 300, Poughkeepsie, New York 12601
Woodstock Publishing Conference at Byrdcliffe, Woodstock Guild, 34 Tinker Street, Woodstock, New York 12498
Write Associates of Western New York Writers' Conference, 471 Burroughs Drive #5, Buffalo, New York 14226

NORTH CAROLINA
Blue Ridge Christian Writers' Conference, Box 188, Black Mountain, North Carolina 28711
Duke University Writers' Conference, The Bishop's House, Duke University, Durham, North Carolina 27708
Wildacres Writers' Workshop, 233 South Elm Street, Greensboro, North Carolina 27401

OHIO

Antioch Writers' Workshop, 133 North Walnut Street, Antioch, Ohio 45387

Cuyahoga Writers' Conference, 4250 Richmond Road, Cleveland, Ohio 44122

Midwest Writers' Conference, Kent State University, 6000 Frank Avenue NW, Canton, Ohio 44720

Skyline Writers' Conference and Workshop, 11770 Maple Ridge Drive, North Royalton, Ohio 44133

Western Reserve Writers' and Free Lance Conference, 34200 Ridge Road #110, Willoughby, Ohio 44094

OKLAHOMA

Central Oklahoma Romance Authors' "Fall in Love" Conference, 1216 Southwest 107th Street, Oklahoma City, Oklahoma 73170

Oklahoma City Arts Center Professional Writers' Series, City Arts Center/Workshop, 1016 Northwest 39th Street, Oklahoma City, Oklahoma 73118

Oklahoma Writers' Federation, Inc., 3617 Meadow Lane, Edmond, Oklahoma 73013

Red Earth Writers' Conference, Center of the American Indian, 2100 Northeast 52nd Street, Oklahoma City, Oklahoma 73111

Writers of Children's Literature Conference, Box 16355, Cameron University Station, Lawton, Oklahoma 73505

OREGON

Flight of the Mind Summer Writing Workshop for Women, 622 Southeast 29th Street, Portland, Oregon 97214

Haystack Program in the Arts, Box 1491, Portland State University, Portland, Oregon 97207

Willamette Writers' Conference, 9045 Southwest Barbur Boulevard, Portland, Oregon 97219

PENNSYLVANIA

Ligonier Valley Writers' Conference, RD #4, Box 8, Ligonier, Pennsylvania 15658

Pennwriters' Conference, 775 Cottonwood Drive, Monroeville, Pennsylvania 15146

Philadelphia Writers' Conference, 830 Montgomery Avenue #406, Bryn Mawr, Pennsylvania 19010

St. David's Christian Writers' Conference, 1775 Eden Road, Lancaster, Pennsylvania 17601-3523

Writing for Publication, Continuing Education Office, Pittsburgh Theological Seminary, 616 Highland Avenue, Pittsburgh, Pennsylvania 15206

RHODE ISLAND
- NECON, Box 3251, Darlington Branch Post Office, Pawtucket, Rhode Island 02861
- Summer Writers' Conference, Creative Writing Program, Roger Williams College, Bristol, Rhode Island 02809-2923

SOUTH CAROLINA
- Anderson College Writers' Conference, Anderson College, Anderson, South Carolina 29621
- Francis Marion Writers' Retreat, Francis Marion College, Florence, South Carolina 29501-0547

SOUTH DAKOTA
- Black Hills Writers' Conference, Authors' and Artists' Agency, 4444 Lakeside Drive, Burbank, California 91505
- Western Women in the Arts Writers'/Artists' Retreat, Route 1, Box 120, Hot Springs, South Dakota 57747

TENNESSEE
- Randall House Writers' Conference, Box 17306, Nashville, Tennessee 37217

TEXAS
- "Craft of Writing" Conference, Box 830688 M/S, C. N. 1.1, Richardson, Texas 75083-0688
- Frontiers in Writing, Box 19303, Amarillo, Texas 79114
- Images of Women in the American West, Community Service Programs, Texas Christian University, Box 32927, Fort Worth, Texas 76129
- Perseverance Precedes Publication, Southwest Texas Society of Children's Book Writers, 111 Moss Drive, San Antonio, Texas 78213
- Society of Children's Book Writers' Conference, 1361 Lakeview Drive, Southlake, Texas 76092
- Society of Children's Book Writers' "Writing for Young People" Conference, 1908 Goliad, Amarillo, Texas 79106
- The Write Attitude, 4245 Calder, Beaumont, Texas 77706

UTAH
- Park Creek Writers' Workshop, Box 226, Pasco, Washington 99301
- Writers at Work, Box 8857, Salt Lake City, Utah 84108
- Write to Sell Conference, Doyen Literary Services, Rural Route 1, Box 103, Newell, Iowa 50568

VERMONT
- Bennington Writing Workshops, Bennington College, Bennington, Vermont 05201
- Bread Loaf Writers' Conference, Middlebury College, West Middlebury, Vermont 05753
- Dorothy Canfield Fisher Writers' Conference, League of Vermont Writers, Box 1058, Waitsfield, Vermont 05673
- Wildbranch Workshop in Outdoor, Natural History, and Environmental Writing, Sterling College, Craftsbury Common, Vermont 05827

VIRGINIA
- Blue Ridge Writers' Conference, 1917 Warrington Road SW, Roanoke, Virginia 24015
- Children's Literature Institute Conference, Curry School of Education, University of Virginia, 405 Emmet Street, Charlottesville, Virginia 22903-2495
- Highland Summer Conference, Box 5917, Radford University, Radford, Virginia 24142
- Shenandoah Playwrights' Retreat, ShenanArts, Inc., Route 5, Box 176-F, Staunton, Virginia 24401
- Shenandoah Valley Writers' Guild Weekend Conference, Lord Fairfax Community College, Middletown, Virginia 22645

WASHINGTON
- Clarion West Writers' Workshop, 340 15th Avenue E #350, Seattle, Washington 98112
- Pacific Northwest Writers' Conference, 17345 Sylvester Road SW, Seattle, Washington 98119
- Port Townsend Writers' Conference, CENTRUM, Box 1158, Port Townsend, Washington 98368
- Seattle Pacific Christian Writers' Conference, Department of Humanities, Seattle Pacific University, Seattle, Washington 98119
- Society of Children's Book Writers' Conference, 3627 South 262nd Street, Kent, Washington 98032

WEST VIRGINIA
- Annual Golden Rod Writers' Conference, 525 Grove Street, Morgantown, West Virginia 26505

WISCONSIN
- Breaking into Magazine Writing and World of Freelance Writing, Writing Seminars, 9409 Voss Road, Marengo, Illinois 60152
- Dillman's Creative Workshops, Dillman's Lodge, Box 98, Lac du Flambeau, Wisconsin 54538

Parting Words

Green Lake Christian Writers' Conference, American Baptist Assembly, Green Lake, Wisconsin 54941

Heartland Writers' Workshop, Mount Mary College, 2900 North Menomonee River Parkway, Milwaukee, Wisconsin 53222

School of Arts at Rhinelander, 610 Langdon Street #727, Madison, Wisconsin 53703

Travel Writing, Editing for Print, and Publicity Writing Techniques, Lowell Hall, University of Wisconsin, Madison, Wisconsin 53703

Wisconsin Institute, Communication Programs, University of Wisconsin, Lowell Hall, 610 Langdon Street, Madison, Wisconsin 53703

WYOMING

Wyoming Writers' Conference, 331 Road 6 RT, Cody, Wyoming 82414

Writers' Colonies

A number of writers' colonies offer writers and other artists the opportunity to live for periods ranging from two to six weeks, or in the case of the Fine Arts Work Center in Provincetown seven months, free of charge or at nominal cost for room and board in settings conducive to artistic production. The colonies vary in the number of artists they can accommodate at a given time. Some are very small and can have only three or four residents at one time. Others can handle up to forty artists. Admission is usually based on the submission of published writing and/or of copies of manuscripts or other artwork in progress. As a courtesy, inquiries should be accompanied by stamped, self-addressed envelopes. The following colonies are among the best known.

Atlantic Center for the Arts, 1414 Art Center Avenue, New Smyrna Beach, Florida 32069

Bellagio Study and Conference Center, The Rockefeller Foundation, 1133 Avenue of the Americas, New York City, New York 10036

Blue Mountain Center, Blue Mountain Lake, New York 12812

Centrum Foundation, c/o Director of Literature Programs, Fort Worden State Park, Box 1158, Port Townsend, Washington 98368

Cummington Community of the Arts, Rural Route 1, Box 145, Cummington, Massachusetts 01026

Dobi-Paisano Project, 101 Main Building, University of Texas, Austin, Texas 78712

Dorland Mountain Arts Colony, Box 6, Temecula, California 92390

Dorset Colony House, Dorset, Vermont 05251

Fine Arts Work Center in Provincetown, 24 Pearl Street, Box 565, Provincetown, Massachusetts 02657

Green River Writers' Retreat, Western Kentucky University, Bowling Green, Kentucky (Write to Ms. Mary E. O'Dell, 11906 Locust Road, Middletown, Kentucky 40243.)
Hambridge Center, Box 339, Rabun Gap, Georgia 30568
The MacDowell Colony, 100 High Street, Peterborough, New Hampshire 03458
Mildred I. Reid Writers' Colony in New Hampshire, Penacook Road, Contoocook, New Hampshire 03229
Millay Colony for the Arts, Steepletop, Austerlitz, New York 12017
Montalvo Center for the Arts, Montalvo Residency Program, Box 158, Saratoga, California 95071
Northwood Institute Alden B. Dow Creativity Center, Midland, Michigan 48640-2398
Palenville Interarts Colony, 2 Bond Street, New York City, New York 10012
Ragdale Foundation, 1260 North Green Bay Road, Lake Forest, Illinois 60045
Ucross Foundation, Residency Program, 2836 U. S. Highway 14/16 East, Clearmont, Wyoming 82835
Virginia Center for the Creative Arts, Sweet Briar, Virginia 24595
The Writers' Community, West Side YMCA Center for the Arts, New York City, New York 10023
Helene Wurlitzer Foundation of New Mexico, Box 545, Taos, New Mexico 87571
Yaddo, Box 395, Saratoga Springs, New York 12866

Additional Print Sources

Children's Authors and Illustrators: An Index to Biographical Dictionaries.
Published biennially by Gale Research, Inc., Dept. 77748, Detroit, Michigan 48277-0748.
Writers who want information and vital details about authors and illustrators of books for young people will be led by this book to sources that give such information as age, addresses, and books published. This resource is found in the reference sections of many libraries and is comprehensive.

Dictionary of Literary Biography. Published irregularly by Gale Research, Inc., Dept. 77748, Detroit, Michigan 48277-0748.
These volumes, which now number in the seventies, provide excellent and extended information about writers and, more recently, about critics of literature. The general editors of this series are Matthew J. Bruccoli and Richard Layman.

Genealogical Periodical Annual Index: Key to the Genealogical Literature.
Published annually by Heritage Books, Inc., 1540 East Pointer Ridge Place, Bowie, Maryland 20716.

Parting Words 157

For those interested in writing genealogy or family history, this resource, at $17.50 a year, is an extremely useful research document. It contains as good an overview as one can find about what is going on in the field.

International Directory of Film and TV Documentation Centers. Published irregularly by the International Federation of Film Archives, Documentation Commission, St. James Press, 233 East Ontario #600, Chicago, Illinois 60601.
The most recent edition of this comprehensive resource appeared in 1988 and cost $45. The directory describes theater collections in more than forty countries and is quite exhaustive.

Owlflight. Published irregularly by Unique Graphics, 1025 55th Street, Oakland, California 94608.
Owlflight is published with fair regularity and has some extremely interesting examples of science-fiction writing. The cost is $10 for three issues. It does not offer suggestions for marketing but might in itself provide a market for some writers who read it.

Publishers Weekly. Published weekly. Box 1979, Marion, Ohio, 43306-2079.
Publishers Weekly has long been the preeminent weekly publication of the publishing industry; writers and publishers depend on it. It has extensive book reviews, most of them appearing weeks or even months before similar reviews appear in other magazines and journals. They identify markets and also indicate books that are in press. At $119 a year, *PW* is not cheap. It is, however, as important to serious writers as a wrench is to a plumber.

Science Fiction and Fantasy Workshop. 1193 South 1900 East, Salt Lake City, Utah 84108.
At $10 year, this monthly publication is a distinct bargain. This publication is rich in specific marketing suggestions for science fiction, fantasy, and horror stories of all lengths. Certainly this is a publication worth looking into.

Science Fiction Research Association Newsletter. Science Fiction Research Association, c/o Ronald Tweet, 3900 Eighth Avenue, Rock Island, Illinois 61201.
Although this publication is limited to members of the Science Fiction Research Association, it is worth seeking out because it has good advice about techniques and markets to which science-fiction writers can send their work.

Theatre Crafts. Published ten times a year by the Theatre Crafts Associates, 135 Fifth Avenue, New York, New York 10010-7193.
This valuable resource provides information about lighting, sound, sets, costume design, and other technical matters. An annual subscription costs $30, which includes the annual directory.

Theatre Information Bulletin. Published weekly by Proscenium Publications, 4 Park Avenue, New York, New York 10016.

Although the annual subscription fee of $100 may be daunting to some, the weekly coverage of the New York theater scene is as complete as one could hope for. Many libraries subscribe. Those who begin reading this bulletin in libraries often become subscribers.

Theatre Times. Published bimonthly by the Alliance of Resident Theatres of New York, Inc., 131 Varick Street #904, New York, New York 10013

The chief emphasis of this magazine, which costs $15 a year on a subscription basis, surveys New York's nonprofit, Off-Broadway theaters and offers excellent information about both the artistic and the financial concerns affecting such theaters. Playwrights can gain good leads from reading this magazine.

Who's Who in America. Published annually by Marquis Who's Who, 3002 Glenview Road, Wilmette, Illinois 60091.

Of all the biographical guides available, this one is probably the most useful, even though it is not the most inclusive. Most notable authors, editors, play producers, directors, and publishers are listed in these two volumes. They are not classified by profession, so one must have the names of people they are interested in knowing more about.

Wonder: The International Magazine of Fantasy, Science-Fiction, and Horror. Wonder Press, Box 58367, Louisville, Kentucky 40268-0367.

Some markets are mentioned in this magazine, but its chief value is in showing the broad range of successful writing that is going on in these three genres. This monthly magazine is quite selective and has high standards.

World SF Newsletter. Published quarterly by the International Science Fiction Association of Professionals, World SF, 855 S. Harvard Drive, Palatine, Illinois 60067-7026.

This newsletter helps to keep its subscribers up to date in the rapidly growing and changing field of science fiction. It identifies some markets and analyzes trends.

The Writer. Published monthly by The Writer, Incorporated, 720 Boyleston Street, Boston, Massachusetts 02116.

The Writer, along with *Writer's Digest*, listed below, is one of the most directly useful monthly publications in helping writers to identify markets. It also contains articles by published writers, editors, literary agents, and other people who know intimately the markets they are writing about. The $23 annual subscription price is likely to be repaid several times over with a new writer's first sale.

Writer's Digest. Published monthly by F & W Publications, Inc., 1507 Dana Avenue, Cincinnati, Ohio 45207.

This monthly publication, which costs $21 a year to subscribe to, features articles that deal with every aspect of writing, with all genres, with both fiction and nonfiction, and with how to break into markets. The individual issues are well balanced, usually containing at least one article on poetry, one on fiction, one on scriptwriting, and one on writing commercially for magazines. The classified advertisements are of particular help to writers seeking assistance, information, and markets. The level of writing in this magazine is generally high and appealing. This publication maintains high standards of professionalism.

Writer's Directory. Published biennially by St. James Press, Inc., 233 East Ontario #600, Chicago, Illinois 60601.

Recent volumes of *Writer's Directory* are in the reference collections of many public and most university libraries. The listings include addresses of writers, pseudonyms, the genres in which they work, and their list of published work with dates of publication.

Year's Best Science Fiction Annual. St. Martin's Press, 175 Fifth Avenue, New York, New York 10010.

This annual collection provides an outlet for those who write in this field but serves its most valuable function by gathering in one place the science fiction that is considered best and that, in many ways, is most representative of what is going on in that field.

Youth Theatre Journal. Published quarterly by the American Alliance for Theatre and Education, Theatre Arts Department, Virginia Polytechnic Institute and State University, Blacksburg, Virginia 24061-0141.

Although this well-presented journal is aimed mostly at those who teach drama and theater, its issues are informative and suggestive for people in all aspects of theater, including playwriting. The subscription costs $20 per year.

RESOURCES
FOR
WRITERS

INDEX

Abbe, George 22
Adkins, Rose, Kirk Polking, and Jean Chimsky 33, 66, 91
Aiken, Joan 69, 94
Ames, Van Meter 22
Andersen, Richard 50
Andrews, C. E. 69
Applebaum, Judith 122
Arbuthnot, May Hill 94
Aristotle 22, 69
Ashley, L. F. 94
Asimov, Isaac 43
Asimov, Isaac, and Janet Asimov 22, 94
Asimov, Janet, and Isaac Asimov 22, 94
Asimov, Isaac, and Martin Greenberg 21
Austell, Jan 61
Avery, Gillian 95

Baker, Augusta, and Ellin Greene 95
Baker, Samm Sinclair 50, 122
Ballanger, Bruce, and Barry Lane 9
Barkas, J. L. 9, 23
Barr, June 69, 122
Barry, Elaine 70
Barzun, Jacques 3
Behn, Harry 70, 95
Belkin, Gary S. 122
Benedict, Helen 50, 113, 123
Bennett, Hal, and Michael Larson 3
Bentley, Phyllis 9, 23
Bernays, Anne, and Pamela Painter 9
Biagi, Shirley 50, 117
Bickford, Elizabeth, Elizabeth Preston, and Ingrid Monke 129
Bicknell, Treld Pelkey, and Felicity Trotman 95
Bingham, Mindy, and Dan Poynter 57
Bishop, Leonard 10
Blackner, Irwin R. 86
Block, Lawrence 23, 24, 108
Bly, Robert W. 123
Bocca, Geoffrey 24
Boggess, Louise 51, 117
Boles, Paul Darcy 10
Bova, Ben 21
Bowen, Catherine Drinker 113
Boyer, Carl, III 116
Brace, Gerald Warner 24
Bradbury, Ray 44
Brady, Ben, and Lance Lee 86
Brady, John, and Jean M. Fredette 10, 24, 40, 44, 96, 123
Bratton, J. S. 96

Braun, Matt 48, 123
Brenner, Alfred 86
Bretnor, Reginald 21, 44, 86
Brooks, Terry 51
Buchler, Justus 70
Burack, Sylvia K. 40, 123
Burgett, Gordon 96, 132
Burnett, Hallie, and Whit Burnett 10
Burnett, Whit, and Hallie Burnett 10

Calvert, Stephen J., and Olga S. Weber 17, 68, 104
Campbell, Walter S. 10, 24
Cane, Melville 70, 108
Card, Orson Scott 44
Carey, Michael A. 70
Caro, Robert A., David McCullough, Paul C. Nagel, Richard B. Sewell, Ronald Steel, and Jean Strouse 114
Carpenter, Lisa 96
Carr, Jo 96
Cartmell, Van H. 61
Cassill, Kay 3, 51, 117, 135
Catron, Louis E. 87
Caws, Mary Anne 71
Children's Authors and Illustrators 156
Chimsky, Jean, Rose Adkins, and Kirk Polking 33, 66, 91
Ciardi, John 71
Clareson, Thomas D. 44, 87
Cleaver, Diane 132
Clifford, James L. 114
Cockshut, A. O. J. 108
Coe, Michelle E. 87, 124, 135
Colley, Ann C., and Judith K. Moore 71
Collier, Oscar, with Frances Spatz Leighton 25, 51
Collins, James L. 48, 97
Colwell, C. Carter, and James H. Knox 108
Conrad, Barnaby, et al. 25
Cook, Albert 71
Cook, Claire Kehrwald 51
Cool, Lisa Collier 52, 117, 132
Cox, Kerry, and Jurgen Wolff 93
Creeley, Robert 72
Croft, Mary K., and Joyce S. Steward 17, 82, 116
Curtis, Richard 133
Cussler, Clive 39

Daigh, Ralph 25
Davie, Elaine 133

RESOURCES FOR WRITERS

Davis, Eugene C. 61
Delany, Samuel R. 45
Delton, Judy 52
Dessner, Lawrence Jay 72, 97
Diamant, Anita 133
Dibell, Ansen 11, 25
Dickson, Frank A., and Sandra Smythe 11
Dictionary of Literary Biography 156
Dillard, Annie 26
Dowis, Richard 11
Drewry, John E. 52
Drury, John 72
Duncan, Lois 11, 97, 109
Dunn, Thomas G., and Frank Pike 66, 129
Dutwin, Phyllis 52

Edel, Leon 114
Edelstein, Scott 52, 124
Editors of Coda: A Poets and Writers Newsletter 19, 38, 59, 121, 135
Egri, Lajos 61
Eidenier, Connie 97
Eliot, T. S. 72
Elwood, Maren 26
Ephron, Henry 87
Esbensen, Barbara Juster 72, 98
Eyerly, Jeannete, and Irwin Hadley 100

Falk, Kathryn 47
Fehrman, Carl 73
Feldman, Elane 135
Feldman, Gayle 12
Fergusson, Francis 62
Finch, Robert 62
Fitzgerald, John D., and Robert C. Meredith 32
Fitz-Randolph, Jane 53, 62, 87, 98
Flesch, Rudolf 3
Fluegelman, Andrew, and Jeremy Joan Hewes 4
Ford, John M., George H. Scithers, Darrell Schweitzer 46
Foster, E. M. 26
Fredette, Jean M. 53, 118, 124
Fredette, Jean M., and John Brady 10, 24, 40, 44, 96, 123
Freedman, Helen Rosengren, and Karen Krieger 53, 118
Freeman, William 4
Frey, Charles, and John Griffith 98
Freytag, Gustav 62
Frong, William 88
Fulton, Len 12, 73

Gabriel, H. W. 53
Gallo, Donald R. 98, 109

Gardner, John 27
Garvey, Daniel E., and William L. Rivers 88
Gee, Robin 125, 133
Genealogical Periodical Annual Index 156
Gibbons, Reginald 73
Giblin, James Cross 45, 99
Gibson, Walker 4
Gilbert, Nan 53, 99, 125
Gittings, Robert 114
Giustino, Rolando 88
Godwin, Gail 109
Goldberg, Natalie 27
Goldin, Stephen, and Kathleen Sky 125, 136
Golding, William 4
Goulart, Frances Sheridan 53, 125
Grebanier, Bernard 63
Greenberg, Martin, and Isaac Asimov 21
Greene, Ellin, and Augusta Baker 95
Greenfeld, Howard 126
Griffith, John, and Charles Frey 98
Griffiths, Stuart 63
Gunther, Max 54
Guthrie, A. B., Jr. 27

Hall, Oakley 28
Hamilton, Anne 73
Hanna, S. S. 126
Harris, William Foster 12
Harrower, Molly 73, 109
Harter, Penny, and William J. Higginson 74, 99
Hatten, Theodore W. 63
Hayes, Helen, Ellen Rolfes, et al. 54, 126
Hendrick, George, and Margaret Sandburg, eds. 111
Henry, Laurie 12, 28
Herman, Lewis 88
Hewes, Jeremy Joan, and Andrew Fluegelman 4
Higginson, William J., and Penny Harter 74, 99
Hildick, Wallace 99
Hill, Archibald A. 74
Hill, Wycliffe A. 13, 28, 89
Hillyer, Robert 74
Hinds, Marjorie M. 99, 126
Hochman, Sandra 74
Holinger, William 28
Holmes, John 75
Hood, Thomas 75
Houseman, A. E. 75
Howells, James F., and Dean Memering 4
Hughes, Riley 13, 29
Hull, Raymond 63, 126
Hunter, Mollie 100

INDEX

International Directory of Film and TV Documentation Centers 157
Irwin, Hadley, and Jeannete Eyerly 100

Jacobi, Peter 54, 118
James, Henry 29
Jarrell, Randall 75
Jarvis, Sharon 45
Jerome, Judson 76, 127
Johnson, Audrey P. 100

Kammerman, Sylvia E. 54, 100
Kane, Thomas S 5
Kelley, Jerome E. 55, 118
Kelton, Elmer 49
Kevles, Barbara 55, 118
Kesselman-Turkel, Judi, and Franklynn Peterson 57, 120
Kirby, David 76
Kissling, Mark 127
Klaus, Carl H., and Robert Scholes 67
Klauser, Henrietta Anne 5
Knight, Damon 13
Knox, James H., and C. Carter Colwell 108
Koch, Kenneth 76
Konner, Linda 55, 119
Koontz, Dean R. 29, 45, 101, 127
Kreutzer, Jame R. 76
Krieger, Karen, and Helen Rosengren Freedman 53, 118
Krook, Dorothea 64
Kumin, Maxine 77
Kunitz, Stanley 77

Lane, Barry, and Bruce Ballanger 9
Lanier, Sidney 77
Lanning, George, and Robie Macauley 13
Larsen, Michael 133
Larson, Michael, and Hal Bennett 3
Lawson, John Howard 64, 89
Leader, Zachary 5
Leavitt, Hart Day 19, 38
Lee, Lance, and Ben Brady 86
Leighton, Frances Spatz, and Oscar Collier 25, 51
Levine, Ellen 134
Lewis, Claudia 101
Lewisohn, Ludwig 77
Lindbergh, Anne 101
Livingston, Myra Cohn 77, 101
Lomask, Milton 115
Lowrey, Marilyn M. 47, 101
Lubbock, Percy 30

Macauley, Robie, and George Lanning 13

MacCampbell, Donald 134
McCormack, Thomas 30
McCullough, David, Paul C. Nagel, Richard B. Sewell, Ronald Steel, Jean Strouse, and Robert A. Caro 114
MacDonald, John D. 39
Macdonald, Ross 41
McGivern, William P. 89
Mack, Karin, and Eric Skjei 5
McLarn, Jack Clinton 13, 30, 102, 119, 134
Mager, N. H., S. K. Mager, and P. S. Mager 55
Maloney, Martin, and Paul Max Rubenstein 55, 89
Malzberg, Barry N. 46
Mann, Thomas 30
Manners, William 127
Manvell, Roger 90
Marks, Percy 14, 30
Marston, Doris Ricker 14, 31, 40, 56, 78, 102
Martin, Valery 14, 31
Martindale, David 56, 119
Mathieu, Aron M. 14, 31, 41, 64, 102
Mau, Ernest E. 56, 119, 128
Maugham, W. Somerset 31, 109, 110
May, Jill 102
Memering, Dean, and James F. Howells 4
Meranus, Leonard S., and Kirk Polking 6
Meredith, Robert C., and John D. Fitzgerald 32
Milios, Rita 110
Monke, Ingrid, Elizabeth Preston, and Elizabeth Bickford 129
Moore, Judith K., and Ann C. Colley 71
Morris, Terry 56, 120
Morris, Wright 32, 110
Morton, William C. 78
Mueller, Lavonne 64
Muth, Marcia 14, 65, 78, 120, 128
Myers, Robert E. 46

Nagel, Paul C., Richard B. Sewell, Ronald Steel, Jean Strouse, Robert A. Caro, and David McCullough 114
Naylor, Phyllis Reynolds 32
Newcomb, Duane 57, 120, 128
Newton, Michael 40, 41, 128
Niggli, Josefina 65, 128
Nins, Anaïs 32, 110
Nolan, William F. 42
Norville, Barbara 42
Nyberg, Ben 15

Oates, Joyce Carol 15
O'Connor, Flannery 15, 33
O'Cork, Shannon 42

RESOURCES FOR WRITERS

Orvis, Mary Burchard 33
Osgood, Charles Grosvenor 78
Osmond, T. S. 79
Owlflight 157

Packard, William 65, 79, 90, 128, 129
Painter, Pamela, and Anne Bernays 9
Paris Review 33, 111
Parsons, Louella O. 90
Paz, Octavio 79
Peacock, Ronald 65
Peck, Robert Newton 15, 39, 136
Percy, Bernard 16, 79
Perlmutter, Jerome H. 6
Peterson, Franklynn, and Judi Kesselman-Turkel 57, 120
Pianka, Phyllis Taylor 47, 103, 129
Pike, Frank, and Thomas G. Dunn 66, 129
Piotrowski, Maryanne V. 57
Poe, Edgar Allan 16, 80
Polking, Kirk 6, 16, 66, 80, 103
Polking, Kirk, Jean Chimsky, and Rose Adkins 33, 66, 91
Polking, Kirk, and Leonard S. Meranus 6
Polti, Georges 34, 66
Pound, Ezra 80
Poynter, Dan, and Mindy Bingham 57
Preminger, Alex 80
Press, John 80
Preston, Elizabeth, Ingrid Monke, and Elizabeth Bickford 129
Price, Reynolds 34, 111
Provost, Gary 16, 20, 42
Publishers Weekly 157

Raphaelson, Samson 66
Rees, Clair F. 34, 58, 121
Rehmehl, Judy 58, 130
Reynolds, Paul R. 58, 134
Riccio, Ottone M. 81
Rico, Gabriele Lusser 20, 34
Rilke, Rainer Maria 81
Rilla, Wolf 91, 130
Rinehart, Mary Roberts 34
Rivers, William L., and Daniel E. Garvey 88
Roberts, Edward Barry 91
Roberts, Ellen E. M. 103, 130
Rockwell, F. A. 58, 132
Rolfes, Ellen, Helen Hayes, et al. 54, 126
Rosen, Michael 17, 81
Rosenthal, M. L. 81, 82
Rouverol, Jean 91, 130
Rowe, Kenneth Thorpe 66, 67, 130
Rubenstein, Paul Max, and Martin Maloney 55, 89

Sandburg, Carl 111
Sandburg, Margaret, and George Hendrick, eds. 111
Sanders, Linda S. 17
Sargeant, Epes Winthrop 92
Schapper, Beatrice 121
Scholes, Robert, and Carl H. Klaus 67
Schumacher, Michael 115
Schwartz, Ted 115
Schweitzer, Darrell, John M. Ford, and George H. Scithers 46
Science Fiction and Fantasy Workshop 157
Science Fiction Research Association Newsletter 157
Scithers, George H., Darrell Schweitzer, and John M. Ford 46
Scully, Celia G., and Thomas J. Scully 59, 131
Scully, Thomas J., and Celia G. Scully 59, 131
Seldes, Gilbert 92, 103
Sewell, Richard B., Ronald Steel, Jean Strouse, Robert A. Caro, David McCullough, and Paul C. Nagel 114
Shedd, Charlie W. 6
Shelston, Alan 115
Shreve, Susan 103
Shulevitz, Uri 104
Silverberg, Robert 46
Simons, George F. 17, 112
Skjei, Eric, and Karin Mack 5
Sky, Kathleen, and Stephen Goldin 125, 136
Smiley, Sam 67
Smythe, Sandra, and Frank A. Dickson 11
Steel, Ronald, Jean Strouse, Robert A. Caro, David McCullough, Paul C. Nagel, and Richard B. Sewell 114
Stein, Gertrude 82
Stern, Jerome 35
Stevens, Serita Deborah 42
Steward, Joyce S., and Mary K. Croft 17, 82, 116
Stillman, Peter R. 116
Straczynski, J. Michael 67, 92
Strickland, Bill 35
Strouse, Jean, Robert A. Caro, David McCullough, Paul C. Nagel, Richard B. Sewell, and Ronald Steel 114
Strunk, William, Jr., and E. B. White 6
Styan, J. L. 68, 92
Surmelian, Leon 17, 35
Swain, Dwight V. 20, 39
Sypher, Wylie 7

Tarliskaja, Marina 82
Tempest, Norton R. 82

INDEX

Theatre Crafts 157
Theatre Information Bulletin 158
Thomas, Frank P. 112
Tobias, Ronald B. 35
Townsend, Doris McFerran 59, 131
Treat, Lawrence 43
Trotman, Felicity, and Treld Pelkey Bicknell 95
Tsujimoto, Joseph I. 83, 104
Turco, Lewis 20, 36

Untermeyer, Jean Starr 83
Untermeyer, Louis 83
Uzzell, Thomas H. 36

Vachon Brian 59, 121
Van Nostran, William 92

Waugh, Hillary 43
Weber, Olga S., and Stephen J. Calvert 17, 68, 104
Welsh, Andrew 83
Welty, Eudora 18
Whallon, William 84
Wharton, Edith 18, 36
White, E. B., and William Strunk, Jr. 6
White, Eric Charles 7
Whitney, Phyllis A. 18, 19, 36, 37, 104
Who's Who in America 158

Wilbur, L. Perry 37, 48, 105, 135
Williams, Joseph 7
Williams, Miller 84
Williams, Nan Schram 37, 112, 131
Williamson, J. N. 46, 131
Willis, Meredith Sue 19, 105, 112
Wilson, Robert N. 84
Wimberley, Mary 48
Wolfe, Thomas 37
Wolff, Jurgen, and Kerry Cox 93
Wonder: The International Magazine of Fantasy 158
Woolf, Virginia 37
World SF Newsletter 158
Writer, The 158
Writer's Digest 159
Writer's Directory 159
Wylie, Max 93, 105
Wyndham, Lee 105, 121

Year's Best Science Fiction Annual 159
Yolen, Jane 60, 106, 131
York, R. A. 85
Youth Theatre Journal 159

Zinsser, William 8, 38, 60, 106, 113, 116
Zobel, Louise Purwin 60
Zuckerman, Suzanne 106